THE
DINGO
TOOK OVER MY LIFE

THE
DINGO
TOOK OVER MY LIFE

by Stuart Tipple with Malcolm Brown

Published by Tablo

Copyright © Stuart Tipple and Malcolm Brown 2019.

Published in 2019 by Tablo Publishing.

Level 1 / 41-43 Stewart Street
Richmond, Victoria, 3121
Australia

All rights reserved.

This book or any portion thereof may not be reproduced or used in any manner whatsoever without the express written permission of the author except for the use of brief quotations in a book review.

Publisher and wholesale enquiries: hello@tablo.io

First Edition

19 20 21 22   LSC   10 9 8 7 6 5 4 3 2 1

To Lindy for staying strong and loyal

To Patricia, Les and Ken for restoring my faith in science

To Long Legs for being my Rock.

Table of Contents

Introduction   1

Chapter One: *Guess Who I Met on the Way to the Shops!*   7

Chapter Two: *From Provincial New Zealand*   25

Chapter Three: *The Dingo Pounces*   37

Chapter Four: *The Frame*   51

Chapter Five: *The Primary Evidence is Bunk*   65

Chapter Six: *The Trial*   81

Chapter Seven: *Conviction? It Ain't Over Yet!*   101

Chapter Eight: *Researching a Disaster*   117

Chapter Nine: *The Political Struggle*   137

Chapter Ten: *The Bitter Stalemate*   155

Chapter Eleven: *Civil War*   167

Chapter Twelve: *Head Butting a Government*   183

Chapter Thirteen: *Lindy Out*   201

Chapter Fourteen: *Repercussions*   211

Chapter Fifteen: *A Tortured Conclusion*   233

Afterword: *The Ferry Master*   253

INTRODUCTION

> *Sometimes the slightest things change the directions of our lives, the merest breath of a circumstance, a random moment that connects like a meteorite striking the earth.*
> - Bryce Courtenay

The Azaria Chamberlain case will go down in Australian history as a disaster, in the league of train smashes, corporate collapses and medical failures. When each of these disasters is scrutinised in the aftermath, it is almost inevitably found that there were contributing factors which could have been recognised well in advance: lack of maintenance, miscalculations, cost-cutting, complacency, negligence, arrogance, recklessness. Such failures individually are often tolerated, to wit with a warning, caution or disciplinary action of some sort, but without upheaval, because other safeguards have been in place. But when a series of individual failures come together and there are no more safeguards, the pieces, as it were, lock into place. How many worksite foremen, viewing the aftermath of a fatal industrial accident, have asked: "Why wasn't this checked?" How many chief executives, pondering a corporate collapse, have asked: "Why didn't I heed that warning?" How many ministers of state, seeing a policy go belly-up, have asked: "Why he did not see that coming?" How many barristers, seeing a client go to gaol, have asked: "Why didn't I pin that Crown witness down properly?" At any point in most sequences of events, safeguards have operated. Things have not worked out in places, but the overall operation has nevertheless proceeded, because other checks and balances have worked. Every time a financial analyst sees a risk in a proposed investment, and that is acted on, then a safeguard has worked. Every time a forensic scientist sees an inconsistency in a test result that casts doubt over the Crown scenario and says there is no confirmation, an effective safeguard has not allowed things to continue.

There are usually multiple safeguards, and sometimes the failure of some of them leads to a rescue operation. Sometimes, just the final safeguard holds up. More than a quarter-century ago a NSW Police superintendent, Harry Blackburn, came under suspicion as the perpetrator of a series of assaults and rapes in suburban Sydney. There were a number of safeguards against a wrongful conviction: the accuracy of eyewitness accounts, the competence of investigating police and of reviewing police, the scrutiny of the Director of Public Prosecutions. All these safeguards failed and Harry was charged and paraded in front of the cameras for all the world to see. As a result of the stress both his wife and daughter-in-law suffered miscarriages and Harry's life was turned upside-down. But the headlong rush to total disaster was stopped in its tracks. A safeguard worked, being the competence of an officer who took over from the original investigators. He was the then Detective Inspector Clive Small. The brief was "full of holes", Small said, in the face of a stiff opposition from superiors, and the prosecution was dropped.

In the Azaria Chamberlain case, a series of safeguards were in place and any blame, whatever it might have been, properly attributed. The couple lost their baby, seized in the jaws of a wild animal at Ayers Rock on 17th August 1980. An investigation followed. To the point of the initial coroner's finding, in February 1981, that a dingo had taken the baby, the safeguards held firm. Then it was reinvestigated. There were further safeguards: the competence of the investigating police and scientific experts, the chance to air all the facts, if it came to that, before another coroner, and again if it came to that, the common sense of trial judge and jury, then perhaps of the Federal and High Courts of Appeal. As it turned out, one of these safeguards might have held, being the view of the case taken by the trial judge, James Muirhead, who saw through the nonsense and virtually begged the jury to acquit. But because of the authority of the jury decision, his urgings were overridden. Another safeguard almost held. Two of the five High Court judges hearing the Chamberlains' appeal, Justice Lionel Murphy and Sir William Dean, found that the appeal should be allowed and the convictions quashed. But they were in the minority on the bench and that safeguard failed. As it turned out, all the safeguards failed. The Chamberlains were convicted, Lindy sentenced to life imprisonment with hard labour, Michael to a suspended sentence, and their lives were torn apart.

As the event was scrutinised, over and over again during the following three decades, it gradually dawned on officialdom – however long that took – that that had happened. The safeguards, or any one of them, should have held up. But with their total failure, the pieces fitted into place, and there was nothing to stop what followed. Then the question was asked, in a royal commission, why this had happened. Contributing factors became readily identifiable: the remote location, making immediate and expert crime scene examination difficult, the incompetence and arrogance of at least some of the forensic scientists, the ruthlessness and irresponsibility of media, making it near-impossible to have put together an untainted jury, the bigotry of the general public and the rigidity of the legal system.

So often, in these disasters, there are warnings. One such warning, had it been properly researched, was an inadequate performance of the principal scientific witness, Professor James Cameron, in a criminal case in Britain. As far as forensic science in general was concerned, there were warnings from previous cases, especially where prosecutions had been based on scientific rather than primary evidence, where evidence had been wrongly admitted or insufficiently tested, where expertise was assumed in an expert judgement when it should not have been. After Michael and Lindy Chamberlain were convicted over their baby's death, the final appeal had to be to the Court of Public Opinion, which is at best fickle. In the Chamberlain case, it worked. But by the time that had been done – the coroner's finding in 2012 reverting to what Denis Barritt had found in 1981 – the lives of everyone in the Chamberlain family had been ruined or severely affected.

Congratulations Australia! A baby is snatched away by a wild animal and the parents are universally vilified, convicted and punished. All those years and years, collectively, of education and training, all that experience of the police officers and scientists and lawyers, all those hundreds of years in which the legal system had been studied, scrutinised and refined, all that money spent on investigation and court proceedings, and yet this happened.

Michael and Lindy Chamberlain had no reason to believe nine-week old baby Azaria was in any danger when Lindy placed her asleep in their tent with their sleeping four year- old son Reagan. From that misplaced confidence, everything went wrong for the Chamberlains.

Having suffered the unimaginable trauma of losing their baby in these horrifying circumstances, they were thrust headlong into a world that was utterly unfamiliar to them, sneered at and pilloried throughout the nation, prosecuted and in Lindy's case, gaoled for life. John Winneke QC, who represented the Chamberlains at one point, was to say it was like Beelzebub going ahead of them all the time, throwing things down which would come back onto them. Leaving aside satanic influences, it was simply a case of the safeguards progressively failing when they should have worked.

Into this mess was thrust Stuart Tipple, a 29-year-old provincial solicitor in New South Wales, retained because he was well-regarded professionally and a Seventh-day Adventist, like his clients-to-be, and in good standing with the Seventh-day Adventist (SDA) hierarchy. With limits to his own experience, he took the brief after the re-investigation was launched and plunged into unknown territory, an unchartered wilderness in which he was to experience frustration, persecution and denunciation. He was often a lone figure, attacked and denigrated over the following years within his own church community, pitching his resources against those of the government of the Northern Territory, which called on experts from the other side of the world. However like other solitary figures, caught in a blitz with nothing going right for them, he stayed calm and planned his moves, set his priorities and battled on. The one thing that went well for him was that both Michael and Lindy Chamberlain recognised his intrinsic value and stayed with him.

I encountered Stuart as a reporter on the *Sydney Morning Herald*. The media did not have a good image in the eyes of the Chamberlains, who had initially been frank and open but soon learned to be very wary. I was tarred with that brush as well. But had had some sort of rapport with them, probably because I was a churchgoer. With Stuart, it was a prickly relationship. Probably the worst moment was when Stuart had private negotiations with Brian Martin QC, then the Solicitor-General for the Northern Territory, about a possible release for Lindy. Stuart told the SDA hierarchy, who distributed the information in a confidential document. That was leaked to me and, in accordance with what I understood to be my obligations as a journalist, I publicised it, and that threw a huge spanner into works as far as negotiations with the Northern Territory went. Stuart once snapped at me in a lift saying I was just another of the reptiles of the press, to which I was about to say: "You're talking about the way I do my job. What about the way you do yours, which is, essentially, winning a case from time to time and keeping some people out of gaol!" I told him a long time later that that would have been my response and even then, he recoiled.

For some years Stuart was harassed by critics urging him to step aside and let another team have a go. The urgings even went to his clients. But the Chamberlains stuck with him, as did the barristers he had retained, but he would scarcely have been human had he not been plagued by the darkest thoughts as to whether his critics were right. His strategy at times took him right out of the legal realm and into that of politics, public campaigns and media coverage. His principal focus was on the scientific evidence, upon which his clients had been convicted and over which he had always held the gravest doubts. He did all this while running a legal practice and a family, and dealing with some of the complications of family life. A royal commission exonerated Michael and Lindy and, after years of dithering, the Northern Territory though its coroner reinstated the original verdict that a dingo had taken the baby. Stuart Tipple had been vindicated even though, in their personal lives, Michael and Lindy Chamberlain had paid a terrible price.

Stuart invited me to join him in writing a book after seeing a play, *Letters to Lindy*, by Alana Valentine, at Sydney University's Seymour Centre in September 2016. He had diary notes and a pile of correspondence that had been sent to him and his clients during more than 30 years handling the case. The letters were from all points of view, some from scientists, others from church members, many from the public, including some that were malicious. That included a couple of postcards to Lindy purporting to be from Azaria in the afterlife and asking her why she had not given Azaria a chance at life too. When I undertook this task, I saw it as Stuart's story but he persuaded me to include some of my own story. This book is the product of what word skills I possess after more than four decades in journalism, coupled with Stuart's learned contributions. This book is the joint effort of both of us. I have referred to myself in the third person, which is a little awkward. The book is meant to be about Stuart's journey, but our journey was so intertwined that I decided it should be both our journeys, but with the emphasis on Stuart. The problem with writing a profile of Stuart, I must say, is that he is absolutely straight down the line, unemotional and tough. He could never be called eccentric or idiosyncratic. He did feel things deeply, but when the chips were down, and the going became very, very tough, Stuart was there, unflappable and unyielding. If anyone could be relied on to see a matter through, it was always going to be him.

In January 2017 when news came through that Michael Chamberlain had died, from some blood disorder, Stuart and I came together again. We attended the memorial service, as did others who had been with the Chamberlains for years, including Andrew Kirkham, who had been one of their counsels, and John Bryson, who had written the ground-breaking book, *Evil Angels*. So were Lindy and the Chamberlain children, her husband, Rick, and Michael's wife, Ingrid, and their daughter Zahra, all in their own way, locking away their own deepest, saddest memories. Michael Chamberlain had said towards the end that he would not want to wish on anyone "the life that I have had". Everyone knew what he meant. This book is an attempt to portray the experience of Stuart Tipple and others as they shared the pain year after year as they grappled with this legal catastrophe.

Malcolm Brown
30th June 2017

Members of my legal fraternity like to tell me "Well the system got it right in the end". They don't like to admit how badly it failed the Chamberlains. The Chamberlains' exoneration was obtained despite the system and would never have been achieved without a combination of extra ordinary circumstances and "people power". I was persuaded by a publisher to write a legal text about the Chamberlain trial as a notable trial. After completing a draft, I attended Alana Valentine's play *Letters to Lindy*. This play inspired me to put the legal text on hold and join with Malcolm Brown to tell this story which allows me to disclose letters I received from Lindy, her parents and key players wrestling with this tragic miscarriage.

Given the important part the media has played throughout I decided this book should be a joint effort with a reporter who has been part of this saga from its beginning. There was no one better suited than Malcolm Brown. Our relationship has often been prickly because as the consummate reporter Malcolm is driven by the need to tell the story whatever the consequences. Nothing was "off the record" to him even when he gave assurances to the contrary. Malcolm wanted this book to be entitled "Representing Lindy" and to be my story. I persuaded him that the better story was to combine our stories and our insights. I accepted the suggested title "The Dingo Took Over My Life". because it better reflects how this case has affected us, our immediate families and so many others who became involved.

This book and the letters reveal not only the pain so many of us felt but also how Lindy remained loyal and true. Lindy addressed all her letters not just to me, but included my wife, Cherie, and my baby son, Jaemes. She recognized before I did how much they would sacrifice and how much I would need their support to see this through.

Stuart Tipple

CHAPTER ONE

GUESS WHO I MET ON THE WAY TO THE SHOPS!

"

To be, or not to be – that is the question
Whether 'tis nobler in the mind to suffer The
slings and arrows of outrageous fortune Or
to take arms against a sea of troubles And
by opposing end them.

– Hamlet

On a fine sunny morning in early September 1981, lawyer Stuart Tipple, was walking along the main street of Wyong on the central NSW coast. At 29 years of age, six years out from Law School, he had no particular worries. He had a fine, sun-drenched lifestyle, a beautiful wife, Cherie, and a good employer: Brennan and Blair, Solicitors, Gosford. A practising Seventh-day Adventist (SDA), Tipple had already established top-level contact with senior members of his church. Among other things he had sat on the board of the SDA Church's hospital, "The San", at Wahroonga, in Sydney's Northern suburbs. Alongside him on the board was Dr Jim Cox, president of Avondale College, Cooranbong, the SDA tertiary education establishment in the Lake Macquarie hinterland on the Central Coast. Tipple in his professional life had taken on tough briefs, as a public solicitor, handling the affairs of hardened criminals. Having seen enough of how that world worked, he had then established himself in a good provincial practice, far enough from Sydney to escape the bustle but near enough not be left out in the sticks. He had fallen on his feet.

There was a cloud, fairly remote, on the horizon: the Azaria Chamberlain case. It interested but it did not affect him. Being a Seventh-day Adventist, his attention had naturally been attracted to it, and he had met SDA Pastor Michael Chamberlain as a boy in New Zealand. At that point he viewed it as someone who might see a storm in the distance. Little did he know that that storm would break over him, and that for decades to come he would be at the centre of a disaster.

At Ayers Rock in central Australia, on 17th August 1980, a nine-week old baby, Azaria Chantel Loren Chamberlain, had disappeared, reportedly taken away in the jaws of a dingo. It had been such an unusual event, seemingly unprecedented and not expected of coyote-type creatures whose normal response to human intrusion was to scuttle away. From the outset there had been doubt, which had quickly evolved into ugly rumours about the parents, SDA pastor Michael Leigh Chamberlain and his wife, Alice Lynne "Lindy" Chamberlain. It was suggested that one or both had murdered the baby and disposed of it. Why on earth she would have done that was a matter of intense speculation. Perhaps the baby had been deformed. Perhaps it had been a human sacrifice, something to do with their religion.

Intense publicity sharpened curiosity, along with the reactions of both parents who appeared on television struck the public as odd. They had not reacted in the way grief-stricken, traumatised parents were expected to react. Lindy's seemingly clinical, dispassionate account of how the dingo might have eaten her baby – "peeling it as you would an orange" – did her and her husband no good at all. Denis Barritt, the coroner found that a dingo had taken the baby. The death certificate filed out soon afterwards said: "Inquest held 20 February 1981 D.J. Barritt Coroner. [Cause of death] severe crushing to the base of the skull and neck and lacerations to the throat and neck."

Barritt had decided to deliver his verdict on national television, because he felt that the hysteria which had given rise to such ugly rumours should be put to rest for good. But he had not succeeded. Barritt's finding, that a dingo was responsible for Azaria's disappearance and death also included a finding that there had been "human intervention" in relation to disposal of the baby's jumpsuit, booties and nappy, found at the base of Ayers Rock a week after Azaria disappeared. He had based that particular finding on evidence that the jumpsuit appeared to have been cut by a bladed instrument. That element of his finding guaranteed, quite rightly, that the inquiry was not over. If there had been human intervention, then who was it? And why?

Tipple, as he walked along the Wyong street that September morning, wasn't thinking about those things. Then Michael Chamberlain turned up in person, in helmet and leathers and on a motorcycle. They greeted each other and chatted for a time. Inevitably they had talked about the events at Ayers Rock and the inquest. At the end of the conversation, Chamberlain said: "Well, if I ever need a lawyer ...."

Michael Chamberlain returned to Avondale College, where he and Lindy had taken up residence after the coroner's inquest. Though they had been exonerated over the loss of the baby, that terrible event, the rumour and innuendo and the inquest already affected them. It was considered appropriate that Michael Chamberlain leave his posting as an SDA pastor at Mt Isa in western Queensland and return to Cooranbong where he and Lindy could do some more study. Michael intended to do a Master's degree in physical education through Andrews University, an SDA establishment in Michigan, USA. With Michael and Lindy were their sons, Aidan, six, and Reagan, four, both of whom had been through the trauma at Ayers Rock.

On Saturday, 18th September 1981, about two weeks after the meeting between Tipple and Michael Chamberlain in Wyong, the storm clouds burst. It started at 8.10 am when police knocked on the Chamberlains' door at Avondale College and Aidan opened it. At the same time, police swooped on the homes of people, in Victoria, Western Australia and Tasmania, who had been witnesses on the night of 17th August 1980 and whose testimony had supported the dingo story. Armed with new scientific evidence and an expert opinion that the baby had in fact been murdered, probably by having its throat cut, the police were on the hunt.

The evidence they were now looking for would come from the Chamberlain' home, and their 1977-model yellow Torana Hatchback. They picked up the Torana at a Central Coast repair shop. What the primary witnesses had said of the events on the night was now to be reviewed. The police took more than 400 items from the Chamberlains' home. They picked up a camera bag which they thought Michael had taken to Ayers Rock. Michael told them it was not the right one and gave them the bag he had taken. The seized items were packed up and sent to the NSW Health Department Division of Forensic Medicine for analysis. Working there was Joy Kuhl, a Master of Science, who was briefed to do the analysis.

News of the raids leaked out and media helicopters started buzzing over the Chamberlains' home at Cooranbong. Michael and Lindy telephoned Jim Cox, who immediately thought of Stuart Tipple. He was unable to reach Tipple just then but he had an instinctive belief in him.

In Alice Springs, Denis Barritt received a telephone call from the NT Solicitor-General, Peter Tiffin, telling him that new evidence had come forward and that Barritt's findings were to be quashed and they had briefed a barrister to represent him. Barritt immediately contacted the barrister, Michael Maurice. He told Maurice he had not been acquainted with the content of any new evidence that might have been available. Barritt said Michael and Lindy Chamberlain ought to have the opportunity to be represented. He had no objection to his findings being set aside if fresh evidence became available, provided it could not have been discovered by due diligence before his own inquiry. Maurice was informed he could not have access to the new information unless he would undertake not to disclose it to Barritt. Maurice felt duty-bound as counsel to discuss all material with his client. Being unable to do this, he withdrew from the case. Barritt's court orderly, Bill Barnes, might have been a little disappointed by the turn of events. He had caught a bucketing from officialdom after Barritt's inquest for presenting the departing Chamberlains with a bouquet of flowers. (Not done, old chap! Court officers must be seen to be detatched!)

In Tasmania, Sally Lowe, who had met Michael and Lindy Chamberlain at the barbecue area of Ayers Rock on the night Azaria disappeared – and had testified that she had heard the baby cry after Lindy took her away and had returned to the barbecue area – was now under intense pressure in the renewed investigation. Under special scrutiny was how long Lindy had been away from the barbecue area. That was now a critical question, because of a possible scenario now being taken seriously by police, Lindy had used her time away from the barbecue area to kill the baby, possibly by slashing its throat. She had then on that scenario secreted the body, washed her hands, changed her clothes and come back to act as though nothing had happened. Then, she had acted out a charade pretending she had seen a dingo take her baby.

Sally Lowe told Tipple later that when interviewed by the police, she had said Lindy had been away from the barbecue area for "a few minutes". The police officer had said: "Surely it would have taken that long just to walk there and back." The police officer had suggested Lindy might have been away "10 or even 15 minutes, or longer". Sally had said Lindy might have taken a few minutes to get to the tent and to put the baby to bed. The police officer had said: "Was it 10 or 15 minutes?" Sally said: "Well, I knew it was not as long as 15 minutes, it was less than 10 minutes." Sally told Tipple. "And so, it went on, until I finally agreed to six to 10 minutes." The questioning had made Sally Lowe feel very uncomfortable. "Not wishing to go back on anything I had made in a statement, I felt it best to say – 'a very short time'," she said.

On Sunday 19th September 1981, the Northern Territory's Chief Minister and Attorney-General, Paul Everingham, announced that a new investigation had begun into the disappearance of Azaria Chamberlain, based on a report by leading British pathologist, Professor James Malcolm Cameron, using technology not available in Australia. Cameron had concluded, from an examination of the baby's jumpsuit, that the child had been murdered, possibly by someone slitting its throat, and possibly holding it upright while the deed was done. It was later to emerge that there had been an extraordinary effort to get evidence to support Cameron's contention, all done in secret, with the Chamberlains blissfully unaware. Cameron had visited Australia and meeting, Paul Everingham and the NT Police Commissioner, Peter McAulay, in Brisbane. After Cameron had presented his findings, the inquiry was reopened. They had had little option. Police regrouped in a new investigation, code-named "Operation Ochre".

Stuart Tipple received a telephone call from Lindy Chamberlain on the Sunday, 19th September. He had never met her but she had been told about him by Jim Cox and by Michael. Tipple drove the 30 minutes from Gosford to Avondale College to meet the Chamberlains in the couple's small and very cluttered cottage. Peter Dean, who had represented the Chamberlains at the coroner's inquest, had flown from Alice Springs and was already there. The Chamberlains were, naturally enough, stunned by what was happening. They were, Tipple said later, "in a state of disbelief". "I suppose like anything you wonder what is going to happen next," Tipple recalled years later. "You wonder what sort of people they really are, what the evidence is against them. I was sensitive to the fact that I did not want to tread on Peter Dean's toes. I saw my role as advisory. I had no idea the case was going to take up the rest of my career." Of Lindy, he said: "She was smaller than I imagined, quite petite. I think the other thing she had a harsh voice which surprised me. But I don't think anyone realised the seriousness of the situation. Certainly, the Chamberlains did not. Why was the case reopened? Obviously, the Chamberlains were "in the gun" and we needed to get information before we could give them advice. Then you do what you always do. You say to your clients don't volunteer anything, let us find out what the police want. We'll ask for any questions they have to be in writing and sent to us."

And what, pray tell, was the alleged crime? It was alleged that a mother, for whatever reason, perhaps in a sudden onset of depression, overstressed perhaps, had killed her baby. A case of infanticide – an event sadly not uncommon, for which in a civilised community mothers are called to account but usually treated with at least a degree of compassion. Surely a crime such as this did not justify going to the other end of the world for expert advice! Would the police and administrators have gone to this much trouble had this occurred in New South Wales or Victoria? Here, it was suspected, the Territory was out to show it could conduct its own affairs and handle even the most difficult criminal investigations. It had the resources of State at its disposal to investigate the case and prosecute. It had police, lawyers and forensic scientists. What did the Chamberlains have? Limited finances and a couple of solicitors. They were two people against an army, and the weight of that army's offensive was likely to brush aside their defences and convict them.

For Tipple, who would for a time be working with Peter Dean, it was to be a massive leap. He would embark on a journey that would take him far and away beyond the comfort zone of provincial solicitor. Lawyers, of course, are required to gain rapid expertise in many subjects – whatever comes through their door. The characteristics of wild animals do not come often.

The dingo, an animal estimated to have come to Australia anything from 3,000 to 12,000 years ago, supposedly related to the Indian Pale-Footed Wolf, was the apex predator in Australia. From colonial times, dingoes attacked livestock and were hunted and killed. Attacks on humans were rare but not unknown. The *Sydney Morning Herald* carried a report in 1902 that an Aboriginal child had been attacked and killed by a dingo. In more recent times, information came to hand that a dingo had killed an Aboriginal baby at Alroy Downs station in the Northern Territory and run off with it but it had not been reported to the authorities because of the legal implications of not reporting a death. Wary by nature of humans, they could be domesticated to some extent, and certainly could become more relaxed in human company over a period of time. But in the context of what was about to happen, when the dingo – a theoretical one in the eyes of the sceptics – was to take centre stage, there was another factor that was far more important. Could they become so relaxed that they could kill a human child?

There was abundant evidence that dingoes had become bolder at Ayers Rock. A Sydneysider, piano teacher Anne Hall, of Beecroft, would say that when she and her husband had visited Ayers Rock in 1979, there were "dingoes everywhere". Julian Carter, of Scottsdale, Tasmania, was to say that on two nights in June 1980 he had been camped there and had seen "a pair of dingoes moving through our tent area, but not both together". He said: "I recall coming out of the shower block and seeing one dingo backing from a tent dragging a carry bag. When I got to the tent area (only a few metres from the showers), it scared before I yelled anything, and it ran in an arc and disappeared into the undergrowth in the opposite side of the shower block. The second dingo ran from another tent, following the first in the same direction into light undergrowth. I yelled after them to hurry both along. All our 23 pyramid tents had door-flaps fixed back and open to permit airing. Apart from half a dozen of my group in the showers, the camp was deserted at that time. The dingoes don't like the presence of people. We did notice these dingoes at a distance earlier and also at a distance on a couple of other occasions while we were at the rock camping ground. Some of the kids were tempted to throw stones at them, but were stopped from doing this. We didn't have any more experience of the animals being in or near the tents. From, later that afternoon we kept all tents closed wherever the bulk of our party was away sightseeing and left one person on the tent site all the time, for reasons mentioned above."

On 22nd June 1980, a Victorian family at Ayers Rock had the traumatic experience of seeing a dingo drag their six-year-old daughter, Amanda, from the family car. Amanda had cried out and the family, intervening, had chased the dingo away. The father, Max Cranwell, reported the matter to Ayers Rock ranger Ian Cawood, who said the dog was "Ding", a semi-domesticated dingo that would have to be destroyed. Cranwell said later that Cawood had said words to the effect that he had shot Ding. Evidence of this particular animal came before coroner Denis Barritt, though not the attack on Amanda Cranwell, which was not on record at the time. Cawood told Barritt that there had been a troublesome dingo, called "Ding" born at Ayers Rock, that had been a nuisance all its life. It had had a habit of going into motel rooms and tearing the furniture, as well as taking possessions. He had shot Ding on 23rd June 1980 and this was confirmed by his wife and a contemporary diary note. A number of people who gave evidence said they had not seen Ding after 23rd June. But in that period, June, July and August, there were seven recorded incidents in which dingoes had harassed children. It was enough for rangers to put up notices in the toilet blocks at the campsite warning tourists not to feed dingoes and seeking permission and ammunition to cull them.

The injunction not to feed dingoes was an attempt to discourage them from coming near people, but there was a dangerous side-effect. Les Harris, president of the Australian Dingo Foundation, an organisation dedicated to upgrading the image of the dingo from that of pest and scavenger and seeking public understanding, was to say that this sudden reduction of a good source created hunger in the dingoes, even more critical at a time they were feeding their puppies. Harold Schultz, of Blenheim via Laidley in Queensland, was to tell Tipple years later that a few weeks before Azaria disappeared, he and his wife had visited Ayers Rock. "We were amazed to see how close the dingoes came to people trying to get food, they appeared to be very hungry," Shultz said. "I warned a tourist who was trying to put her hand on one which made a rush on her trying to bite. I have been in the country all my life, born 67 years ago, and have had a lot to do with our wild life and their habits. The dingoes here would not come near people. You have a job to see them in the bush. That is why most people think a dingo would not take a baby. People who have not been there don't know the situation at that time at Ayers Rock. The way those dingoes hang around the camping area, that dingo knew the baby was in the tent and took its chances when the tent flap was open to go in."

On 16th August, the night before Azaria disappeared, Lorraine Beatrice Hunter, a tourist from New South Wales, at Ayers Rock with her family, saw a dingo attack her son, Jason. According to her later sworn evidence, she heard him screaming and saw a dingo standing over him. She charged at the dingo and the dingo had been slow getting away. That same night, Judith West, a tourist from Esperance in Western Australia, saw a dingo pull at the arm of her 12-year old daughter, Catherine, who had cried. Judith had intervened and the dingo had run away. She had also hunted a dingo away when it pulled at clothes on her clothes line. Greg Lowe, a Tasmanian tourist was at the campsite with his wife, Sally, just before Lindy raised the alarm, said he had seen a dingo at the outside of the barbecue area and had told his daughter, Chantelle, not to pat it because it might be dangerous.

Not all these accounts were known at the time Denis Barritt took evidence, but there was enough for him to form a view that the dingo was a prime suspect. He also had evidence from Judith West and her husband Bill that they had heard a dingo growl a few minutes before Lindy raised the alarm. He had evidence before him of dingo prints found outside the tent, and marks on a sand hill indicating that a dingo had been dragging something, which it had put down briefly, apparently to change its grip, and left an imprint on the sand consistent with the fabric of a baby's jumpsuit. There was plenty of evidence to support a dingo attack, together with the total lack of evidence that anything else could have happened.

Some people were not satisfied and inquired further. There were serious questions as to whether there had been a dingo at all, and if something else had in fact happened. Now, in September 1981, that safeguard, being the finding of a competent coroner, was failing. The entire case that there had been a dingo attack which had cost baby Azaria her life was unravelling.

Stuart Tipple had a difficult path to negotiate. There were many obstacles in his way, the first being the Northern Territory. The Territory was very much the wild frontier of Australia, where everything was from time to time extreme and the resources for coping were limited. The Territory had an interior so dry that a stranded traveler might die of thirst. It had a "Top End" so wet that a stranded traveler might be drowned, or die of hunger. Even those in more temperate regions were affected by the changes of season. There were only two seasons in the Top End: Wet and Dry. In the change of seasons, when the air was pregnant with heat and moisture, there was a greater incidence of domestic violence. The Top End had had the devastating cyclone in 1974. The Territory was Australia's front line in world conflict. Darwin had been heavily bombed by the Japanese and the area was still wide open to any invader from the north. And there were the crocodiles, box jellyfish and taipans.

The Aboriginal people were more concentrated in the Top End than anywhere else in Australia. Many were closer to the way they had always lived than Aboriginals elsewhere. There was an ugly history of racial confrontation and the deprivation of land and culture had reduced others to the status of demoralized fringe-dwellers. That was reflected in incarceration rates. Some of the more vulgar whites would joke that the best way to solve the Aboriginal problem was to put a whole lot of them into the back of a truck with a flagon of red wine and a dozen machetes, and leave them to it. On one occasion in Alice Springs, someone placed a bottle of alcohol in the grounds of the John Flynn Memorial Church where Aborigines congregated to drink. The alcohol was laced with arsenic and an Aboriginal woman died.

On 20th July 1980, at Ti Tree, 200 kilometres north of Alice Springs, two police officers forced a car containing eight Aborigines to stop, on suspicion that the driver was highly intoxicated. A scuffle developed. One police officer opened fire, killing one of the occupants and seriously wounding another. Five of the surviving Aborigines were then charged with serious offences and one of the police officers went on trial for murder and serious wounding. Media reporting of the incident so angered local police that an ABC reporter, Terry Price, complained that he was being tailed wherever he went. Price rang the inspector and said that if the tail on him was not removed, there would be a national story that he was being harassed. The inspector got the message. The police officer who fired the shots was acquitted but because of the emotion that had been aroused, the trial of the five Aborigines was transferred from Alice Springs to Darwin.

The Northern Territory had originally been administered from South Australia and the state continued a close association with the Territory. The Commonwealth assumed responsibility in 1910. The Commonwealth amended the legislation in 1947 to allow the Territory to have its first Legislative Council. The council was replaced in 1974 by an elected Legislative Assembly. Paul Everingham had been a solicitor in Alice Springs and had worked closely with Ian Barker, then practising in the Northern Territory, and Brian Martin, also a lawyer. The three knew each other, had mutual respect and were all to become involved in the Chamberlain case. Everingham had served on the Alice Springs Town Council, won a seat in the new assembly and in 1977 became leader of the National Liberal Party. In July 1978, when the Commonwealth granted the Territory self-government, Everingham became the Chief Minister. A passionate advocate for the Territory, Everingham pushed for many things, including a university. If the Territory were to be regarded as a side issue in national politics, it was not going to be for lack of effort on his part. The Territory was not going to be dictated to on how to run its affairs, conduct its police operations or run its judicial system.

The next obstacle Tipple confronted was what might be called anthropocentric arrogance, the feeling that we are masters of everything around us and that animals recognise that. The refusal of so many to accept the dingo story can be written down at least in part to this attitude. Far beyond the rest of the animal world in intellectual capacity, humans have always tended to regard themselves as not only above their fellow species, but in command of them. There is even a biblical injunction, in Genesis 1, verse 28: "And God said to them, 'be fruitful and multiply and fill the earth and subdue it, and have dominion over the fish of the sea and over the birds of the heavens and over every living thing that moves on the earth'." They were at the beck and call of Man, or otherwise allowed to follow their own lives, unless those lives and activities brought them into conflict with Man, who would then hunt them away or kill them. The Thylacine came into conflict in Van Diemen's Land, so it was eliminated. Children were brought up to regard all animals and their interests as subordinate to the interests of Man. Who has not seen a tiny child presume to exert authority over a dog which outweighs it and could, if so inclined, kill the child?

There is sometimes a shock when the seemingly docile animal retaliates. Often it is because of a basic misunderstanding or disregard of the psychology of the animal. A good-hearted person thinks it inappropriate for the dog to eat something it has in its jaws and tries to remove the item, then gets bitten. A mother living in Mt Colah, north of Sydney, was to write to Tipple: "When ordinary domestic dogs, jealous household pets, savage or kill babies, as has happened often enough in Australia – why be so disbelieving when a wild dingo does the same?"

This anthropocentricity has extended to dealing with animals far bigger and more dangerous. We see in the film, *Jurassic Park*, how actor Wayne Knight's character got lost on a rainy night, encountered a dinosaur and tried to sweet-talk it: "No food on me!" Of course, from the dinosaur's point of view, he *was* food. A tourist in Yellowstone National Park in the United States fed a grizzly bear and, deciding the bear had had enough, withdrew the food and said: "Sorry, feller, that's enough!" The bear thought otherwise and the man was seriously injured. At an Australian circus, a handler gave an elephant a treat and had more of it in her hand but decided to keep it till later. The elephant reached out with its trunk to get it and the handler moved it away. After a few unsuccessful attempts, the elephant drew its trunk back and with a mighty jerk of the head and trunk knocked over and killed the handler – "removing the obstacle", an animal psychologist said – and thereby solving the problem. When it came to the case of a dingo allegedly snatching a tiny baby from its crib in the central Australian desert, hearing and smelling a tiny mammal in a vulnerable position, the reaction of so many Australians was: "Oh no, a dingo would not do *that!*"

This disinclination to accept the dingo story was the background upon which the reinvestigation was mounted. Initially it was led by the evidence of a forensic odontologist, Dr Kenneth Ayelsbury Brown. He told Denis Barritt that he did not think the damage to the baby's clothing was caused by canine dentition and was more likely caused by deliberate cutting. Brown's evidence had been rejected by Barritt on the grounds that Brown did not have experience of bite marks through clothing. Brown denied that he felt humiliated by Barritt's finding and wanted to pursue the investigation because of that. However, he did take the jumpsuit, with the permission of the Northern Territory police, to the eminent British forensic pathologist Professor James Malcolm Cameron, of the London Hospital Medical College. To be fair to Brown, there might have been some disdain at the coroner's remarks but he was a professional dissatisfied that a problem had not been solved and he resolved to pursue it. Cameron, after an examination of the jumpsuit and examining the patterns of bleeding, ruled out a dingo attack, opting instead to advance a theory of murder. So in through that portal marched a legion of forensic scientists.

Forensic science was the third great obstacle in Tipple's way, though it should not have been. At least from the days of Sir Arthur Conan Doyle's fictional detective, it had become the essential tool of criminal investigation. People could lie and dissemble but traces left behind at the scene of the crime, or carried from that scene, could not be denied. So many crimes had been solved using that science. A tiny spot of blood the killer had not cleaned from the murder scene, a hair follicle that should not have been there, a footprint, a trace of paint, all could point to the offender. The Locard Principle had it that when any two objects collided, microscopic particles would be transferred from one to the other. It became much harder for a criminal, even if he or she ensured there were no witnesses, to be confident that no physical traces remained that could link that person to the crime.

Forensic science could also be used to prove the negative. It was not the suspect's blood at the scene. It was not the suspect's fingerprints. The footprints did not match the suspect's shoe size. If an innocent person is accused, then forensic science should be relied on to prove that innocence. That, accordingly, was the third safeguard. The problem was that this safeguard could fail under the impact of flawed science or incompetent or biased practitioners. Forensic science was not infallible, and when scientific evidence was the mainstay of a prosecution, in the absence of convincing primary evidence, there was danger.

In practice, in almost all successful prosecutions, the scientific evidence backed up primary evidence. When heart transplant pioneer Victor Chang, was shot dead in 1991 during an abduction attempt, one of the would-be abductors had helped police considerably by dropping his wallet at the scene. Other inquiries pieced together the story, but what sealed it was the transfer of paint between Chang's Mercedes and the offenders' vehicle, which the offenders had used to stage a minor accident to get Chang to stop. When Sef Gonzales, a student, murdered his family in Sydney in 2001 and painted "Fuck Off Asians KKK" in blue paint on a wall of the house, to turn suspicion elsewhere, a faint smear of blue paint was deposited on his jumper. There was other evidence to convict him. The blue paint was just another piece, to wit strong evidence. Scientific evidence can play a vital role when police have a great deal of evidence but just cannot get the piece that seals it. In Crows Nest on Sydney's north shore in 1983, John Robert Adams gave a lift to an intoxicated Mary Louise Wallace. His story was that they had had sex in the car, he had then gone to sleep and when he woke, she was gone. She was never seen again. Adams maintained his innocence for decades, but in 2013, police founds strands of hair in the boot of his car which could be linked to Mary Wallace. That confirmed what police had always thought, that he had killed her and put her body in the boot of his car. The hairs had remained even though it was on record that Adams had been seen carefully cleaning his car soon after Wallace disappeared. Adams was charged with murder and in 2017 he was convicted.

Popular television series, such as *Crime Scene Investigation* focus on the seeming infallibility of forensic science. Television's Detective Columbo burrowing away at what has been left behind seems to always get his man. Such has been the enthusiasm for forensic science that juries have sometimes been inclined to overlook deficiencies in primary evidence, questions of motive and whatever else, and rely on the what they see as cold, hard facts, or supposed facts, coming from scientific observation. In the London Hospital Medical College, Professor James Cameron told his students the forensic laboratory was the "Temple of Truth". Tipple said later: "The way I see it is that people are quite willing to accept that other people make mistakes. However, they see every bit of scientific evidence as infallible. It is a big problem. What people don't realise is that even fingerprint evidence is subjective."

Occasions when convictions obtained largely on scientific evidence had left people unsettled and there were convictions that had been, or were to be, overturned because of changing views on the scientific evidence. On 15th September 1964, a hotel waiter, Alexander McLeod-Lindsay, returned home in Sylvania, in southern Sydney, in the early hours to find his wife, Pamela, and son, Bruce, had been savagely assaulted by someone wielding a jack pick. McLeod was charged with attempted murder because the pattern of blood spatter on the wall of his bedroom apparently matched blood spatter on his jacket. McLeod-Lindsay said the blood had got there when he picked his wife up. He was convicted, though there was no evidence of motive, and the sighting of him that night by work colleagues, together with his seemingly untroubled demeanor at work, suggested he was totally innocent. McLeod-Lindsay was sentenced to 18 years gaol for attempted murder. There were protests about the conviction but McLeod-Lindsay failed in his appeals. He was released on parole in 1973 and set out to rebuild his life as best he could.

In Adelaide, a spray-painter, Edward Charles Splatt, was convicted of the murder of Rosa Amelia Simper, 77, killed violently in her home in the early hours of 3rd December 1977, because trace elements such as paint, metal and timber fragments found at the home matched trace elements found at Splatt's home and on his clothes. The case had some worrying problems. There was no primary evidence, no apparent motive, no evidence that Splatt even knew Rosa Simper, and no evidence that he had tendency towards violent homicide. The police, at the start of their investigation, had only the trace elements to work on. They decided that the obvious source of the paint and metal fragments was a structural steel manufacturing factory, W.E. Wilson and Sons, Pty Ltd, diagonally opposite Simper's house. In their investigation of W.E. Wilson employees, police singled out men who worked at the factory, did a forensic search of their homes and settled on Splatt, where it was alleged there were so many trace elements matching those in Simper's home it had to be Splatt. On 24th September 1978, Splatt was convicted and sentenced to life imprisonment. His appeals failed and police said proudly that it was "all done on forensics". One of the forensic investigators, was Sergeant 1st Class Barry Cocks, of the South Australian Police Technical Services Division, was to become involved in the Chamberlain case. But as at September 1981, there was a challenge to Splatt's conviction, led by an Adelaide *Advertiser* journalist, Stewart Cockburn, whose articles the previous May had annoyed officialdom and prompted a review of the case, led by the very man who had been the prosecutor, and together with a colleague from the SA Law Society, had rejected the need for a review. However, that was not going to be the end of the matter.

James Malcolm Cameron, on whose opinion the entire Chamberlain inquiry would reopen, was a graduate of Glasgow University. He had joined the London Hospital Medical College in 1963. Cameron was described as having an "extraordinary insight into casework" and a "low threshold of suspicion when confronted with sudden death". He was unafraid to speak his mind. In the 1960s and 1970s he took those qualities into what had been regarded as "taboo" areas of forensic medicine, child abuse. He was co-author of a paper on battered children in 1975, *Guide to Baby Battering*, which had been circulated to hospital staff, instructing them how to recognise signs of baby battering. It became a standard text. When it came to offences against children, naturally the community was outraged, even the prison community who would usually exact their own revenge, and the forensic scientist who exposed the perpetrator tended to be a hero.

Cameron had developed forensic techniques which had brought him fame because of his ability to crack cases that might have escaped traditional investigative work. In 1977, he had worked on the case of a murder victim whose head and hands had been removed. Working on what was left, he identified the victim through the curvature of the spine, and as a result, two men were convicted of murder and sentenced to life imprisonment. In the late 1970s, according to author Colin Evans in his book, *A Question of Evidence*, the British Society for the Turin Shroud invited Cameron to examine the shroud. In his report, Cameron said: "The image of the face is of one who has suffered death by crucifixion." He found "deep bruising of the shoulder blades, indicating the angle at which the beam of the Cross might have been carried" and the scourge marks on the body would be "consistent with the flagrum, a short-handed Roman whip with pellets of lead or bone attached to its thongs …The image indicates to me that its owner – whoever it might have been – died on the cross, and was in a state of rigor when placed in it". Cameron did pull back from saying that this was definitely evidence that it had been the shroud of Christ. How was it possible that so much could be read into stains on a piece of cloth which was at least centuries old, if not millennia? One theory was that the Turin Shroud was a medieval forgery, in which the vague Christ-like image had been painted. But he was proud of his interpretation of the Shroud. Was Cameron even then showing a tendency to go well beyond the bounds of what he could reasonably deduce?

Serious problems relating to forensic science had arisen in Britain when forensic science gurus were shown to be all too fallible. Sir Bernard Spilsbury (1877 – 1947) had been a profoundly influential British forensic scientist. His authority filled the courtroom. Regarded as a virtuoso in the witness box, he was skilled in persuading juries of his viewpoint. Knighted in early 1923, he had been approved by the Home Office and had lectured in pathology at the London Hospital Medical College, which was to become the base for James Cameron. However, he became dogmatic and inflexible, conveying the impression that he was infallible, and causing concern within the judiciary. Doubts were being expressed publicly by 1925, and later these doubts were emphasized and the opinion was expressed in some of the major cases in which he was involved that his unwillingness to engage in academic research or peer review, might mean there was sufficient doubt as to produce an acquittal. His domination of the courtroom threw doubts on the jury system.

Further material was to come to light that Cameron himself had had a significant failure. In October 1975, the Appeal Court in Britain quashed the convictions of a youth and two boys for the murder of a homosexual prostitute, Maxwell Confait. Confait's body had been found after a fire in a house in Catford, in south-east London, in April 1972. The three were gaoled, the youth for life, one of the boys for four years and the other detained under the *Mental Health Act*. But it became clear in later inquiries there were large discrepancies in the evidence that convicted them. The three had allegedly confessed to the crime, never a good look for someone claiming to have been wrongly convicted. In the light of the facts that became known, it did not appear possible for them to have carried out the killings at the time alleged. Cameron, it turned out, had not taken a rectal temperature which would have put Confait's death two days earlier than stated. It also transpired that Cameron had failed to notice discolouration of the abdomen, which should have indicated to him that the victim had been dead for some days. There was a degree of *rigor mortis* at the time Cameron examined the body. He had said the fire had sped up the onset of *rigor mortis*. But in fact, there had been *rigor mortis* for some time, and it was just starting to wear off.

At the very time of the renewed investigation into the disappearance of Azaria, attention had been focused in Britain on the case of one John Preece, convicted in 1973 of rape and murder of an Aberdeen housewife, Helen Will. Evidence against Preece had been given by a forensic pathologist, Dr Alan Clift. Preece had examined blood and semen, hair and fibres. There was no evidence that Preece had ever met the victim. But science, it was thought, had the answer. Clift had analysed a semen stain on Helen Will's underwear and concluded that the killer had been a blood group A secretor. A secretor was someone who secretes detectable levels of their blood in their bodily fluids such as saliva and semen, which allows their blood group to be analysed from such stains. But what Dr Clift did not mention was that the victim had the same blood group, and with that to work on – DNA technology then being in the future – it was not possible to say that the blood, and for that matter the semen, came from Preece. When this came out at Preece's appeal in March 1981, Preece, who had spent eight years in gaol, was exonerated and Clift condemned. Three hundred and thirty cases where his evidence had sent people to gaol were then reviewed and Clift hustled off into early retirement.

Cameron's report, in which he advanced a theory that Azaria had been murdered, would turn out to be another in this stream of disastrous forensic investigations. It destroyed the safeguard of the coroner's finding and had it held would have stopped the looming disaster in its tracks. For the Chamberlains, some of the pieces that would condemn them were locking into place. But there were still safeguards to go.

The announcement of the reinvestigation of the baby's death unlocked the feelings of the mob. When the reinvestigation of Azaria's death was announced, many Australians were already skeptical about the dingo story. Some were not ready to give them any benefit of the doubt. There was belligerence provoked to a large extent by perceptions of the Chamberlains and their religious faith. There were those who, seeing a couple at a disadvantage, were ready to leap upon them. This might be called the "yobbo mentality", which is a worldwide phenomenon, the outlook of loutish, uncultivated people, who sneer at and ridicule things beyond their comprehension. They join in a mob mentality and seek out a publicly available target. This is present in varying degrees in many people. It can be seen in any school yard in the country, where a pupil who is a little "different", and uncompetitive, is singled out for abuse and bullying. It can be seen in attitudes towards migrants. The Seventh-day Adventist Church was not widely understood. There was a widespread feeling that it was just a cult and it was often confused with Jehovah's Witnesses. "There was a survey done about attitudes towards religion," Tipple said. "I was shocked to find that some people thought Adventists wore special underpants." More ominous suggestions had it that the SDA's practised black magic, even child sacrifice. None of that was true, but it was difficult to dispel.

When Lindy Chamberlain cried out in the central Australian desert on 17th August 1980, that "a dingo's got my baby", then appeared on television with Michael seeming strange and distant, even cold, that was enough to set tongues wagging. Their faith was not readily understood, nothing about them, not even the name they had chosen for their daughter, added up. Denis Barritt was aware of that, and took pains to telecast his finding, itself unprecedented, in order to quell such rumour and innuendo forever. The televised finding had the opposite effect. It appears to have humiliated the NT Police, the NT Government, individuals such as Kenneth Brown, and the Northern Territory as a whole. It appears to have filled the NT Government and police, ~~northern Territory Government and police~~ with a determination to continue the investigation. When the renewed inquiry was publicly announced, the mob applauded.

When Stuart Tipple, a New Zealand boy who had settled to life as a provincial Australian solicitor, took this case on, he looked immediately, as any lawyer would, to the safeguards still in place. The police reinvestigating the case might have found the original explanation was correct after all. Or they could have found insufficient evidence of foul play. The forensic scientists engaged by the Crown similarly might not have come up with seemingly incriminating evidence. If there were to be another inquest, the view the new coroner might take was potentially another safeguard. There were many safeguards still ahead, including a possible jury and appeals courts. If the Chamberlains were innocent – and Tipple was sure they were – then that had to come out somewhere along the line. Tipple was entitled to have some confidence and optimism.

Tipple's experience was relatively limited as might be expected of any young professional only six years out from training. Although hardly a babe in the wilderness, he had no idea that all the safeguards in place ahead of him were going to fail, one by one, and that Lindy was going to be rushed headlong into a life sentence for murder and Michael convicted of a related crime. To unravel this mess was going to take much of his remaining professional life. Where, in the normal course of things, he would have led a successful practice in Gosford New South Wales and enjoyed a peaceful life, he was to be plunged into the national, even international battleground and be forced onto the ropes where he would have to contend, not only with flawed operations which put his clients at such disadvantage but also with sustained attacks on himself from his clients' supporters for supposedly failing them. Many tears were to be shed, including some of his own.

CHAPTER TWO

FROM PROVINCIAL NEW ZEALAND

"

When we are children we seldom think of the future. This innocence leaves us free to enjoy ourselves as few adults can. The day we fret about the future is the day we leave our childhood behind.
— *Patrick Rothfuss*

Stuart Tipple and Michael and Lindy Chamberlain were all innocents: New Zealand-born, Seventh-day Adventists and churchgoers. They were to encounter each other, and that experience, which would take up the prime of life for all of them and leave them badly affected by a world that had taken away that innocence and left them wounded. Nothing that any of them had ever done had brought upon them what was going to happen. They might each have thought as the crisis deepened, how good it would have been to have returned to their lives in provincial New Zealand and start again. However, the harshness of life was set to descend on them before they ever left New Zealand.

It might be said, if we were to probe a little deeper, that there were other, more subtle, undercurrents in their lives that in some strange way brought them together. Both Stuart Tipple and Michael Chamberlain saw tragic, premature deaths in their families when they were very young, followed by grieving and a search for spiritual rejuvenation. Stuart lost his father through complications from an asthma attack when he was 13 years old, Michael his brother, Geoffrey, though illness when Michael was only seven. Even Lindy, though not having tragedy in her early life, had it in her family history. Her mother, Avis Murchison, was only four years old when her father died and in her early teens when she lost her mother. This obliged Avis to become housemother to two brothers and it might have left her with a strident, authoritarian streak, passed on to Lindy. Both Tipple's parents belonged to the Seventh-day Adventist (SDA) Church. Michael's mother, Greta, brought up a Baptist, converted to Seventh-day Adventism following family trauma. Michael turned to Adventism because of another traumatic experience.

Lindy's father, Cliff Murchison, was an SDA pastor. The church was established in Australia in January 1886, when 29 members met in Melbourne. It was established in New Zealand in October 1887 at Ponsonby, an inner suburb of Auckland. That year, Ellen White, an SDA pioneer from America, co-founded Avondale College, Cooranbong, as the "Avondale School for Christian Workers". Cooranbong, in the Lake Macquarie hinterland, was on flat, rather marshy countryside, idyllic in some ways but rather isolated, perhaps a good place for a spiritual retreat and contemplation but hardly outward-looking, though the trainees were to go out into the world. The college's primary purpose was to train missionaries and school teachers to move out into other parts of Australia, New Zealand the South Pacific rim and sow the seeds of its education and health message in the context of "apocalypse now".

The SDA church, a New World church coming so lately onto the scene in Australia and New Zealand, after Old World Christian churches had established themselves, made headway as a revivalist movement. The SDAs preached the imminent Second Coming and the need for Humanity to be prepared for it. They were to live good lives, abstain from alcohol, preferably practise vegetarianism, observe the moral principles of their Christian faith, keep physically fit and turn themselves out neatly. The SDA Church stuck to the letter of the biblical text by observing the Saturday Sabbath, a point where the mainstream churches differed, saying the SDAs were taking the Fourth Commandment about observing the Sabbath to an extreme and it did not matter when the Sabbath fell.

Stuart Graeme Holden Tipple was born at Blenheim, on New Zealand's South Island, in 1952, a third-generation New Zealander. His grandfather, John Tipple, an Anglican, had fought with the British Army in the Battle of the Somme, showing great proficiency as a sniper. In 1924, John migrated from Suffolk to New Zealand and took up employment as a builder. John Tipple's wife died when his son, Frank, was very small. John brought up his two children by himself. Hearing about a new principal, sporting a Master's degree, coming to the local SDA school at Papanui in suburban Christchurch, he sent Frank there. Frank finished his schooling and then went to Longburn College, an SDA establishment at Palmerston North on New Zealand's North Island. At this time, Frank decided to become a Seventh-day Adventist. He met his wife-to-be, Margaret Gardener, a Seventh-day Adventist and a direct descendant of the great Scottish Reformation theologian, John Knox. The couple fell in love and they were married in Wellington. A son, John, was born in 1948, followed by Stuart in 1952, David in 1955, Trudi in 1958 and Barbara in 1964.

The Tipple family moved to Christchurch where Frank, not confident that the building trade he was engaged in could give him a steady income, decided to study for a Master's degree in Education. The years Frank spent studying were difficult for the family because everyone had to be quiet at night while Frank studied. Frank graduated in 1961, joined the Education Department and was posted to Fairlie in rural New Zealand, near Lake Tekapo, looking out on New Zealand's Southern Alps. Being the only Seventh-day Adventist family in town, the Tipples were looked at a little askance, but the family came to love the Fairlie community and because the family lived on a rural property, Stuart took quickly to the outdoor life. He also took a fancy to table tennis. The family didn't have a table tennis table so his father set Stuart up a small table the father had used to help with his wallpapering. Because the table was small, Stuart had to acquire faster reflexes, and that enabled him to win the Fairlie junior table tennis championship.

After two years, Frank Tipple was transferred back to Christchurch, where the family settled in the suburb of Papanui. The fifth child, Barbara, was born in 1964. Frank became Geography master at Avonside Girls' High. Stuart went to the Papanui SDA Church where, at the age of 11, he met Peter Chamberlain, younger brother of Michael, who was about the same age, and they struck up a friendship. Stuart was invited to the Chamberlains' farm where Stuart met 21-year-old Michael. Stuart saw that Michael, a very presentable young man, was doted on and pampered by his mother. Stuart and Peter began hunting ducks, rabbits, hares and deer.

Michael Leigh Chamberlain was born in Christchurch, on the South Island of New Zealand, on 27th February 1944. His great-grandfather, William Chamberlain, had built one of the local Methodist churches and had, reportedly, raised a militia in New Zealand to send people to fight in the Boer War. Michael's father, Ivan Chamberlain, was a warrant officer at the time, serving as a pilot instructor in the Royal New Zealand Air Force. Ivan married Greta and after the war took to farming and served as a Methodist Church trustee. Michael, their first-born, was given the middle name "Leigh" probably in memory of Samuel Leigh, the great Methodist missionary.

Michael was brought up an 81-hectare farm on the Canterbury Plains outside Christchurch. He had ill health as a child, surviving a bout of tuberculosis. He had a younger brother, Geoffrey, born with *spina bifida*, who died in 1951. Michael was to write: "I was too young to understand. I just saw the tragic consequences of my mother Greta's spiritual struggle to keep Geoffrey alive. She was searching for an answer: What's wrong with us? Why is this happening? Why is an innocent struck down? (These were questions I too had cause to answer later in life). My mother was a very religious Baptist woman. In her quest for hope, mother attended all sorts of spiritual experiences, some weren't Christian. My father didn't want to know about my mother's spiritual search. I don't think he knew how to deal with it. It was too painful. My mother even went inadvertently to a spiritualist who used charms, pendants and pendulums, hoping they could somehow save Geoffrey."

Peter Chamberlain was born in 1952, and life resumed. Even that – a child born replacing one who had died – was to be repeated in Michael's life. In the meantime, Michael went to Lincoln High School in Christchurch, where he became a prefect and represented the school in athletics, Rugby Union, tennis and cricket and was the captain of the 1st X1. Michael finished his schooling at Christchurch Boys' High School and in 1963, he enrolled at Canterbury University in a Science degree, thinking he might become an industrial chemist.

Greta Chamberlain in her quest for spiritual fulfilment settled on Seventh-day Adventism and took Michael and Peter with her to the SDA church. In 1963, Michael suffered a serious motorcycle accident. He was counselled by an SDA pastor. During his convalescence, he thought about the serious issues in life and as a result decided to convert from Methodism to Seventh-day Adventism. He completed a second year of his Science degree in 1964 and then in 1965, at the age of 21, elected to become an SDA pastor and to travel to Australia and study theology at Avondale College.

At the time Michael Chamberlain embraced Adventism, the SDA church was changing. As author Lowell Tarling was to observe, the church was then seven or eight generations old and was "growing up". It had dropped its sectarian characteristics and was becoming a proper denomination. Michael Chamberlain was to point out in his book, *Beyond Azaria, Black Light/White Light*, that in the mid-1950s two American protestant theologians had concluded that the SDA Church was not a cult at all. The problem was – and this was to come out later – the Seventh-day Adventists were still regarded as separate and to some extent exclusive; they were right, others were wrong, they would achieve salvation, others would not.

The problem facing Adventists was further compounded by the fact that they tended to stay with their own kind. Tipple said: "Most Adventists live their lives in a bubble. They are born SDAs, they go to SDA schools and many of them end up working for the SDA church. The thing about Catholics is they are encouraged to go down to the pub and have a few beers." But that was the life Michael Chamberlain had decided for himself. He went into it with his eyes open.

Stuart Tipple and his brothers helped Frank in his building work which he undertook during school holidays. Frank converted a property into flats and had half-completed the renovations of the family home when in December 1965 he died suddenly. Margaret, with five children, including a baby, was hard-pressed. Stuart remembers how the local SDA community moved in and began a project to finish the renovations of the family home. With Frank's life insurance payout and income from leasing of the flats, the family was able to get by. And in the long, hard road ahead of her, Margaret became more spiritual. "She told me that when Dad died, she made a covenant with God," Stuart said. "She asked God to become father of her fatherless children." Stuart for his own part made a decision that he would "never ask Mother for a dollar". He earned his own pocket money by delivering groceries by bicycle.

Stuart Tipple and Peter Chamberlain continued to get on well. Peter said: "We could talk freely with each other and often with different points of view. Yes, we argued but never in anger. We soon became great mates. Stuart was an honest clean-mouthed friend, and was there to back you up when needed in argument or fight. We were baptized into the Adventist Church at the same ceremony." Stuart was without a male mentor or role model, so he learned to be self-sufficient, though Margaret kept the family on an even keel. Peter said: "Margaret enjoyed finding out what you thought, or how you ticked. She never would harp on your bad points, but would soon give her shilling's worth if you questioned her better judgement. I respected Margaret, a special person and having to bring those Tipple boys and girls up single-handedly and with a baby in arms still. I admired her guts.

"It wasn't easy for the family to lose a dad so young or suddenly. My mother Greta was more of a follower, while Margaret was her own person, and I feel this helped this family to seek out the vocation they preferred in life. One of Stuart's better points in life, was he waited and listened before he spoke. I was the opposite. I knew I was no saint like Stuart. He was a great mate in my early youth and probably helped me stay on the straight-and-narrow more than I helped him. Yes, we enjoyed duck hunting on the farm, social rugby and a little deer recovery to make a bob or two. We met some outdoor hardships together but were able to laugh about them later."

Stuart Tipple finished his schooling at Shirley Boys High School but felt no inclination to do Law. He believed that a prerequisite for Law was Latin and because he had not studied Latin, he did not consider it as a possibility. Awarded a bursary to do teacher-training, he decided to follow his father into Education. When he went to enrol at Canterbury University in Christchurch, he discovered that Latin was no longer a prerequisite. He enrolled in Law. It meant he lost his bursary and to get himself through, he realised he would have to work part-time. His first job was cleaning windows. He made extra money shooting with Peter and selling deer carcasses to butchers. Then he did a tradesman's course and worked as a drain-layer's labourer, installing stormwater and sewerage pipes. "He worked hard for his extra dosh," Peter said. "Often, I'd see him come home covered in dirt from drain laying for Stan Brown, our social Rugby coach."

At Avondale College, Michael Chamberlain, having a better time of it, living a clean, healthy life and studying theology, became friendly with another theology student, Phil Ward. "I quite respected Phil – he was a highly creative preacher," Michael said in *Beyond Azaria*. "His sermons were completely different, out of left field."

On 4th March 1948, Alice Lynne "Lindy" Murchison was born in Whakatane, on the North Island of New Zealand, daughter of an SDA pastor, Cliff Murchison, and Avis. Lindy's paternal origins were in the Isle of Skye off Scotland. Her great grandfather, Malcolm Murchison, arrived in Australia in 1852 with wife Flora and an infant son, Alister, and settled in Geelong, Victoria. Flora ran the toll booth gate in Geelong. Alister died very young but their next child, Alexander Murchison, took to the land and set up sawmills and creameries in Victoria. He married Isadora Kate Marr, of Irish convict stock who was the proprietor of the Post Office Tea Rooms and Accommodation in Hobart. The couple settled in the Otway Ranges where Alexander started pioneer farming. Alexander was heavily involved in the Victorian Conservation Commission.

The Murchisons had a son, Clifford, or Cliff. They lived next door to another Cliff, Cliff Young, who became his friend and would become known throughout Australia for his long distance running in gum boots. When Cliff Murchison was very young, he accepted Christianity and decided to become a Seventh-day Adventist, the first in his family to do so. He also decided, in his teens, to become an SDA pastor. He left home and worked in rural Victoria selling books door-to-door to raise the money to go to Avondale College. He worked in

Melbourne for a short time. Cliff was at Avondale College from 1933 till 1938. He worked in the college dairy during the terms and eventually got permission to start a local milk round, on foot, with the excess milk that had formerly been thrown away. His enterprise was so successful that the college bought a horse and cart to expand the service.

In 1939, Cliff Murchison was posted as an SDA pastor to Christchurch in the South Island of New Zealand. He met Avis Hann, a New Zealand-born girl with English-German-Spanish heritage, who came from Stratford on New Zealand's North Island. They married on 15th October 1941. A son, Alexander, was born on 20th August 1942 at Rotorua. Lindy arrived in 1948. She was 20 months old when the family settled in Victoria in 1949. Both Alexander and Lindy were brought up as Seventh-day Adventists. Alexander went to school in Melbourne. "Lindy started school when we were in South Gippsland," Alex said. "She was a happy, cheerful creature but I found out that when I teased her even at an early age, she would stand up for herself."

Cliff Murchison continued at various appointments around Victoria. At one of those postings, at Benalla, Lindy went to High school with and subsequently dated Alex Gazik, who went on to Avondale College to study theology. Cliff Murchison's pastoral travels took him north of the border, to Broken Hill in New South Wales. At Avondale College, Michael shared a room with Alex Gazik, who was still dating Lindy Murchison and had put up a large colour photo of her on the wall. Alex consistently "promoted" Lindy to Michael as someone he should meet. Michael said: "I gave in, accepting his word on a fateful hitch-hiking race to Broken Hill." Soon afterwards Lindy and Alex broke up. Michael visited again the next year with Lindy's cousin. Everything else followed. "Lindy and I fell in love, and I courted her by letter," Michael said. "We spent 19 full days together before we got married, such was the insulation of college life." Michael graduated in 1969 and married Lindy at the SDA church in Wahroonga on Sydney's North Shore. Michael was posted to Tasmania, where he was very active in the community and wrote radio scripts. A son, Aidan, was born in 1973. Michael was ordained as a pastor just before they were transferred to North Queensland around Christmas 1974.

Phil Ward graduated in Theology and showed aptitude during his college years. He did not become a pastor but instead began work as a TV news camera man and started a publication, *Small Business Letter*, which was successful. He used his skill as a camera man by taking a film of Michael and Lindy's wedding which he edited and gave to them as a wedding gift. It is necessary to mention Phil here because he was to loom much larger in the lives of Michael and Lindy at a later time.

Stuart Tipple graduated in Law in New Zealand in 1975. Setting out to work there presented difficulties. The country was, in Tipple's words, "in a pretty bad way". "I think about 40 of us graduated but there were only two positions available for articled clerks," he said. "I managed to get one of them." Tipple was accepted by the firm, Harper Pascoe and Company, in Christchurch, unusual in that he was "an Adventist boy when everyone else in the firm had been to Christ's College". Stuart pointed out to a senior partner that he was the only lawyer the firm had ever employed who had not been to Christ's College. The partner thought long and hard before replying: "That is not right. In 1942, we employed someone who had been to St Andrew's, the Presbyterian College."

That same year, Michael, with Lindy and Aidan in tow, was posted to North Queensland as an SDA pastor. Reagan was born in Bowen on 16th April 1976. From 1977, Chamberlain ran a radio program, called *The Good Life*, on two radio stations in North Queensland. He also wrote columns for the *Cairns Post*, and he took no pay for his columns.

Tipple was admitted as a solicitor of the Supreme Court of New Zealand in 1976. But by then he was looking further afield. He decided to go to Australia because his girlfriend had gone there. He arrived in Sydney in February 1976 and found employment as an administrative assistant at the Sydney University Law School. He also lectured part-time in Law at an institute for the Commonwealth Department of Foreign Affairs. From there, he joined the NSW Public Solicitors' Office, in Bent Street, Sydney, and was assigned to the Indictable Section, dealing with serious crime, such as murder, manslaughter, robbery, rapes and serious assault.

Tipple was learning the criminal law from the bottom up. Being a Public Solicitor made him a "poor relation" in the legal establishment, but the work was far from boring. He went to Katingal, the maximum-security prison at Long Bay Gaol, to consult with Russell "Mad Dog" Cox. A week after Tipple took instructions from him, Cox thought a more expedient way than waiting for a court appearance was to escape. His escape from Katingal was one of the more famous of the state's gaol breaks. "In Katingal, they would let you out for exercise so many hours a day," Tipple said. "The only area not under surveillance was behind the door that opened out into the exercise yard. It was a cage. He had obtained a hacksaw blade and every time he went through the door, he jumped up and sawed at a bar. On the day he escaped, he cut right through the bar, got up and out. They shot at him." The matter was mentioned in court the following week and Tipple remembers telling the judge, Justice Yeldham: "I was having difficulty getting instructions."

Tipple also took instructions from James Edward "Jockey" Smith, who was a notorious bank robber and prison escapee, who was alleged to have shot at and tried to murder police officers. Smith had complained loud and hard about what he claimed was police corruption. "This case of Jockey Smith was a watershed moment for me," Tipple said. "He was not a violent criminal, before he was labelled Public Enemy No 1. When I went to see him in Parramatta Gaol, I thought I was about to see this big, tough criminal. Instead I met this small man who sobbed about police corruption and how he had been fitted up." According to Tipple, Smith claimed the police had said, 'We will get you, you little bastard'." When Tipple got into Smith's case, he realised that the case against him was "full of holes". "Smith had been identified by a police officer in court but he had failed to identify him from wanted posters in his police station," Tipple said. "I saw this was dodgy. This identification evidence should not have been admitted." When Tipple tried to speak to the Senior Public Defender, Howard Purnell, about it, Purnell was still inclined to write him off as Public Enemy No 1. This was a significant moment in Tipple's development as a lawyer. Sure, the criminals are cunning and deceptive, and to meet that the police have to develop cunning themselves. There is a tendency for them, and the prosecutors, to stray beyond the bounds of professional objectivity.

There comes a point where the prospect of conviction/acquittal becomes a contest between individuals. Years later, Lindy Chamberlain would tell Tipple a police officer had told her: "We'll get you, if not this time, we'll get you next time."

Tipple persisted in his advocacy for Smith. Whatever Tipple might have thought of him privately, Smith had rights. "You have to look at this case!" Tipple told him. Tipple persuaded Purnell there was merit in what he had to say. Purnell took up the case and Smith was acquitted, and it was another lesson for Tipple. "We had a wonderful win," Tipple said. "Smith's convictions for the shooting of a police officer, Jeremiah Ambrose, and the murder of bookmaker Lloyd Tidmarsh, were overturned. I realised then that no matter how skilled and experienced your barrister is, even a junior solicitor can have influence."

In his work with Purnell, Tipple was appearing in the High Court and the Court of Criminal Appeal two days a week. In one case, he worked with the then Public Defender, Michael Adams, with whom he was to have later acquaintance. Tipple became involved in a case where an osteopath, Petronius-Kuff, had gone with a friend to Ron Hodgson Motors and produced a cheque as payment for a Jaguar car they drove off in. Kuff asked the dealer to hold the cheque because the money was still coming through. They later gave the dealer another cheque, which bounced. Kuff was charged with obtaining property through false pretences. Adams and Tipple argued that under the terms of the contract, Kuff never would never have gained legal ownership of the car until he had paid for it, and because Kuff didn't pay for it, he was not guilty. The court decided obtaining possession of the car was enough and Kuff was convicted. "If they are against you, they are against you," Tipple said later. "If a court decides your client is the bad guy and undeserving, it's very difficult to win, no matter how good your legal arguments are."

During his two years with the Public Solicitor's Office, Tipple visited his sister, Trudi, who was working at the Sydney Adventist Hospital, "The San", in Wahroonga. During one of those visits, he chanced upon another nurse "a beautiful girl", Cherie Kersting, whom he asked out. One night, about to go to a law lecture, Tipple suggested Cherie should look for an engagement ring. "She had found one by the time I got out of my law lecture," he said. After they were engaged Cherie graduated from her nursing course and moved to Melbourne to live with her parents. She began modelling and her agency urged her to enter the Miss World competition. Cherie decided not to because it would have delayed their wedding plans. The agency persuaded another model in their agency to enter and that girl went on to become the Miss World runner up. Stuart and Cherie married at the St John's Uniting Church at Wahroonga on 5th December 1978.

As a married man, Tipple found the demands on his time exacting. He was constantly in court or going to prisons. His clients were for the main part, as legendary Sydney solicitor Bruce Miles put it, "the hopeless and the helpless", and the nastiness of what he had to deal with started to wear. "What finished me was having to take instructions from a man who had killed a woman and had not told anyone about it so he could keep getting Social Security benefits," Tipple said. "I saw these awful crime scene photographs and then had to interview this man, who happened to be suffering from tertiary syphilis. That was not the romantic criminal law that as a young lawyer you like to imagine. I thought there had to be better ways." When he was on his honeymoon, Tipple saw a position advertised for a solicitor with Hickson Lakeman & Holcombe, a Sydney law firm, and applied for it.

Accepted by the firm, Tipple did general litigation work, acting most of the time for insurance companies. By now he was conscious of financial pressures. House prices in Sydney were rapidly rising and he feared, though he was now getting a professional salary, that he and Cherie might not be able to afford a home. So, where else could he go? Way out in the backblocks of the state? Or somewhere near to Sydney where the prices were lower. He looked to Gosford, where he had recently appreared in court. The Central Coast, which was a developing area and had good prospects, suited him and he bought a home in 1979. A friend sent him an ad by the Gosford law firm, Brennan and Blair, which was seeking a solicitor. He got the job and, as he realised, started at the bottom, "doing all the work nobody else wanted to do".

The Chamberlains in north Queensland were living a full pastoral life. Michael went jogging every morning, it being the ethos of Seventh-day Adventists to be physically fit. Michael's other great interest was photography. He carried a camera in a bag beneath his legs as he was driving, so he could whip the camera out at any moment. He was broadcasting and writing a column on health and fitness in the *Cairns Post*. On 17th June 1979, 15 kilometres south of Port Douglas on the North Queensland coast, Michael and Lindy Chamberlain picked up an accident victim, Keyth Lenehan, bleeding from lacerations to the skull. They put him into the car through the back. According to Lindy, he was lying with his feet in the hatch area of the car, with his shoulders on Lindy's lap, and his head between the two front passengers' seats. The blood might have flowed down between the two seats. Michael drove to Cairns Hospital where Lenehan was taken in as a patient. It was obviously a Christian thing to do, and which anyone with a sense of humanity would have done. Lenehan's blood might well have run down the side of the passenger's seat and onto the floor, where it would remain as dried flakes.

In January 1980 Michael Chamberlain was posted to Mt Isa in western Queensland to be the SDA pastor. Michael continued his writing on health, religion and community for the *Mt Isa* Star. Azaria was born on 11th June 1980, the family decided on a holiday to the Northern Territory, including a stopover at Ayers Rock. They took their holiday in August 1980, when temperatures in the Australia inland were cooler, and tragedy struck at Ayers Rock, when Azaria, nine weeks and four days old, was reportedly snatched for the family tent by a dingo. A police investigation followed, then the first coroner's inquest, which confirmed a dingo had taken the baby. After Stuart Tipple and Michael Chamberlain met on the Wyong street in September 1981, the three individuals – Michael, Lindy and Stuart – all fine, upstanding individuals who had nothing to answer for, came together and would, in essence, be locked together for forever after. Total innocents who had all the vitality and health of a New Zealand upbringing, nurtured in Christian households, they were to spend a major portion of their remaining lives unscrambling a mess they were not responsible for, but which had been created by the muddle, incompetence, bigotry and inflexibility of others.

CHAPTER THREE

THE DINGO POUNCES

"

I hear your laughter in the night
Enjoy it while you can
The party's just got under way
Laugh awhile white man
You weren't invited to this place
My heart is one huge stone
But if you stay and eat and drink
Don't leave that child alone

My spirit rises with the dusk
As it has done before
And when I come and take and steal
I'll leave you ripped and raw
You'll never laugh like this again
My mark is stamped right through
And anyone with any heart
Will share your pain with you

I hear your sad knock on my door
I open it with shame
Welcome to the desert
Michael is your name
The evil bone is pointed now
The spirit has been sent
Wait beside the fireside
My thief is in your tent

– Lowell Tarling

The Chamberlain family arrived in Mt Isa in January 1980, and were only meant to stay there for 12 months. The plan was that the family would then move to Victoria where Michael would receive training in various aspects of the church's health ministry. Mt Isa was a wealthy mining town founded after the discovery of one of the world's richest deposits of copper, lead and zinc in 1923. Mining had been extensive, enormous wealth acquired, and as with all mining towns, the debris of mining, in particular copper dust, drifted across the landscape and deposited itself on every available surface. It settled onto the Chamberlain's possessions, into their house, into the yellow Holden Torana Hatchback, and into Michael Chamberlain's camera bag.

On 11th June 1980, Azaria Chantel Loren Chamberlain was born at Mt Isa Hospital. Michael was reportedly making a nuisance of himself, insisting on taking photographs in the labour ward. The name Azaria was of Hebrew origin, and it meant "Blessed of God". There was one incident, when Azaria apparently tumbled from a shopping trolley in a Mt Isa supermarket. However, a quick check with the family GP, Dr Irene Milne, showed she had not suffered any significant injury. In August 1980, the Chamberlains set off on a holiday to the Northern Territory. Michael loved the outdoors and wanted to go to the Top End. "I wanted to go to Darwin to catch barramundi," he said. "But Lindy had been to Uluru [the Aboriginal name for Ayers Rock, now in general use] before, at the age of 16, and wanted to go again. We meant to spend three days there, then go on to Darwin."

The family arrived at Ayers Rock on Saturday, 16th August 1980. The motels at the site were rudimentary but there were facilities for aircraft and radio telephones were available, even though they were unable to be operated during certain times of the day. Perhaps the white, civilized, modern people who went there, fresh from air-conditioned luxury, really did not appreciate that they were coming into a place where there were fewer safety nets. People driving into the desert might run out of petrol, be nonplussed about what to do and find themselves in a situation where death is a distinct possibility. In remote areas, people with medical conditions could not just call for an ambulance. Someone bitten by a snake had a problem. Further north the problem was much the same. An out-of-towner found an inviting pool of water in the vast northern flatlands and plunged in, realising only in the last seconds of his life that he has chosen the domain of a crocodile. His body was later taken from inside the crocodile, in nine chunks. The Aboriginal people, so often disregarded, had a collective wisdom which had ensured their survival over millennia. But how many visitors referred to it?

The Chamberlains spent Sunday exploring the Ayers Rock area, during which Michael took the famous photograph of Lindy holding Azaria on the side of the rock. Michael and Lindy were in the camping area on the Sunday evening talking to two Tasmanian tourists, Greg and Sally Lowe, Lindy holding Azaria in her arms. Sally said later: "One of the few things that stands out in my mind after we were introduced to Lindy was, we asked what the baby's name was. (Something I usually do to give you an idea if it's a girl or boy – sometimes saved offending proud mums). The baby's name was offered and so on. About this time Lindy had said how they had hoped for a girl and were so happy when the baby was a girl. The conversation stayed on babies for a while. Although we love Chantelle [Greg and Sally's child], Greg and I wanted a boy. I think some mention was made of this. As I have some memory of Mike or Lindy saying something like – boys are easy, it's harder to try for a girl (as though girls were special because of that). Our conversation went on to bushwalking, Tasmania and New Zealand and then on to Greg's studies. Greg and Mike were talking about study at the time of Lindy's return to the barbecue. Being more or less left out of the conversation, my ears were free."

As they talked a dingo surprised them by leaping out of the darkness and grasping a mouse near their feet.

Greg Lowe, in a letter to Tipple a long time later, said he had offered Michael Chamberlain a beer which Chamberlain had declined, on the grounds he did not drink alcohol. "Lindy then offered the information that 'a drinker doesn't realise the effect it has on the family, that he ought to think not only the possible injury to his health but the effect this would have on his wife and children's future'. (I think she disapproved of my casual attitude to beer-drinking)," he said. "This does indicate that she was concerned with future family health and welfare." In the tent next to the Chamberlains' tent, Bill and Judith West, a couple from Esperance in Western Australia, heard a canine growl which they took to be from a dingo, perhaps the growl of an animal warning another off.

On Lindy's account she left the barbeque area with Azaria in her arms and Aidan beside her the and returned to the tent. After putting Azaria in the crib, Aidan announced he was still hungry. Lindy went to the back of the car, got a can of baked beans out and returned to the barbeque area with Aidan. A minute or so after that, Michael Chamberlain, Sally Lowe, and another camper, Gail Dawson, heard what they thought was a baby's sharp cry from the direction of the tent. When Michael remarked on it, Lindy went to the tent to have a look, and according to her account, saw a dingo come from the entrance with something in its mouth. She could not make out what it was carrying. Her first instinct was to go into the tent to check the baby. The baby was gone. She raised the cry which transformed her from a housewife to a headline: "A dingo's got my baby!"

Michael and the Lowes immediately ran to the tent. In his later account in a letter to Stuart Tipple, Greg Lowe said his wife Sally found a pool of blood – she estimated 8 by 16 square centimetres in area – on the floor of the tent. The blood was spread over articles of clothing, sleeping bags and other items. Writing to Tipple years later, Sally said: "I know there were several spots and I saw them in front of me and to the right. The immediate priority on the night, was to find the baby. Michael Chamberlain and Greg Lowe went in the direction the dingo was thought to have gone." Greg said: "Then we extended the search pattern to a grid on the whole of the sand hill area to the east of the tent and other areas. I indicated to Mike that night that if I were a dingo, I would do a circuit and wait in the bushes near the scene of the tent. We searched extensively 'close to home' in quite a large radius."

Other campers went immediately to search the sand hills, and were soon joined by rangers. A local Aboriginal elder, Nipper Winmatti, on his later account saw dingo tracks outside the tent and he followed them. He said he saw blood in the sand. "We first tracked the dingo from the back of the tent," he said. "It came around and went inside the tent." He had followed the dingo tracks towards the tiny Ayers Rock township, which comprised a collection of motels and other buildings. The dingo had apparently been carrying a burden, but the tracks had petered out in the spinifex. Others saw evidence of dingo tracks in the sand. The head park ranger at Uluru National Park, Derek Roff, went tracking that night with a local Aboriginal, Ngui Minyintiri. They followed the tracks and drag marks for 15 metres before losing them, then traced them back to a point 17 metres from the tent and in direct line with the tent. He had backtracked to within 12 metres of the road running beside the camp site.

The Chamberlains stayed near the tent in the freezing cold for several hours waiting for news. About midnight they were persuaded to go to a nearby motel. A local police officer and the camp nurse, Bobby Downs, helped them transfer clothing and bedding from the tent into the car and the police four-wheel drive vehicle before driving them to the motel. Greg Lowe told Tipple later that they might have unwittingly transferred some of the spilled blood onto their clothing. The tent remained as they had left it. Greg Lowe posed the question in a letter to Tipple much later: "Could any of these blood-stained articles ... and effects account for any alleged traces of ... blood in the car, especially if they were bundled into the car before the Chamberlains left for the motel?"

Word went out nationally that a baby had been taken by a dingo at Ayers Rock. Reporters scrambled to get there. People scratched their heads and wondered. A dingo?

On the Sunday morning, a motel employee at Ayers Rock, Elizabeth Prell, took breakfast to the Chamberlains. She later said she saw a blood stain on a sleeping bag that had been removed from the tent. The stain was "about three inches" in diameter. At Ayers Rock, Aboriginal trackers scoured the area further out from Ayers Rock. They found dingo tracks at the base of Ayers Rock, then argued among themselves about their significance. Tracks made by the searchers on the night and next day complicated things. At the tent, there seemed much clearer evidence that the dingo had been there. Constable Frank Morris, the police constable stationed at Ayers Rock, found dingo tracks along the tent. He also saw paw prints when he lifted the bottom edge of the tent where it had ballooned out near where the bassinet stood.

Two police officers who arrived from Alice Springs, Inspector Michael Gilroy and Sergeant John Lincoln found paw prints immediately behind the tent together with a wet patch in the sand which they thought might have been saliva. They took photographs and a sample of the wet sand but the photos did not turn out and the wet sand was never properly tested. Gilroy looked carefully at the baby's bassinet and found animal hairs which he thought might be dingo hairs. A camper, Murray Haby, found an impression in a sand dune near the camping area which appeared to him to have been made when a dingo put something down. He showed it to Derek Roff. The imprint on the sand reminded Roff of crepe bandage or, as he said later in evidence, "very consistent with elastic band sort of material". It was a perfect description of the material of the jumpsuit Azaria was wearing.

That, surely, should have been enough. A dingo had been there. As in all police investigations, the first thing to look for is what the perpetrator has left behind. In this case it was tracks, the drag mark and the imprint of fabric on the sand. That in combination with, the dingo growl, the baby's cry and Lindy's report of seeing a dingo, should have been enough. Of course, in the initial period, it was. The principal objective now was to find the baby – or more probably its remains – and, if possible, the dingo.

Word was now well and truly out. Lindy's parents, Cliff and Avis Murchison, were retired and living in Nowra on the NSW south coast. Alex Murchison was working for Shoalhaven Shire Council, as it then was, laying sewerage pipes, when his foreman approached and told him the news.

At Ayers Rock, the searching continued all Monday, during which Michael was at pains to get black-and-white photographic film so he could take pictures for a newspaper that had contacted him. His actions were, he said later, to warn people what might happen, but some people even in those early stages were mystified by his actions, wondering about his priorities. On the Tuesday, Aboriginal trackers followed dingo tracks for six kilometres from the campsite into sand hill country but found it doubled back and then the tracks became lost near the reservoir at the township. That day, Michael and Lindy Chamberlain, left for Mt Isa. There were still people searching and their decision to leave raised eyebrows. Michael and Lindy had decided there was no hope of finding the baby alive. Michael Chamberlain, having a traumatised family, decided his priority now was to look after them.

In the meantime, police packaged up the Chamberlains' tent and its contents and put them in a cardboard box to be taken to Darwin for scientific examination. It was, in retrospect, a clumsy way of handling evidence, some of which, like any blood spray on the tent wall, was fragile, hard to see and easily destroyed. It must also be taken into account that all this had happened in a remote area. Distance was difficult. Communications were difficult. The radio telephone cut out for several hours each day. At that stage there was only the vaguest thought that one of the family might have been responsible for the child's death, but the second safeguard, the expertise and professionalism of investigating police, was starting to fail.

The Chamberlain family arrived at Mt Isa and was now the centre of attention. Lindy's parents, Cliff and Avis Murchison, and Lindy's brother, Alex Murchison, went to Mt Isa. Alex said: "I remember mum held up the space blanket and there were muddy paw-prints on it. I could see the tiny pin-holes of light shining through where the dingo's claws had gone through the space blanket. There was mud on the paw prints, the soil was still caked on."

At Mt Isa, the gossip and rumour-mongering had begun. Members of the local SDA Church rallied around the Chamberlains. Lindy was also consoled by a close friend, Jennifer Ransom, and told her that she would be reunited with her baby in Eternity. According to Mrs Ransom, Lindy said: "I know that if I am true to the Lord for the rest of my life, she will be back in my arms as pure and beautiful as when I put her down to sleep". A dry-cleaner at Mt Isa, Jennifer Prell, said Michael Chamberlain had brought in a sleeping bag which had "seven or eight" stains on it and had said he wanted it cleaned. The stains, potentially, constituted more evidence that blood had been spilled in the tent.

The Chamberlains' tent arrived in Darwin at the bottom of a cardboard box on Thursday 21st August. The box was handed to Myra Fogarty, a police officer who had had three months' experience in forensic work but no formal training. Her superior, Sergeant Bruce Sandry, told her to look for hair and blood. Fogarty unpacked the box and examined it. She was not told about any blood spray on the tent wall and did not see it. She assumed she was looking for human hairs and plucked some of her hair out to use as a control. She did not do any "lifting", using adhesive tape to pick up what particles there might have been on surfaces in and on the tent. What she did say when she made her report was that there was less blood than she would have expected had there been a dingo attack. That was a careless comment on her part. It carried a number of assumptions, principally that the dingo would have torn the baby's flesh and tossed it around in its jaws, spilling blood. If a dingo had snatched a baby in the way it apparently did, it would more likely to have been quick, a second or two. The baby would then have been whisked away by the dingo. Its teeth would all probability have occluded the blood in the wounds, preventing much of it from spilling. Her comment about expecting more blood was to rebound on her.

The next development came on Sunday, 24th August, when a tourist, Wallace Victor Goodwin, found Azaria's jumpsuit, singlet and nappy at the base of Ayers Rock, 3.5 kilometres from the campsite. It was 20 metres from a dingo lair, though at the time not even the rangers knew the lair was there. There was no sign of the body. Goodwin reported the find to Constable Frank Morris. Morris, moved the clothing before photographing it to see whether there was anything inside it. In hindsight, a lot of controversy would have been avoided if the area had been sealed off and everything photographed before it was touched or moved. Morris must surely have wished he had done that. To be fair to him, the suggestion there had been a murder was a long way off. After examining the clothing, Morris laid it out in the way he thought he had found it. Goodwin did not agree with the way Morris did it. He said the description of the clothing, "neatly folded", was not accurate. Morris claimed the jumpsuit was basically open except for a couple of studs at the bottom which he undid. Goodwin heard

Morris ask Roff whether there were other dingo lairs in the area and Roff had said there were three. The second safeguard, preserving scientific evidence of a dingo attack, was failing.

Back in Mt Isa, Michael and Lindy Chamberlain started to hear the first poisonous talk about them, which was to rise to a crescendo. There were stories floating around that the SDA church practised black magic, or child sacrifice. The national mood itself became darker when on 29th August, Dr Eric Milne, brother of Lindy Chamberlain's doctor, Dr Irene Mile, rang the police and told them that "Azaria" meant "Sacrifice in the Wilderness". It was enough for the NT Police to send Constable Jim Metcalf, to the Mitchell Library in Sydney to research the meaning of the name. He came up with nothing but the rumour persisted.

The stories kept coming – that Azaria had been kidnapped by Aboriginals, or for that matter aliens. One extraordinary story was that Lindy had spear-tackled Azaria in the Mt Isa Supermarket, that a blood transfusion had been ordered on the baby and the Chamberlains had refused because the SDA church did not believe in blood transfusions, and that the baby had died and the dingo attack at Ayers Rock had been a charade, with SDA accomplices at Ayers Rock to back up her story. There was not a scrap of truth in this, though Azaria had had a tumble from a shopping trolley. The Chamberlains were at a disadvantage because of their religion. When questioned on television about the supposedly neat state of the baby's clothing, Lindy said: "If you've ever seen a dingo eat, there's no difficulty at all. They never eat the skin. They use their feet like hands and pull back the skin as they go – just like peeling an orange."

If only she had not said that! It caused audiences across the nation to recoil, at the supposedly clinical way in which she spoke about her lost baby. What Lindy said was accurate enough. Anyone who has ever owned a dog would know that dogs do not eat like pigs. They are quite delicate, even fastidious, eaters. But such was the developing hysteria that Lindy's remarks did not go down well. There were other suggestions being put about, that the mother had done away with the baby, that it had been buried in the sand, dug up and reburied, and the jumpsuit placed near where dingoes were known to be. The Chamberlains were not helped by the findings of David Torlach, an agricultural scientist, called by the police to analyse soils at Ayers Rock to find the source of sand found in the jumpsuit. He found that soil in the campsite area had the same acidity as sand in Azaria's jumpsuit and was different from the sand at the base of Ayers Rock.

The rumours escalated. When Malcolm Brown, as a reporter on the *Sydney*

Morning Herald, rang Lindy at Mt Isa on 3rd September 1980, Michael had resumed his ministerial duties and was on a four-day conference for SDA ministers at Townsville. She said Aidan had come home crying from school, after receiving cruel jibes from other children. A friend's phone had been "running hot" with unsympathetic inquirers. "The latest rumour going around is that my husband has been charged with murder, and that the baby was a sacrifice for our religion," she said. "People say this memorial we want put up to Azaria at Ayers Rock is part of this sacrifice thing." When she went shopping, and was unrecognised, she heard the gossip. "They're liking the case with the Jonestown massacre and with the Spear Creek murders at Mt Isa 12 months ago," she said. "I think three people were killed then. We were not even in Mt Isa. People say Azaria was sickly. They even say she was spastic. She wasn't." In October 1980, police conducted an interview with Aidan Chamberlain at Mt Isa. While they were doing that, Constable Barry Graham searched the Chamberlains' car using a Big Jim torch. He reported: "I examined the interior of the vehicle, including the front and rear sections, seats, console, dashboard, glove compartment and hood. I did not find any suspicious staining in those areas." He later admitted that he was also looking for a possible weapon and found none, not even scissors. His report would not be disclosed till years later. Neither the Chamberlain's nor their legal team were told of this search until the Royal Commission years later.

Michael and Lindy Chamberlain gave statements on 1st and 2nd October. On 15th December, represented by an Alice Springs solicitor, Peter Dean, and later Phil Rice QC, from Adelaide, they appeared at the coroner's inquest before Denis Barritt. Barritt was a genial 54-year-old former Victorian detective, then barrister, who had come to the Northern Territory 2-1/2 years before as a magistrate and coroner. He was from several perspectives the right man for the job. He had taken pains to educate himself in traditional Aboriginal law and culture. Interviewed by Malcolm Brown, he said that on one occasion an Aboriginal youth had stolen a car in Alice Springs and driven out towards an outstation in the desert. When he was a long way out, he had heard a noise in the back seat, had a look and found a little boy had been sleeping there. The youth brought the boy back to Alice Springs. He tried to get away but was caught. Barritt said: "The rules of the bench prevented me from stepping down and hugging that young man! He could have just ditched the boy somewhere. But he did the right thing." Barritt did not say what penalty he had imposed for illegal use of the car, but it would probably have been a good behaviour bond, possibly with no conviction recorded. Barritt had a similar common-sense view towards the evidence that was now presented to him.

Appearing in the witness box, Lindy Chamberlain was well aware of rumours and suggestions that she had been involved in the baby's death. She told Ashley Macknay, counsel assisting the coroner, that she could not entertain a scenario other than a dingo taking the baby. She said: "To consider that it was done with something other than a dingo brings in such a range of coincidences with split second timing that it seems impossible." Greg and Sally Lowe gave evidence of what they had seen and heard, all exculpatory of the Chamberlains. Bill and Judith West gave evidence of hearing a dingo growl before Lindy raised the alarm.

Six-year-old Aidan Chamberlain's statement totally supported the account his mother gave. He said he had been with his mother during the entire period from Lindy Chamberlain being at the barbecue area with Azaria and the moment she had raised the alarm. He said: "While we were in the tent, mummy put bubby in the cot and then I went to the car with mummy and she got some baked beans. I followed her down to the barbecue area. When we got to the barbecue area mummy opened the tin of baked beans and daddy said, 'Is that bubby crying?' and mummy said, 'I don't think so'. Mummy went back to the tent and said, 'A dingo's got my baby!'."

All the evidence was pointing to a dingo attack. Aidan's evidence, together with that of Sally Lowe, provided a barrier to any suggestion that there had been foul play. But the ugly rumours would not go away, and the yobbo mentality had been stirred. When the inquest resumed on 9th February 1981, after the Christmas break, it was decided, in the light of a number of anonymous telephone threats that had been made against the Chamberlains, that they should have a bodyguard. The man assigned to the task, Constable Frank Gibson, might have been under instructions to pick up anything about the Chamberlains that could be used in evidence. Whether that was true or not, Gibson became very positive in his attitude towards the couple. Others never became positive. The fact that the Chamberlains were "different" became the focus of national attention. Pastor Wal Taylor, the SDA Church's legal liaison officer, said: "Had this involved the Methodist or Baptist Churches, there may not have been the same misunderstanding. There are the mainstream and fringe churches and many people have tended to put us on the fringe."

In the resumed inquest, the focus was on scientific evidence. From the start, the Chamberlains were at a disadvantage. A South Australian forensic biologist, Andrew Scott, confirmed there been a spray of blood on the tent wall. That was critical evidence that the baby had been attacked in the tent. By the time Scott tested the area he failed to get a positive result, possibly because the material had been affected by the waterproofing compound in the tent wall. Scott concluded that it was probably not human blood.

Other evidence potentially raised suspicion. Rex Kuchel, a forensic botanist from Adelaide, a part-time scientific adviser to the South Australian Police, had examined sand and vegetation embedded in the jumpsuit. He had been looking for pulled threads which he expected had an object covered in the jumpsuit material been dragged through vegetation. Rather, he thought, the jumpsuit – presumably with the baby's body in it – had been buried in sand hills east of the campsite, then dug up and carried to where it was found at the base of Ayers Rock. In his experimentation, he had arranged for an effigy of a baby to be dressed in a jumpsuit and dragged through vegetation at Ayers Rock. The result, he said, was quite different. It was pointed out by Ashley Macknay that he had made his observations taken from pictures by a professional photographer rather than direct observation. There had been damage to the undergrowth by the person dragging the effigy. But he had not been on the spot and had not been able to determine what other people had been through that area.

Kuchel agreed under questioning that wild animals, and even domestic animals, sometimes buried their prey. But if the clothing was buried, where? Dr Barry Collins from the Minerals Department of South Australia said that 90 percent of the soil found on the baby's clothing was consistent with the soil found at the site of the Chamberlains' tent and 10 percent from the area round Ayers Rock. That seemed to support the burial theory. Had a dingo done the burying? Or had it been done, for whatever reason, by a person or persons? Sergeant Barry Cocks, of the South Australian Police, fresh from his involvement in the Edward Charles Splatt case, gave evidence supporting human intervention. From ruptures in the jumpsuit, he had concluded that a "bladed instrument", a knife perhaps, or a pair of scissors, had been used. Kenneth Brown said he had examined the clothing and also examined dingo skulls and had concluded that a dingo's teeth could not have done the damage to the baby's clothing. So that laid it squarely on the line that there had been human intervention. Had it been someone at Ayers Rock? Or had it been the parents? And if so, why? Was it to fabricate evidence of a dingo attack?

A dingo expert, Dr Eric Newsome, senior researcher at the CSIRO Wildlife Research Division, said it was unlikely a dingo would have taken the baby but he did not discount the possibility. He said crows or eagles could have taken the clothing to where it was found at the base of Ayers Rock. That left open the possibility that a dingo had taken the baby but that person or persons had intervened afterwards. Another possibility, never brought up, was that in the week since Azaria disappeared and when the clothing was found at the base of Ayers Rock, an animal might have got at it and moved it of its own accord. Nevertheless, Macknay was not persuaded by much of the scientific evidence. In his submissions to Barritt on 19th February, he was particularly critical of the evidence of both Kuchel, Cocks and Brown, according to a report of proceedings by the *Sydney Morning Herald*. "What has happened, I submit, is that [they] were in pursuit of finding points to support the theory that no dingo had any part to play in this," he said. The three rejected that suggestion, maintaining that at all times they were professionally objective.

Denis Barritt, satisfied that the baby was dead and that she had been taken by a dingo, decided that the issues raised by the suspicion and gossip surrounding the case should be addressed. He abided by a request from a television crew to telecast his findings nationally. Appearing before an international audience on 20th February 1981, he said neither of the parents, or for that matter their two sons, had had anything to do with the baby's death, but there had been "human intervention" in relation to the damage to the clothing and the way it was handled and deposited after the dingo took the baby. Barritt accepted the primary evidence that a dingo had been responsible. He did not find the scientific evidence to the contrary convincing. Of Kenneth Brown's evidence, that a dingo had not caused the damage to the jumpsuit, he said Brown had admitted he did not have expertise in bite marks made on clothing, so it would be "dangerous to accept his evidence in that regard".

Barritt was severely critical of the police, whom he believed had been biased in their investigation, a bias fuelled by a disbelief in Lindy's story. He was particularly harsh on Myra Fogarty, whose evidence on finding less blood than might be expected from a dingo attack had been in his view a tacit attempt to advance the murder theory. Constable Fogarty had not been taught the principles of scientific observation and had been given a critical examination which was beyond her competence. Supervision in the section, Barritt said, had been "negligent in the extreme". Sergeant Sandry, he said, appeared sceptical of the dingo theory when he interviewed dingo experts, according to a report of the finding in the *Sydney Morning Herald*. Sandry and Fogarty had, like Morris, not appreciated just how critical what they did would become. In different circumstances their performance would not have been remarked on at all. In professional terms, they were in the wrong place at the wrong time. But Barritt was adamant that the police should have done better. "Police forces must realise, or be made to realise, that courts will not tolerate any standard less than complete objectivity from anyone claiming to be making scientific observations," he said.

These deficiencies in the police investigation had compounded the problems of the Chamberlains who had been subjected to "probably the most malicious gossip ever witnessed in this country". Barritt said he had had advice from a Hebrew expert that "Azaria" meant "With the Help of God", and that the name for "Sacrifice in the Wilderness" was similar-sounding but different. Another meaning for Azaria given at the inquest said it meant "Blessed of God". The confusion probably arose because directly under the definition of "Azaria" was "Azazel", which meant "Devil", "Bearer of Sins", or the name of a demon in the wilderness to whom a goat was sent.

Barritt said the NT Parks and Wildlife Service had a responsibility to protect human life, particularly in circumstances where there had already been dingo attacks on children. The service had a responsibility to protect children coming into national parks and where there were dangerous animals, they should be eliminated from parks or at least those parts where there was a high frequency of visitors. He acknowledged that the service had a responsibility to preserve wildlife. If there were laws forbidding the destruction of particular wildlife, then the inherent danger of these creatures should be publicised. The death of a baby, he said, was a high price to pay for conservation. And that, it seemed, was that. The safeguard, of the balanced, objective look of an experienced coroner, had worked.

Michael and Lindy Chamberlain emerged from the courthouse and displayed an enlarged picture of Lindy holding Azaria, then returned, it was hoped, to resume their lives as an SDA pastor and wife. Azaria's death certificate registered at Alice Springs on 6th March 1981 read: "Inquest held 20 February 1981 D.J. Barritt, Coroner. Severe crushing to the base of the skull and neck and lacerations to the throat and neck."

In Gosford, Stuart Tipple had followed the case with intense interest. He was aware of the rumours that there had been foul play. He did not think Michael would have done anything like that, or been party to it in any way. It was with "a feeling of great relief", he said later, that he heard Barritt's finding which exonerated the parents.

Of course, the inquiry was not over. If, as Barritt said, there had been human intervention, then who was it? The person or persons responsible could face several charges: of interfering with a corpse, unauthorised burial and failure to report a death. It was a matter for the police to answer that unsolved question. The NT police held onto the jumpsuit and other exhibits from the inquest. A senior police officer at Alice Springs said, quite justifiably: "The hearing can be reopened in the future if fresh information comes to light." There were other factors too. The NT Police had their noses totally out-of-joint. The NT Conservation Commission did not like his remarks either. The NT Government appeared anxious to demonstrate it could handle its affairs as well as anybody else. The case acquired a political significance which it would never have had the same event occurred in New South Wales, Victoria or any other states. Cases like the Ananda Marga prosecutions or the Blackburn case in New South Wales, or the Cessna-Milner case which involved allegations of improper conduct, had embarrassed the governments but had hardly threatened their hold on power.

In Darwin, Myra Fogarty resigned from the NT Police Force. In Adelaide, Kenneth Brown wanted to continue the inquiry. He later denied that he had felt humiliated and wanted to vindicate himself, and to be fair the criticism of him was not damning. It was just a point made from the bench about one corner of his professional expertise, but it was stated in front of an international audience. He did think more could be found out, and perhaps he should seek the advice of a world authority, Professor Cameron, who had invited Kenneth Brown to work in his laboratory in 1975. It would also be possible to consult Bernard Sims, who lectured in forensic odontology at the same college, and who had written book, *Forensic Dentistry*, which had been regarded for years as an authority on the subject and which Brown himself had referred to in his work in South Australia. Brown asked the NT Government for the baby's clothes, and he received them on 27th May. He travelled to Britain with the clothing. He was going to what he might have thought was the forensic "Privy Council", the London Hospital Medical College, to have matters reviewed. The safeguard of Barritt's finding, the common-sense view of a genial worldly-wise former frontline detective, was now under threat.

CHAPTER FOUR

THE FRAME

> "
>
> *I think Beelzebub must have gone through beforehand, throwing down all these items that people might pick up and use against the Chamberlains.*
> — John Winneke QC

> *I think ... that if I had been a Catholic, showing grief like a Catholic, I probably would have had 45 percent acceptance in Australia. But because I was acculturated in to Seventh-day Adventism, expressing Seventh-day Adventist grief, I probably got only five percent acceptance out there in the community*
> — Michael Chamberlain

Despite Denis Barritt's finding in February 1981 on the disappearance and presumed death of Azaria Chamberlain, and the pains he took to put rumour and innuendo to rest for good, there was general dissatisfaction in at least part of the Australian community, and the dingo story continued to raise doubts. At an official level, the case had not been closed. Barritt had said there was "human intervention" in relation to the disposal of the clothing. The police were obliged to keep the file open and try to discover what that human intervention was.

Phil Ward, successful in his newsletter publishing business, decided the police had not done enough. To his mind the answer on the human intervention question was the key. There had been dingoes on the scene. There had been people living at Ayers Rock township. What did those people know? Ward's business newsletters, published by the Business Newsletter Group, based in Epping in north-western Sydney, were full of sometimes quick-fire but by no means valueless advice, such as in one issue he trumpeted the merits of buying off the plan in new developments. Ward had a following. He used his newsletter to support a newly-formed Australian Small Business Association. Ward would branch into a newsletter venture giving advice on health, at one point declaring there were "100 new health ideas in each issue". He also produced a newspaper, *Adventist News*, not endorsed officially by the church but purportedly telling Adventist laypeople what was really happening. The Chamberlain case was "like manna" to him, Tipple said.

As with all his other enterprises, Ward provided unrelenting drive. He told his readers there was evidence that a dingo could remove a baby's body from the clothing and leave the clothing virtually intact. The evidence, from a CSIRO scientist, was that when a dingo kills, "it peels off the skin from the head to the back feet. If it was removing a jumpsuit and singlet from a dead child, it could peel them off in the same way. This would leave the clothing largely undamaged, leave the baby's booties still inside the legs of the jumpsuit, and leave very little blood on the clothing because it had pulled the clothing over the wound on the head".

Kenneth Brown was on another tack. He gave the jumpsuit to Professor James Cameron with a briefing on what he believed were the salient points in the case. Brown said that only two press-studs had been undone on the jumpsuit when found, and the clothing had been left in a neat bundle. Cameron asked for a transcript of the inquest evidence which the NT Solicitor-General, Brian Martin QC, duly dispatched on 3rd September 1981. Cameron examined the jumpsuit blood staining. He concluded that had a dingo attacked the baby, it would not have caused bloodstaining like that. The bloodstaining was more consistent with the neck having been cut, possibly in a circumferential fashion. He believed that a dingo could not have opened its mouth wide enough to have seized a baby by the head. It would not have extracted the body leaving only two studs undone, and it would not have left the clothing in a neat bundle. He subjected staining on the jumpsuit to ultraviolet fluorescence, a very up-to-date technique, and he discerned what he believed to be three hand impressions, from a small adult.

When word got back to the NT administration that Cameron was asking serious questions about the disappearance of Azaria Chamberlain, Detective-Sergeant Graeme Charlwood was called back to take charge of the inquiry. Charlwood, a lithe, intelligent man had the reputation of a brilliant investigator.

It was said of him that if a man committed an offence in the Northern Territory, he had better not have Charlwood after him. On 27th August, Charlwood met NT Police Commissioner, Peter McAulay, for a briefing. Neither Tipple nor Michael Chamberlain knew when they met on the street in Wyong a week or so later what was going on.

On 9th September, Charlwood met Kenneth Brown. Cameron made his report on 11th September and briefed Charlwood. On 14th September 1981, Cameron met NT Chief Minister Paul Everingham and NT Solicitor-General Brian Martin in Brisbane. Cameron went through his report. He rejected the dingo theory and outlined his reasons. After the three met again the next day, Martin passed Cameron's report to an eminent Brisbane counsel, Des Sturgess, for an opinion. Sturgess, a gravelly-voiced, towering man with a quite formidable presence in court, said there was apparent substance in the report and that the inquiry should be reopened. As a result, the NT Police formed a task force for the operation, which was code-named Operation Ochre. On 17th September, Charlwood met Sydney CIB Detective Sergeant Dennis Gilligan. The two went to the Sydney magistrate, Kevin Waller, to obtain a search warrant for the Chamberlains' home at Cooranbong.

Even at that very early stage, anyone taking an independent, objective view of Cameron's report would have been entitled to ask some searching questions. Cameron might have been a brilliant pathologist, but when he wrote his report, he was 20,000 kilometres from the scene. What he was looking at was a tiny, pathetic, dirty scrap of baby's clothing, a rag which in other circumstances might have been thrown into the rubbish without a second thought. But in those grubby marks he believed he saw, as he had with the Turin Shroud, things that might have escaped anyone else. Human handprints? Bloodied ones? A Queensland bushman, Harold Schultz, was to say in a letter to Tipple a long time later that from his experience the supposed handprints were probably the pad marks of a dingo after it had seized the baby and was holding the jumpsuit in place while it extracted the body.

Some of what Brown had told Cameron was not accurate. He told Cameron only two studs had been undone but that had never been established. Nobody in the coroner's inquest had said so. When later shown a photo of the clothing found at the base of Ayers Rock – or at least the clothing as re-laid by Constable Morris – Cameron agreed that it was not in a neat bundle. There was to be considerable doubt whether Cameron could ever have made out three human hand impressions on the baby's jumpsuit. Even had there been one, what was later to emerge was that it was not even blood. It was red dust. Cameron had only assumed that it was blood. He had read what Dr. Andrew Scott had said about examining blood on the jumpsuit and from that had assumed that the supposed hand-impressions comprised blood. He had not tested to confirm that, yet his report concluded it was a bloodied handprint. "I am satisfied beyond all reasonable doubt that there is little if any evidence of involvement with the jump-suit with members of the canine family," said the good professor.

It did not stop there. Later, after examining the towel taken from the Chamberlains' car, he reported: "On the back of the towel there are additional marks that suggest blood staining, until proved otherwise". The use of the phrase, "until proved otherwise", was extraordinary. Here, he was making an assumption and putting the onus on the Chamberlains and in Lindy's case on someone facing a life sentence – to prove they were innocent. In such circumstances, a forensic scientist is not privileged to assume anything and it is dangerous to do so.

Cameron believed that the circular pattern of the blood around the top of the jumpsuit was consistent with a cut around the neck. But common sense has to prevail here as well. How can anyone say materials behave in a certain way? There is the glorious unpredictability of materials. Anybody who drops an object on the floor knows that the object, potentially, can go in any direction. NSW prosecutor Roy Ellis recalls an incident when the "Rumpole"- style Sydney lawyer, Bruce Miles, was defending a woman charged with the burning death of a toddler after there had been a fire in a caravan. An expert was called by the prosecution to indicate the path the inflammable liquid would have taken after it left the canister. "Miles suddenly jumped up, picked up a carafe of water and poured it over the bar table," Ellis said. "'They think they can tell where a liquid will flow?' Miles told the startled jury. The woman was acquitted."

Even from a layman's perspective, there could have been a number of explanations for the bloodstaining on the jumpsuit. More explanations of the blood pattern were to come. Dr James Ferris, Professor of Forensic Pathology at the University of British Colombia, was to say that the bloodstaining did not support either a dingo attack or a cut throat. Instead, he thought the blood had come from an accumulated pool and on the balance of probabilities had flowed after death.

But all that was for the future. The NT Police believed that they were probably pursuing a cunning, manipulative killer and her accomplice. They thought they had already been vindicated and poured scorn on Denis Barritt, calling him "Ding-a-ling Denis". When the police arrived at the Chamberlains' home on 18th September 1981, they presented their warrant and searched the house. Simultaneously they interviewed primary witnesses across the nation, to prevent any possibility of witnesses contacting each other to discuss what they were going to say. Lindy Chamberlain was to write later that she was driven to a police station at nearby Toronto and that, unbeknown to her at the time, Charlwood was equipped with a tape-recorder. According to Lindy, Charlwood indicated that he thought she was guilty. Charlwood later denied that, and because the tape-recorder apparently malfunctioned, it was her word against his.

In this case, the primary facts were like square pegs, the police, presented with the round hole that Cameron's report represented, were obliged to try to make them fit. There was great difficulty with this, and another way of looking at it, even then, was that Cameron was completely wrong and the primary witnesses, supporting the account of the Chamberlains, right. The authorities, however, were of the view that there was more to be discovered. In the NT Supreme Court on 20th September 1981, Justice John Toohey formally quashed the findings of Denis Barritt on the grounds of new evidence and ordered a new inquest. NT magistrate Gerry Galvin was appointed the coroner. The safeguard represented by Barritt had been brushed aside. Now they had to look to what sort of safeguard Galvin was to represent.

Dean and Tipple compiled a letter to Charlwood on 20th September: "As you know, we act for Pr. and Mrs. Chamberlain. We understand you wish to interview Pr. And Mrs. Chamberlain and to obtain their handprints. We are instructed to advise you that on legal advice, Pr. and Mrs. Chamberlain decline to give you the handprints or an interview. We are also instructed to advise that if you wish to submit to us a written list of questions for Pr. and Mrs. Chamberlain, it will be given consideration. If you wish to make contact at all with Pr and Mrs Chamberlain, please do so through the writer or Mr. Stuart Tipple ... We also understand that you have some advice from a Professor of Forensic Medicine, a Professor Cameron. We would be obliged if you would make a copy of his report available to us as soon as possible." Dean got no reply.

There were some seemingly startling discoveries in the car. Jim Metcalf, attached to the forensic section of the NT Police, felt under the dashboard and felt something "sticky to the touch". It appeared to be a spray pattern. There could be no criticism of Metcalf in doing this. He found something and reported it. It was up to others to decide what it was. The suggestion, of course, was that it was blood, and that would lead to the question of how it was deposited. And the answer to that was it had spurted. And how had it spurted? From a severed artery? The immediate objection from a lay point of view was how it could ever have been blood and to have been still there and "sticky" 13 months after the baby was allegedly killed? How long does it take blood to dry? A few minutes? That obviously depends on how much blood there is and how thick it is. But a spray of blood? Not very long at all. Five minutes? Certainly not 13 months, especially when deposited on a metal or vinyl surface and exposed to the heat of Mt Isa. It would surely have become little more than dust, and fallen off.

The spray pattern noted on the tent wall immediately after Azaria disappeared might well have resulted from a spurt of blood, but the chance to analyse it was lost. It had been missed at the forensic section in Darwin and when examined by Scott it had become too denatured to allow a proper analysis. That, as it was to transpire, was a vital piece of evidence lost, like the faint scratch marks that the dingo might have left on the space blanket of the Chamberlains' tent, subtle traces of an event that would have taken only a few seconds to be destroyed, not to mention the police photos of the paw prints around the tent that could not be developed, or the wet patch, thought to be saliva, that was never properly tested.

Samples of the spray pattern under the dashboard of the Chamberlains' car were removed by Dr Tony Jones, an NT pathologist.

When the Chamberlains learned that blood had apparently been discovered in the car, Lindy's reaction was: "Oh, they've found Keyth Lenehan's blood!" The understanding that Lenehan, the accident victim the Chamberlains had picked up two years earlier, had shed blood in the car became an accepted fact from that time on, and the entire battle between Crown and defence revolved around the question of whose blood had been found. Had Lenehan ever been in a position to shed blood in the front of the car? Yes, he might well have. According to Lindy, he had been lying with his feet pointing towards the boot of the Hatchback and his head near the front seats. From the Chamberlains' point of view, any blood found in the vicinity of the front seat was his.

Joy Kuhl had a busy workload and this was just another inquiry. The NSW Health Division of Forensic Medicine laboratory was busy. It was involved in an average of 600 crimes a year and doing anything from 20,000 to 50,000 tests. Because of the volume of work, the laboratory had adopted a policy of not keeping slides or photographs of its tests, which would have involved employing staff to ensure the records were kept and intact. Normally the word of the forensic scientist would be accepted. Joy Kuhl had given evidence many times. She was regarded as competent. She was not used to having her work seriously challenged. She felt quite up to the task of doing an analysis of the blood samples taken from the car, first confirming they were blood, then checking whether they contained foetal haemoglobin, which meant that the blood had most likely come from a baby under the age of six months.

While Joy Kuhl's investigation – on which the whole case would ultimately swing – got underway on 21st September, so did the media coverage. The media was not first to be off the mark in breaking the news, the police were. Bill Allen, then the Deputy Police Commissioner of New South Wales, told the *Herald* that the car was "full of baby's blood". The *Herald* declined to run the story on what Allen had said because it was potentially very defamatory, but other media was galloping ahead. The *Australian* reported the ultraviolet fluorescence technique Cameron had used to find three hand impressions on the jumpsuit. On 22nd September, Channel Seven announced that Cameron had done an investigation and had concluded that the baby's neck appeared to have been cut in a circumferential fashion, and that the baby might have been decapitated. It also said that there were impressions of human hands on the jumpsuit and that the baby might have been held upright as she bled to death. The genie was out of the bottle. News swept the nation that the baby had been murdered. Any hope Michael and Lindy Chamberlain had of getting a fair trial was effectively swept away. Lindy Chamberlain became a figure of evil. In Sydney, an artist painted and exhibited a series of "dark" portraits of her, including one depicting her with fangs.

There was no lack of news in the Northern Territory. On 23rd September, the *NT News*, published in Darwin, reported on Cameron's finding that "because of bloodstaining and blood patterns on the clothing, human hands were holding her as she bled on the night of her death." The same day the *NT Star* newspaper reported that Cameron's findings were backed by at least two other forensic scientists regarded highly throughout the world. Malcolm Brown contacted the *NT News* asking about the story, which was apparently hot from the lips of local police. The *NT News* reporter said police had been through the sequence of events on the night Azaria disappeared and had found there was an "eleven-minute window" when Lindy could have done it.

Many in the general public had already made up their minds. One writer said in a letter to Michael and Lindy: "Dear Sir and Madam, All Australia knows you are guilty of murder, and that you will eventually be charged, and convicted. Why not confess now, and save a lot of unnecessary Police investigation and Government expense?"

From all appearances, it was a race against time. While Tipple and Dean were scrambling to organise the defence, the public, through the media, were laying siege to the Chamberlains. On 1st October, the *Sydney Morning Herald* reported: "Pastor and Mrs Chamberlain remain at Avondale College, the Seventh-day Adventist academic, residential and health food complex in the quiet countryside round Cooranbong, near Morisset. They are very aware both of the developments in the case and the media people who wait each day outside the college gates should they decide to make a media comment. They have said they are not making any comment to the media but may do so later. All media inquiries are directed to their solicitor, Mr Stuart Tipple, of Gosford, who has consistently refused to accept them."

If Tipple was trying to do the right thing, to take the issue out of the public forum and direct it to the courtroom where it belonged, the public was not prepared to wait. Endless jokes were circulating. One had two dingoes outside the tent, deciding whether to "eat in or eat out". Another had it that to bring up a baby at Ayers Rock, all one needed to do was "kick a dingo in the guts". Still another posed the question of what an Irish dingo would do. It would eat the tent. Some theories about what happened were half-joking. Some were apparently serious. Tipple and Dean were appraised of some of them. One person told Dean that the baby had either been taken on walkabout by Aborigines in Arnhem Land or had been sold into white slavery in South-East Asia. What really threw Tipple was when he got into a Sydney taxi on his return after the Inquest was adjourned. The driver, not knowing who Tipple was, told him the latest "Azaria joke". There was a new Azaria Doll you can buy for Christmas, if you cut its head off, it says: "Mummy did it! Mummy did it!" "I was shocked. Taxi drivers are a barometer of the public opinion and it made me realize how difficult it was going to be," Tipple said.

The police and Crown law advisers were not going for way-out theories. What they were putting together was a murder scenario, where Lindy had a "window of opportunity" – a period of perhaps 11 minutes when she left the barbecue area with the baby and Aidan and committed the foul act. On their scenario, Lindy slipped into her family car and cut the baby's throat, then secreted the body, probably in the camera bag which Michael had with him at his feet on the driver's side of the car, washed the blood off her hands somehow, then returned to the barbecue area with Aidan and a can of baked beans and pretended that nothing had happened. She had then turned to go back to the tent and had claimed to have seen the dingo leaving with something in its mouth. She had then told Michael, who immediately agreed to help her cover it up. The Chamberlains were meant then to have buried the body, retrieved it at a later time and disposed of it.

In the cold light of day, it all seemed so incredible as to have been utterly unrealistic. How could a couple like this, for all the world normal and very presentable, loving parents with a family, have been even capable of doing these things? It was so contrary to the evidence of the primary witnesses. Greg Lowe, in a letter to Tipple, said that when he joined Michael Chamberlain to do a search in the immediate area of the campsite, "at no time did I see anything remotely resembling freshly-dug sand." Lowe added: "Surely a [compilation] of visual observance of both parents could be obtained for the complete period of time from the disappearance to the departure of Michael and Lindy – they must have been in view of the public at all times, whether searching, consoling each other, or generating support for the search. Same thing for the motel and next day."

But the forensic scientists were on a roll. The one concession to common sense was that there was no discernible motive. On 23rd October, an expert wrote in a letter to James Cameron: "Dear Taffy, Des Sturgess and I have continued to hold lengthy discussions about the Dingo case, and the trouble has been to come up with a motive. We have explored the possibility of the throat cutting being a *second* assault on a child already dead from an impulsive act of child abuse by a mother who is at the end of her tether. There is suggestive evidence of a previous assault on the child (the shopping trolley incident). Facts are that after a hot and tiring day, Mrs C. arrived back at the camp site, and later carried the baby to the barbecue area. Here she spoke to a Mrs Law [sic], who states she saw the baby – covered – move its leg or legs. After a while Mrs C. take the baby back to the tent and later returns to Mrs Law and Mr C. at the barbecue. Shortly Mr C. and Mrs Law hear a baby's cry – a strange cry Mrs C. says she does not hear it. Mr C. tells her to go back to the tent and see the child. This she does and very soon raises the cry –'A dingo has taken my baby!' There is confusion and a search gets under way, and over the sand hills, away from the tent, in the area where Mrs C. says she saw the dingo go. I'd like your medical opinion on medical aspects of this explanation.

"When Mrs C. returns to the tent from the BBQ on the first occasion, she attacks the baby by some form of suffocation. The child rapidly loses consciousness and leaves it for dead and returns to the BBQ. But the child is not yet dead – as we know in asphyxia, cyanosis and 'going limp' occur before death – death appears to have taken place before, in fact, it has. Incomplete obstruction to breathing need not be immediately fatal. Taylor (p33 Vol 1) says that infants tolerate suboxia [a low concentration of oxygen] better than adults. In some asphyxiation states, especially in neonates, death is delayed for a period during which secondary changes develop, especially in the C.N.S., sufficiently to precipitate death. My theory is that this 'latent' period occurred between the time Mrs C. attacked the child and the time the 'strange cry' of a child was heard by Mrs L. and Mr C. at the BBQ. The 'cry' was an inspiratory gasp, a reflex action triggered by a rise in the pCO2 and a fall in pO2 in the arterial blood – a final reflect attempt by the child to survive.

"When Mrs C. returned to the tent after the cry, she found the child dead – she also saw a dingo – (completely innocent) – and raised the now famous alarm. The subsequent actions of both Mr and Mrs C. were designed to foster the dingo theory and protect themselves. The throat cutting of a dead child is one explanation of why no spurting of blood was in evidence in the tent – just evidence of a flow of blood. The child was then placed in the C's car through the driving side door; later buried in loose sand near the tent, exhumed and disrobed, then laid to its final rest. Taffy, I cannot accept post-natal depression or schizophrenia on the part of Mrs C., nor sacrificial action on the part of both of them. I think it is was an unpremeditated act of aggression on the child, with an unfortunate result which, in panic, Mrs C. was stuck with. Their actions after the death are the only bizarre part of the deal – and are still going on. The theory is OK only if the physiology holds up. Peter McAulay will see you before you receive this letter – he leaves for an Interpol conference on Monday. Des and I write to you with the theory rather than relay it through Peter. He will be up-to-date on the Police side of it."

Prosecutions strive to find and prove a motive even though there is no legal requirement to do so. Even with their best efforts the police were never able to come up with any reason or motive as to why Lindy would have harmed Azaria.

An anonymous correspondent cut to the quick with a letter to Lindy which said: "The net is closing in, Lindy. You will not escape justice this time. Very soon you will be on trial for murder."

On 29th October 1981 Tipple received a most extraordinary letter, and perhaps it should be related in full, not because it had any grain of truth, but as an example of what one person appeared to have held as a sincere belief. A correspondent from Cremorne in Sydney suburbia said: "My conscience is pricking me with regard to the Azaria case, because I observed something in the Press about three years ago which seemed to indicate that the culprit was a lion, not a dingo. It was a photo of two cows drinking from a stream, not normally putting their head down, but by crouching for a drink, and they obviously had lions' bodies. That indicated that they were cross-bred. As regards the human hand print, a lion may have eaten a man, and the result may have been a man with golden eyes. Another indication there was a little girl of about two/three whom I saw at Circular Quay about that time, too. She had golden eyes, so I assumed she had had the experience of being taken by a lion. I think that the indications are so obvious that I am surprised that you even think of dingoes.

"And that brings up what you would think it necessary to do for prevention in the future. Seeing withholding suggestions, they do not get across, it would seem a lion-hunt would be more successful than a dingo-hunt. The caves in the western end of Ayers Rock is the most likely end that they would hole up, because the Rock seems to be approached by tourists from the southern side, judging by photos, so the west and north would be least under observation by visitors. It makes you wonder how the dingoes escape from them, too. I wish to apologise for my lateness in writing regarding this, but apparently nobody else thought along these lines, though I expected it to be discovered in the press articles at the time, and apparently no-one thought of it. Wishing you success and best wishes." The correspondent added: "By the way, I am reluctant to write letters because of nieces who like to take the credit for anything I do, and it may be the same this time. Seventeen is the house I actually live in, but people trying to contact me always speak from Nineteen, next door. The proprietors live there, and are very nice people, so do not disturb them. It just seems a scheme in my own family."

But how less laughable was all the speculation on the mental state of Lindy Chamberlain, depicting her as deranged or evil?

On 24th November, a team of NT police had arrived at Ayers Rock with picks, shovels and sifting equipment in an attempt to find the remains of Azaria Chamberlain. If Lindy Chamberlain had cut the baby's throat, she must have had blood on her and must have found a place to wash it off. The police searched the basin of the motel room the Chamberlains had stayed in on the night Azaria disappeared and checked around the sink to see whether they could find any blood, the theory being that when the couple went with their boys to the motel on the night Azaria disappeared, Lindy might have washed the blood off herself there. That day, Gerry Galvin the NT coroner nominated to conduct a second inquest, rang Dean, in response to an earlier call Dean had made. Galvin spoke about the proposed new inquest and about a media release being made through the NT Chief Minister's Office "to stop various newsagencies hounding him for information". Dean told him that he had not spoken to anyone from the NT Department of Law and the only information he had about the proposed inquest came from press releases. A QC, Phil Rice would be coming from Adelaide to make an application for an adjournment once the inquest had been formally opened.

Dean had again briefed Phil Rice. Rice, a bluff, thickset man with quick wit and ready sense of humour, seemed right for the part. Initially, Rice, meeting Tipple, thought he was "some sort of padre". Rice had all the ruggedness and earthiness an appearance in an outback court called for down to the piece of rope he used as a belt. But he was very old school and insisted on getting his instructions in writing so he knew exactly what was required. Rice said he would like a chance to interview Cameron. Dean applied to the NT Crown Law Department to do that.

On 25th November, Dean sent a telegram to NT Department of Law asking for permission to interview Professor Cameron. Peter Tiffin replied: "Prof Cameron is not presently available for interview, and I see no reason to endeavour to make him available. It is proposed that he give evidence in due course before the coroner, as will other witnesses. I see no reason to make any disclosure sooner. I consider the proper place for all evidence to be made public is before the coroner on oath. It has been decided that none of the evidence proposed to be placed before the coroner will be disclosed to anybody except those assisting the coroner."

On 26th November, Dean sent a further telegram to Egerton, Sandler & Summer, saying Rice might want to try to talk to Cameron notwithstanding the NT Government's strictures. He also asked the firm whether it could find out whether there was anyone in the world who had the same status as Cameron in forensic pathology. Dean asked whether there was any information it could find out about Cameron which would be useful in cross-examination. He also asked whether there were any new textbooks on forensic medicine available in London and whether any journals could be found that had particulars on the ultra-violet photography technique.

Egerton, Sandler & Summer contacted James Cameron, and finding he would not cooperate with an interview, it approached Professor A.K. Mant at Guy's Hospital Medical School in London to discuss Professor Cameron's report with him, and was also unsuccessful. In a telegram to Dean on 2nd December 1981, Mr G.F. Dunn, from Egerton, Sandler & Summer, said: "[Cameron] feels that a discussion with us or our expert would be useful and would be usual and permissible under UK law. But he is under instructions from NT Crown not to speak to us or our expert. He also feels that when his report findings and opinions are known to you at the inquest you will require advice from one or two experts. I infer that on cross-examination Cameron may be able to give the answers necessary for you to obtain and adjournment as in his opinion as an expert used to court work you cannot be expected to deal with his report without expert advice which you could not obtain beforehand since he could not release information as he would do formally. Mant, before we approached him, discussed Cameron's findings, report and opinions with Cameron in detail. Mant would act for us only with Cameron's agreement. However, Mant says he agreed with everything Cameron says in his report."

Dunn said he had received "non-forensic advice" that if the only physical evidence as to the way the child died was the state of the jumpsuit, then it would have to be demonstrated that it was based on one of two things: that the blood had low oxygen content, suggesting that the breathing had been obstructed in some way; that there might be traces of adult skin on the jumpsuit, left by the adult holding the baby down. Possibly, the advice was, baby could have been held down and its breathing obstructed.

Surely that was more speculation upon speculation. Dunn did not say whose speculation that was, but the idea of the baby being throttled and held down while it bled to death was both macabre and useless. Cameron's scenario had it that the baby had been held by bloodied hands. And that also was speculation. The second inquest into the disappearance and presumed death of Azaria Chamberlain was formally opened on 30th November 1981, then adjourned. On 4th December, a NSW police officer delivered a summons to Tipple's office in Gosford requiring both Chamberlains to give evidence at the inquest. The summons came with two return air tickets. According to Tipple, the officer smirked as he served the summonses and said, "the Chamberlains won't need the return tickets". Tipple went with the Chamberlains to Alice Springs on 14th December, with word going ahead of him that he was "a church lawyer". As junior counsel, Dean chose Andrew Kirkham, a lean and intense Melbourne barrister who added a touch of big city sophistication. Kirkham, meeting Tipple, had expected a little greying docile man to come through the door and got rather a shock when he saw Tipple. But he fixed Tipple with his steely blue eyes, making Tipple uncomfortably aware he was under assessment. He passed the assessment. Both Rice and Kirkham quickly realised that Tipple was good value. It was never, of course, going to be the church on trial, but such was the hysteria of the time that the SDA Church was lumped in with it. And there were many, many more misconceptions to come.

CHAPTER FIVE

THE PRIMARY EVIDENCE IS BUNK

> *O, what a tangled web we weave*
> *when first we practise to deceive!*
> — Walter Scott

It was perceived by those entrusted with the enforcement of law in the Northern Territory that Michael and Lindy had probably enacted a huge deception, that they had taken the benevolent coroner, Denis Barritt, for a ride and the whole country with him. Now there was a chance to unravel that deception and get it right. Of course, for anyone engaged in untangling a deception, there is always the risk of weaving an even bigger one.

At the surface, there was nothing deceptive at all at Alice Springs when the mob — to put it bluntly — turned up at Alice Springs for the beginning of the second coroner's inquest in December 1981. For all the world, it was re-run of what had happened 12 months before. Nothing had changed in the surroundings. The ancient MacDonnell Ranges slumbered outside town, the wide sandy breadth of the Todd River remained at their foot, with its gums and small groups of Aborigines sitting all day in a tight circle. The sparkling new casino was doing well with the foreign trade and on the banks of the Todd River a young Aboriginal man lay drunk. People even with passing acquaintance with the Northern Territory had all heard stories of insipient violence in parts of the Aboriginal community, of attacks on each other with *nulla nullas*, which were Aboriginal hunting sticks. There was still a big gap between Aborigines and other Australians in average life expectancy. Malcolm Brown heard a piped rendition of *Joy to the World* in the Alice Springs mall. In the early morning – while the music was being piped – he saw an inebriated Aboriginal man stumble along a footpath, see a beer can on the ground, pick it up, shake it and drink the dregs. What did Christmas cheer mean to him? Brown heard of positive moves to improve the lot of Aboriginal people and no doubt these were genuine, but he did not see much response to it in the people he saw. There seemed a far bigger tragedy in process than the death of a little girl. What could anyone do about that?

Just before the inquest started, a group of journalists joked about what Michael Chamberlain would do when he could no longer escape the media. One said not to worry, because in a while Michael Chamberlain would be running around in a Northern Territory gaol saying: "Where do I go? Where do I go?" Michael and Lindy Chamberlain, with Tipple and their counsel, Phil Rice QC and Andrew Kirkham, were a lonely, isolated group after they arrived and took up residence, joining Dean in Alice Springs. Peter Chamberlain arrived from New Zealand to be beside his brother. He was joined by Colin Lees, a friend of Michael's, and Irene Heron, a friend of Lindy's from Hervey Bay in Queensland. Against them was the world. It was generally assumed that the Chamberlains would be committed for trial. Counsel assisting the inquest was Des Sturgess, the Brisbane barrister.

When the hearing began on 15th December, before coroner Gerry Galvin, Sturgess called Michael Chamberlain to the witness box. Kirkham objected that Chamberlain was being called before he had heard the new evidence and had time to consider it and was granted an adjournment to provide legal advice. One radio station reported that Michael Chamberlain had declined to answer questions on the grounds that he might incriminate himself, which was untrue. Michael Chamberlain went back into the witness box and accepted that blood had been found in the car, but he said whatever had been found had an innocent explanation: from Keyth Lenehan, or from minor family incidents where blood might have been spilled, or when Reagan injured his forehead and when Aidan had had a nose bleed.

Then came the evidence that would cruel the Chamberlains' chances. Joy Kuhl told the inquest she had found blood in numerous places in the Chamberlains' car and on their possessions. In the Chamberlains' car, she had found "a lot of flakes of dried blood ... It was just virtually suspended there between the hinge and the vinyl of the front passenger's seat." She had taken samples from the spray pattern under the dashboard. Kuhl prepared extracts from the samples she took and applied Ortho-tolidine tests, being a presumptive

THE DINGO TOOK OVER MY LIFE

test for the presence of blood, then cross-over electrophoresis and Ouchterlony tests to confirm if it was blood and its origin. The Ortho-tolidine test did not definitely confirm that blood was present. Other substances, such as rust, soap and copper oxide, could give positive reactions as well. But the Ortho-tolidine tests were the first step, and Kuhl obtained strong positive reactions. She had then set out to see whether foetal haemoglobin was present in the samples. For the crossover electrophoresis and Ouchterlony tests, she used an anti-serum which was supplied by a German company, Behringwerke. If she obtained a positive reaction, that was confirmation that it was most likely blood from a baby, because babies' blood contained foetal haemoglobin for some time after birth.

Kuhl said she had found foetal haemoglobin, or "foetal blood", on smears on a towel and on chamois and a chamois container that had been found in the car. She had detected blood in a stain, she estimated had been about five millilitres in volume, beneath the front passenger's seat in the car. Material extracted from the carpet below the front passenger's seat showed a positive reaction to a test for foetal blood. The foetal blood had been discovered when she cut into and tested the spray material. She had found foetal blood below the front passenger's seat on the carpet, in the console box and in areas of the floor. She had found a 10-cent coin encrusted with material that she concluded was foetal blood. Congealed matter from under the dashboard had also given positive results for foetal haemoglobin.

After testing a pair of scissors found in the console box, she reported the presence of foetal blood even though the test controls had failed. She counted this as one of twenty-two positive results. Tipple later said Kuhl's initial testing was on anything that might have been used as a weapon. She was given a knife the police found in the Chamberlains' house. There was no evidence the knife had ever been in the car, and the tests on that produced negative results. So, the scissors became, by implication in the murder scenario, the weapon she had used. Tipple commented: "On one hand they were saying how cunning and devious the Chamberlains were. On the other hand they said they left a blood-stained towel and scissors in the car." The Crown was more settled on the "deviousness" perspective. "When the police searched the Chamberlain home, Lindy gave them two [canvass] hats with stains on them," Tipple said. "When they tested the staining, it turned out to be gum arabic. When it was found not to be blood, they accused her of trying to mislead them."

Joy Kuhl told the inquest she had spent four days examining the camera bag that had been in the Chamberlains' car. There had been nothing visible on the surface of the camera bag but she had obtained samples by rubbing blotting paper on it. These attempts to confirm the presumptive presence of blood had been "generally unsuccessful", but she had obtained a strong reaction to the presumptive presence of blood in the right-hand bottom corner and base in particular. With the zipper, she had not just a positive result for the presumptive presence of blood but confirmation of blood and a positive result for foetal haemoglobin. From that, it could be extrapolated by the layman that the positive results for the presumptive presence of blood indicated that there had in fact been blood there and the surfaces had been carefully cleaned, and who were the potential jurors, but lay people?

So, what did all that amount to? It was evidence supporting the contention that Lindy Chamberlain had sat in the car with the baby on her lap, or holding it down, and had slit the throat, and that there had been an arterial spurt onto the under dash. The evidence on the spray pattern, Tipple said, was quite devastating to the Chamberlains. But the pieces were nevertheless being relentlessly put into place. She had then hidden the body? Where would that have been? The camera bag? There was camera equipment in the bag but there were sponges, material that protected the camera equipment, which it was surmised could have soaked up the excessive blood. The implication of the failure to confirm the presence of blood on other parts of the bag was that the bag had been washed. And that bag, mind you, was an item that Michael Chamberlain had volunteered rather than let the police take away the wrong bag.

The evidence was reported nationally. Everywhere, people were shaking their heads and saying words to the effect: "I always knew there was something in it! Fancy this bitch trying to fool us with that dingo story!" Somewhere in the midst of all this, Michael Chamberlain invited Malcolm Brown to go jogging with him early one morning. He was looking for an ally in the media and Brown, who was a churchgoer, was the closest he could get. Together with his brother Peter and Colin Lees, they jogged along the side of the Todd River in the dawn light, the town of Alice Springs on the other side of the river just stirring. Brown saw Michael for who he was, a small individual dragged out of his quiet and agreeable private life and thrust into a world quite alien to him, his name reported throughout the world, with so many now wishing him and his wife to hell. Brown said later: "We reached the end of the run, and I felt then that he would have wanted to just keep running, to let the desert swallow him up. But he turned around and jogged back."

In his motel room, Stuart Tipple rose, looked at his multitude of files and wondered how on earth his clients were going to get out of this.

The Chamberlains had been relying on the evidence of the primary witnesses – people who had been at the campsite – but now it was being overridden by people from distant laboratories who thought they knew better. Anyone taking an objective look at the primary facts would have asked some serious questions about that. If there was so much blood in the car, why wasn't any of it on Lindy? The police scenario was that she must have changed her clothes in that 11-minute window of opportunity and cleaned her hands. But where and how would she have done that? What water had she used? If there was all that much blood in the car, why hadn't any been transferred to Bobby Downs, a nursing sister who had sat in the Chamberlains' front seat the night Azaria disappeared? Nobody had noticed blood in the car on the night, or the next day. The implication was that the scissors had been used to cut the baby's throat. Leaving aside the appropriateness of using such an implement as a murder weapon, why would Lindy have left the murder weapon in the car at all? For the police to have searched the car the day after Azaria disappeared and found the scissors might have been fair enough. But 13 months later?

Joy Kuhl gave a robust performance during cross-examination by Andrew Kirkham. Yes, she said, she had destroyed her test plates, in line with the laboratory practice, because preserving and filing test plates and photographs would have required extra staff. She had not disclosed that in her test on the scissors, the controls had failed. When questioned on this, she said: "I have not reported that there was definitely foetal blood. I said I, 'indicated that the blood was of foetal origin'." To a lay person, hearing that foetal blood had been identified elsewhere, the evidence that there were "indications" of foetal blood would probably have been enough to conclude there was foetal blood on the scissors especially when it was counted as one of the positive results.

Phil Rice protested that the inquest was a "de facto prosecution" of the Chamberlains but Des Sturgess shrugged off the objections. Rice objected to the Crown calling Dr Kenneth Brown, whose evidence had been rejected by the first coroner. This too was shrugged off. Brown told Rice he had not been motivated by a desire to justify himself when he had brought overseas experts into the case. "I was concerned with the presentation of my evidence and I wanted to consult with my professional colleagues," he said. He agreed that Barritt had rejected his evidence because of his lack of expertise in bite marks through clothing, but no, he said, that had not stung him. Brown remained of the view that a dingo had not caused the damage to the jumpsuit.

After a day of devastating evidence, Tipple and Michael Chamberlain went off to play a game of tennis. "The stress was so great, we needed to have something to do," Tipple said. "A photographer took a photo with a telephoto lense of Michael as he grimaced after playing a poor shot. We knew nothing about it until the photo appeared in the papers next day."

What was apparent was the extraordinary lengths the Crown had gone to prove its case. No avenue of inquiry had been overlooked. Every rabbit had been pursued down every burrow. The Crown had flown in three experts from overseas, Professor Cameron, Bernard Sims, and Ray Ruddick, chief medical photographer at the London Hospital Medical College, who had taken photographs for the other two, and who occupied the witness box for four minutes. James Anthony Gothard, of the NSW Health Commission, took a similar time to say that the two stains on canvass hats belonging to the Chamberlains were not blood but "a substance like cellulose." Darryl Michael Cummins, a science graduate who worked in Sydney for Bonds Coats Paton, travelled to Ayers Rock to occupy the witness box for three minutes, enough to confirm that Azaria Chamberlain's jumpsuit was one of his company's products. The *Sun-Herald* reported that weekend: "The evidence this week reduced itself to discussion of the stomach contents of three ants at Ayers Rock." (The question being whether insects might have consumed at least some of the blood on the baby's clothing). Detective Superintendent Neil Plumb, was sitting in the inquest ensuring the multitude of Crown exhibits were properly presented. Why a superintendent? Was the evidence so important that it needed the personal attention of such a senior officer? The *Sun-Herald* article and the questions it asked was a lonely cry in the wilderness. For the general public, the Chamberlains were being written off as guilty. A postcard arrived at Lindy's home wishing her a merry Christmas and showing a female dingo with her cubs. The card said: "They have their own babies. Why should they want yours?"

When the court resumed in January 1982, after a wretched Christmas at Cooranbong, Michael and Lindy Chamberlain had become targets for just about anyone, in particular the media. When they arrived at Alice Springs airport, Dean met them and escorted them to a mini-bus, then transferred to a car and left by a side-entrance to the airport, with collaborators waiting to spring an ambush on the pursuing media by suddenly driving vehicles across the road and blocking them. The primary witnesses, whose evidence so supported Lindy's story, were now on the back foot.

Sally Lowe, who had heard the baby cry when on the murder scenario she should have been dead, said in a later letter to Tipple: "I had not liked being drawn into giving an exact shape and number of spots of blood at the second inquest. To me when I had seen them in the tent, they were just spots of blood, when added to the pool of blood would have meant a lot of blood. At the time, I didn't take in the exact number. (I didn't count them or get a ruler or draw a graph around them)." One way or another, the evidence of blood in the tent, which was direct evidence of an attack on the baby, was disregarded. Andrew Scott said the spray was too denatured for him to obtain an accurate analysis of it. He couldn't prove it was human blood. Although he conceded it was impossible to be certain with negative results, he concluded it was probably not human blood."

What was of interest to the inquest was where blood had been found, or supposedly found, in the car. An NT forensic biologist, Tony Jones said a spray under the glove box of the Chamberlains' car had parallel lines and the spots had tails, consistent with the spurt of the blood from a severed artery of an animal or a small child. "It is a fine spray and I would say from a severed artery," he said. "The heart would have still been beating." Tipple said later: "When I reviewed Tony Jones' evidence, he said he would do further tests. There is no evidence he ever did further tests." Andrew Scott said blood on the jumpsuit appeared to have come from the back and he also said that the spots were consistent with blood spurting. According to Scott, the pattern of bleeding indicated that the body had been held upright at some stage. Professor James Cameron said he had found three hand imprints on the jumpsuit and that was consistent with the jumpsuit having been held upright with the body in it. "The sand-staining of the garment I would suggest is consistent with the blood having dried, the two top studs being undone and the clothing with the body still in it coming into contact with the sand," he said. On the pattern of blood staining, he said: "It would be reasonable to assume it was a cutting implement, possibly encircling the neck or cutting the main blood vessels or the structure of the neck."

Professor Malcolm Chaikin, head of the Faculty of Applied Science and head of the School of Textile Technology at the University of New South Wales, was a very proud man who liked the limelight. He said he had examined 28 tufts obtained by vacuuming the Chamberlains' car and found that six of them could have come from Azaria's jumpsuit but he couldn't say they definitely were. Three tufts taken from Michael Chamberlain's camera bag could also have come from the jumpsuit. He concluded that the tufts he found could only be produced by a cutting action and most probably with a pair of scissors. Holes in Azaria's jumpsuit could have been produced by an object with a cutting edge or by a blunt object though he conceded that it was possible the blunt object could have been the tooth of a dingo. Chaikin warmed to his subject and spoke with such enthusiasm that Sturgess had almost to beg him to stop so he could ask another question. He was followed by forensic odontologist, Bernard Sims, who said he did not think a dingo had caused the damage to the baby's jumpsuit. Sturgess asked: "Is it your opinion that there is no evidence that that a member of the canine family, either by tooth marks or the presence of saliva, had anything to do with damage to Azaria Chamberlain's clothing?" Sims replied: "That is so."

The world seemed to be closing in on Michael and Lindy Chamberlain. On 23rd December 1981, Sturgess told Galvin that Joy Kuhl had done more tests on Michael Chamberlain's camera bag and on a hunting knife found in the Chamberlains' home. That day Rice, Dean and Tipple held a crisis conference. Dean said: "I may be on the wrong track but I feel that Cameron's authority is such that we really need an absolutely top man on a world-wide basis." Rice replied: "Oh don't think I'm overlooking that, I think though that we have to have a springboard advisor, that's all. That's not necessarily going to mean he'll be our witness but that's the approach we make. "

Joy Kuhl gave evidence on her investigation, most of it involving tests, most of which were cross-over electrophoresis tests. Of her, Tipple said: "Joy Kuhl at the second inquest was a very impressive witness and the way she was dressed – down to her scarf – made a really big impression. She had this air of incredible confidence. She was saying how old the baby was, how old the stain was. It was pretty technical evidence. No one else wanted it." Everything Kuhl said was highly publicised. When she didn't obtain positive results in her testing, she often referred generically to the results as being "soap reactions". It was a misleading term, implying there had been an attempt to clean the particular surface or item. Tipple took steps, ultimately successful, to have her stop using that term. But Joy Kuhl was unfazed. According to Tipple, she said: "I am so experienced I can tell if a positive presumptive result is really blood. I would not have been fooled by a false positive."

Others were not prepared to take a submissive attitude to Joy Kuhl. Tipple got a telephone call from a medical biologist, Patricia Fleming, working at Westmead Hospital in Sydney's western suburbs, suggesting he get a copy of Kuhl's work notes. When she was asked in open court to produce her work notes and make copies available to the defence, she appeared to agree graciously. Joy Kuhl photocopied the work notes while Tipple stood with her at the photocopier. But within herself, Joy Kuhl was seething. An implied challenge like this was utterly unpalatable. "I could feel her hostility. In court she was everyone's friend, but not now," Tipple said. "No one had ever asked her for her work notes."

The work notes looked to Tipple like "hieroglyphics, and there were few others who could understand them". Dr Vernon Pleuckhahn, a forensic pathologist of the Geelong Hospital in Victoria, passed them onto his own staff to examine. "Pat Fleming also had a look at them and taught me how to interpret them," Tipple said. "She pointed out a number of discrepancies where the controls had been failed, inadequate controls had been used, and clearly Kuhl's evidence indicated she did not have a good understanding of the topic. She did not know that Azaria would have had some adult haemoglobin. And there were other bloopers." Tipple went to Kirkham's home in Victoria to talk about it. While they were there, Pleuckhahn arrived. "He said he had shown Joy Kuhl's notes to his staff and they had said it was good quality work," Tipple said. "I said, 'Hold on, what about the scissors test when the controls failed?'". "It just shows you how much rubbish you get told," Tipple said.

Tipple and Kirkham worked on the cross-examination of Joy Kuhl, but it was so complex that at times they were on the back foot. Questioning Kuhl on a reagent, he asked whether the presence of water would have made a difference. She replied that it was "prepared in water". "When she was under stress, she was like this," Tipple said. "We had to back right off. The cardinal rule in cross-examination is never ask a question you don't know the answer to." Joy Kuhl was open to criticism, but it was going to take a lot of work to put her in a position where she was seriously challenged. Sturgess told Galvin that such questions should be reserved for a trial. What Kirkham had raised was "a defensory thing that has no business here", he said. Sturgess submitted that Lindy Chamberlain be committed for trial for murder and Michael for being an accessory after the fact.

Tipple realised that Joy Kuhl's evidence was the key to the case. He and Kirkham worked intensely the night before Rice was to submit to Galvin that there was no case to answer. It did not help their mood when, instead of joining them, Rice wanted to go to dinner and urged Kirkham to go with him. Rice went, Kirkham did not. But next day, Rice made a spirited submission to Galvin that the evidence did not add up to a *prima facie* case. There was too much doubt about it. Of the supposed bloodied hand impressions on the jumpsuit, he said that was just Cameron's interpretation. If one tried hard enough, he could make out "Father Christmas, occasionally". But Galvin in his finding on 2nd February 1982 said there was a *prima facie* case and a significant question had been raised that could only be resolved by a trial. So, the next stop would be the Supreme Court of the Northern Territory. The safeguard of the second inquest had failed, now the Chamberlains would have to look to the safeguard of a jury trial.

When Tipple and the Chamberlains returned to Sydney, then to the Central Coast, Tipple had the weight of the world on his shoulders. How could such an event, an isolated incident in which a wild animal killed a child, have blown up into something like this? And what were the chances, given the hysteria that had been generated, of the Chamberlains ever getting a fair trial? The day after the committal, Chamberlain supporter, Marion Jones, wrote to the then chairman of the Law Reform Commission, Michael Kirby QC, complaining about the extraordinary attention being paid to the case. She wondered whether there were matters here that the commission could take up. Kirby replied on 9th February: "I too am surprised at the tremendous media coverage given to the 'isolated homicide case' to which you refer." However, he said that inquiring into the law governing coroner's inquests was not in the brief of the commission and that she should contact the Federal Attorney. Kirby remained well aware of the prejudicial effect of the publicity and was later to make a public statement about it, about the almost impossible prospect of finding an unbiased jury. Malcolm Brown, in a private conversation with the former coroner, Denis Barritt, raised the same question. Barritt expressed confidence in the "common sense of juries", but Brown had doubts whether any potential jury would be unaffected.

Joy Kuhl, realising she was being seriously challenged, returned to Sydney and began testing more than 230 bloodstains, from adults and babies. She recorded the results, photographed her test plates and confidently asserted that no sample of known adult blood had ever produced a false reaction to her antiserum for foetal haemoglobin. These results confirmed her conclusions that the stains she had tested from the Chamberlain's car and items came from a child less-than six months old.

When it was announced that Sydney barrister, Ian Barker QC, a former NT solicitor-general, would be leading the prosecution, Tipple received a call from John Agius (later an SC), whom Tipple had seen frequently in Sydney while instructing the Senior Crown Prosecutor. Agius said: "I see Barker is going to be the prosecutor ... he'll be a dangerous opponent."

Tipple wanted Kirkham to stay with the case. Kirkham and Rice were in different cities and he had not quite forgiven Rice for going to dinner the night before final submissions at the second coroner's inquest. In retrospect, Rice might have been the better man, because of his common touch, which would appeal to a Northern Territory jury. But it was not to be. Andrew Kirkham referred Tipple to John Phillips QC. In a profile of Phillips in the *Sydney Morning*

Herald, journalist Jefferson Penberthy painted a picture of a very sophisticated, urbane metropolitan gentleman. Phillips was also an outstandingly successful criminal lawyer. "Although he is only 46, colleagues say there is 'something of the old world about him', he is a member of a choir, and likes to sing grand opera in a magnificent and highly trained tenor voice," Penberthy said. "He is married and lives with his wife and two children in Melbourne's solidly-establishment suburb of Kew. Each day he rolls down the Johnson Street hill to the city in a lovingly-preserved 1950s model Bentley, often humming or singing an aria as he goes."

In that very profile lay the seeds of trouble to come. Phillips, and some of the experts he was to call, were all part of the Melbourne "establishment", the distant big brother to the Territorians, not well acquainted at all with the living conditions of Territorians or the problems they had to face. Phillips was impressive to meet. A spruce, good-looking man, he quickly instilled a feeling of confidence in his clients. He travelled to Gosford for his first conference, with the Chamberlains. Lindy turned up with a wig which she was preparing for a function and groomed it throughout the interview. Phillips felt the case could be answered. He had the primary witnesses, whose evidence fully supported Lindy's version of events, and as for the scientific experts, he could assemble an expert in each instance to rebut what the Crown put up.

The most efficient way to prepare for the trial, was to compartmentalise the work. "I was given the blood and that was my real part in all this," Tipple said later. "Phillips and Kirkham had gone around interviewing people, Sally Lowe and others." Phillips and Kirkham went to the Northern Territory to interview the Aboriginal trackers. "They decided not to call Nipper," Tipple said. "Kirkham said to me, 'I have had a lot of experience in the Territory and I know that Aborigines do not fare well in our criminal justice system and they [he and Phillips] felt the trackers evidence could be broken down and they had an excellent witness in Roff.'" Even though this was not his decision, Tipple would receive a lot of criticism because of it.

With regards to the blood, Tipple knew his clients needed someone "really good." Tipple asked Scott who might fill that role. He recommended a number of forensic biologists including Dr Patrick Lincoln, who worked at the London Hospital Medical College, where Cameron worked. Ultimately, Tipple decided on Lincoln. "I travelled to London in May and was dead scared when I went through customs with the blood-stained clothing. It appeared to Tipple that Lincoln had little time for Cameron. "His office was just down the corridor," Tipple said. "I remember sneaking past Cameron's office."

Of critical importance was that Lincoln had tested the same anti-serum used by Kuhl and found it reacted with adult haemoglobin in the Ouchterlony test. This confirmed that the anti-serum was not specific to foetal haemoglobin in the ouchterlony test. However, he did not get a false reaction with adult blood when he used it in the cross-over electrophoresis test.

Tipple said: "Lincoln went through the Kuhl's work notes and thought her tests established there was foetal haemoglobin on the chamois, its container and camera bag. It was clear that he did not like to criticise the work of fellow scientists and he was sympathetic to Kuhl. He could not believe we were going to all this trouble to test her work. He got negative results in his tests for foetal haemoglobin, on everything we gave him including some samples from the under-dash spray. But he warned that you can't rely on a negative result because of the age of the samples. They may have just denatured."

Disappointed in this, Tipple looked elsewhere and he turned to Professor Barry Boettcher, an immunologist and head of the School of Biological Sciences at Newcastle University. Boettcher was a very knowledgeable and skilled scientist. "I went to see him and for the first time I immediately got answers," Tipple said. "I found it ironic that we went searching the world for answers to our questions and the guy who was able to offer the answers was less than an hour's drive away." Tipple sent a copy of Joy Kuhl's notes to him, together with photographs of the jumpsuit and nappy, and the matinee jacket Lindy said Azaria had been wearing. Boettcher carried out tests similar to Kuhl and Lincoln and he obtained positive reactions to adult blood with the ouchterlony and the cross-over electrophoresis test. Tipple decided not to call Lincoln for the defence, because it would have created a situation where two defence experts were arguing with each other. Boettcher did give the impression to some people of having a touch of intellectual arrogance and being rather aloof, which would not appeal to Territorians. Tipple said: "He was actually a very humble guy. But he was confident and we both believed that once he presented his evidence, that would be the end of the trial. He felt that the whole case rested on his shoulders."

Of all the places where blood was supposed to have been deposited in the car, it was the under-dash spray that proved the biggest headache for the defence lawyers. There was a question from the outset whether it was blood at all. Tipple's consultant at Westmead Hospital, Pat Fleming, pointed out that Joy Kuhl's work notes showed she had not used adequate controls. "That was clear to me from Kuhl's work notes," Tipple said. "If you had relied on her work notes, that evidence would have been thrown out." More significantly, an SDA pastor, Webber Roberts, rang Tipple to say that he had a similar spray pattern under the dashboard of his own Holden Torana. Tipple obtained the plate and passed that onto Phillips, who went with Kirkham to the GMH factory at Port Melbourne. "GMH kept the plate and said, 'We will ask a few questions and see if we can help you'," Tipple said. "But after a few days they rang back and said, 'There is nothing we can do'." It was a common reaction, Tipple said. "People didn't want to get involved." And the moment passed. In fact, with the advantage of hindsight, it might be seen as the tip of the iceberg. It suggested Joy Kuhl had found foetal haemoglobin in material that was not even blood.

On 11th March 1982, the Chamberlains made an application to have the trial held in July or August. The Crown said their British witnesses would not be available at that time. "In fact, I was told it was put off because Cameron wanted to attend the swimming at the Brisbane Commonwealth Games," Tipple said.

The Chamberlains had no money to speak of. "I realised this was going to be a great financial burden on them so I applied for Legal Aid," Tipple said. The trial was finally set for 13th September and, in an attempt to get a jury that had not been influenced by the saturation publicity surrounding the case, the venue for the trial was shifted from Alice Springs to Darwin. This sort of thing had been done before. In prosecutions in 1980 that followed the scuffle at Ti Tree, where a police officer had shot two Aborigines, the trial had been shifted from Alice Springs to Darwin.

Tipple was well and truly in the hot seat. He was plagued by letters and messages from all and sundry, some being humble offers of support, some drawing on religious sources. Others were on the lunatic fringe. One large envelope, postmarked 22nd March, arrived at his office. "I heard my secretaries scream and went out to see what it was," Tipple said. Out had plopped a garment soaked in fresh blood. With it was a note saying that Azaria had been "kidnapped by a vicious woman who wanted a baby girl". It went on to say that the writer had carried out an experiment using blood from three slaughtered chickens to see how much blood was needed to produce the blood pattern on Azaria's jumpsuit. Apparently, it was not much, and the good soul thought it would be appropriate to send Tipple the actual evidence in the post.

In April 1982, Lindy Chamberlain confirmed she was again pregnant, which was going to complicate matters. Michael and Lindy Chamberlain, now supported by the church, continued the best they could at Avondale College. But now they were being continually pestered by the media, whom the college administration told not to come onto the grounds. The media virtually camped on the footpath outside the college. Tipple made an announcement that all media inquiries were to be directed to him. But the media stayed. On one occasion, a student on duty at the gate lost his temper when a television crew turned up saying they wanted to see the principal, Dr Jim Cox. They did not really want to see Dr.Cox, they wanted a leg-in to Lindy. Seeing the student's dummy-spit was likely to be reported, Cox drew himself up to his diplomatic best and defused the situation. But nobody saw Michael and Lindy. Michael Chamberlain said later that an afternoon newspaper reporter, frustrated by the continual blockage, fabricated an entire interview and had it published.

If the Crown had had its way, that torment would have continued a lot longer. Because Lindy was due to give birth in November, the Crown applied to have the trial delayed till after the birth, for fear of aborting the trial. The Chamberlains did not want to wait. If it was set to start in September, they wanted to get it over. At a closed court on 11th August 1982, NT judge, Justice James Muirhead, who would be presiding over the trial, declined to delay the trial.

Two days later, utterly frustrated by the failure of the Legal Aid office to respond to his request made the previous April, Tipple demanded to speak to Legal Aid's acting assistant director. He expressed his concern and reminded Legal Aid of the imminence of the trial. On 19th August, he received a reply: "I wish to assure you that the officers handling this matter have spent considerable time in relation to it and have been endeavouring to facilitate an early decision concerning the provisions of assistance to your client." On 23rd August, he finally received qualified approval. The letter he received said: "The Australian Legal Aid office will not be responsible for any preliminary work performed prior to commencement of the trial." Legal Aid would also fund just one solicitor, not two that Tipple felt was needed. John Phillip dictated a letter in reply: "I must say I was appalled at the terms the terms of the Legal Aid grant conveyed to us today and to the adequacy of the fees and allowances granted to us but I am much more concerned that the grant of legal aid extends to only allowing one instructing solicitor. Mr. Tipple has carried out extensive preparatory work and it is vital that he continue to instruct us throughout the trial. Mr. Dean on the other hand, has been involved in this matter from the First Inquest and has been identified by the media as the Chamberlains' legal adviser. I fear that unless he continues to act there will be a repetition of the speculation which followed the departure of Mr. Rice QC which was widely and wrongly ascribed to the lack of confidence by him in the Chamberlain cause. In addition, at the most critical time of our preparation we are to be faced with the task of instructing a new solicitor from Legal Aid about a case that is the most complex I have encountered in 23 years at the Bar." Tipple said: "Legal Aid was unmoved. The Chamberlains decided to retain me and dispense with Peter Dean." Dean, a solid, conscientious performer, principally remembered in the inquests for wearing a pith helmet during excursions to view the areas under discussion, had to bow out, and Tipple, though he was part of a very good team, was only too well aware of what he had realised in time as a Public Solicitor, that the instructing solicitor is vital.

On 24th August, Tipple interviewed Malcolm Chaikin, who resented anyone who had the effrontery to question him. "He conceded that marks on the nappy could have been caused by a dingo but insisted the damage to the jumpsuit could only have been made by a bladed instrument, most likely scissors," Tipple said. "He was adamant that dingo teeth could not cut like scissors or produce tufts. He emphasized that it could not be proved that the six tufts (cotton loops) recovered from the camera bag and vacuuming's from the car were definitely from Azaria's jumpsuit only that they could have come from the jumpsuit or from a similar material." Here was one scientist, very proud, expecting instant acceptance, who was not going to back down easily when challenged. As with many other experts called to court cases, one issue is what they have to say, another is their credibility. The experts lined up, with their lawyers and supporters, in Darwin in September 1982, ready for the mother of all jousts in a bid to persuade the jury they were right. The jury was there, somewhere in the urban sprawl of Darwin, solidly saturated for the previous two years with news and speculation – "seething", as a later jurist would describe it – and in those 12 was the safeguard upon which the Chamberlains were obliged to put all their hopes.

CHAPTER SIX

THE TRIAL

"

Once a jolly pastor camped in a caravan,
Under the shade of a kurrajong tree,
And he sang and he prayed as he watched the baby's bottle boil,
"You'll be a Seventh-day Adventist like me."

Seventh-day Adventist, Seventh-day Adventist,
You'll be a Seventh-day Adventist like me.
And he sang as he prayed as he watched the baby's bottle boil,
"You'll be a Seventh-day Adventist like me."

Down came Lindy to snatch up Azaria,
She picked up the scissors and stabbed her with glee,
And she smiled as she shoved the baby in the camera bag,
"It's fun being a Seventh-day Adventist with me."

Seventh-day Adventist, Seventh-day Adventist,
It's fun being a Seventh-day Adventist like me,
And she smiled as she shoved that baby in the camera bag,
"It's fun being a Seventh-day Adventist like me."

Out came a dingo mosing (sic) round the camp fire,
Lindy winked at Michael and said, "It wasn't me."
What happened to the baby you put in the camera bag,
Give it to the dingo and you'll get off scot free.

…

Give it to the dingo,
Give it to the dingo,
Give it to the dingo,
And you'll get off scot free.

Up jumped the dingo and ran past the camera bag,
"You'll never blame her murder on me."
And Azaria's ghost may be heard as you pass by the kurrajong tree,
"Mummy was the one who did away with me."

– Anonymous

So, there we all were at Darwin on Sunday 12th September 1982. It was awkward, changing weather for the north, between the Dry and the Wet, when humidity increases, tempers fray and incidents of domestic violence increase. The first two weeks of the Wet Season are known to locals as "Suicide Season". In fact, one of the court orderlies assigned to the Chamberlain trial committed suicide in the first two weeks. There were patches of beauty in the Darwin landscape. The Bougainvillea was in bloom, Darwin Harbour lay flat and green. Darwin Prison sat quietly on the southern outskirts of the city, surrounded by the flat damp country of the North, wet and unattractive. To the normal, law-abiding person, a prison merited barely a second glance as one passed by. That was another world, another universe, a world reserved for a certain type of person – a prisoners' universe of personal purgatory – hidden from view. But now, Michael and Lindy Chamberlain were looking at the place differently. Was that prisoners' universe going to envelope them?

Michael and Lindy Chamberlain were greeted in Darwin by Graeme Olson, the SDA pastor in Darwin, who accommodated them at the rear of his residence a kilometre or so from the central business district. Olson, a former South Australian policeman, was not destined to get on well with the Chamberlains. They were all committed Christians, and it was more of a personality clash than anything else. Olson had sympathy for the difficult work police had to do and knew some of the policemen, including Sergeant Barry Cocks, who would be giving evidence. Malcolm Brown was later to say: "The pastor and the policeman battled within Graham, and I am not sure whether the pastor won." But Olson nevertheless formed a firm view towards the end of the trial that the Chamberlains were innocent. The accommodation for the Chamberlains was very ordinary. It was a separate building in Olson's grounds that had been used for Sabbath School. They would rather have been in a hotel. But Olson was a good bodyguard. When he was present, the Chamberlains were safe.

Tipple, along with John Phillips QC and Andrew Kirkham, moved into the Travelodge Motel a block away from Olson's residence, in Mitchell Street. Legal Aid refused to fund two solicitors. The Chamberlains were forced to choose Tipple or Dean. They chose Tipple and Dean had to go. In Dean's place they were assisted by a lawyer provided by Legal Aid, Greg Cavanagh. Arrangements were made to pick up and transport Michael and Lindy to the court in Cavanagh's Mazda so Tipple could be with them to protect them walking into and out of court. Ian Barker QC arrived to lead the prosecution. For the time being he was being assisted by Des Sturgess. Barker's junior was a genial counsel and sometime actor, Tom Pauling. Instructing solicitor was Michael O'Loughlin, a fit, muscled young man, very much a macho man, sporting a tattoo, who had once been on a road gang but had been persuaded to make better use of his brains. The media flocked into town, many staying at the old Darwin Hotel across the road from the Supreme Court, a sprawling establishment reminiscent of the legendary Raffles Hotel in Singapore. Like Sydney radio reporter Sean Flannery, they were full of beans, very active, and very intrusive.

Tipple got word from Sturgess that the trial would take at least three months. That was terrible news. It meant that Lindy would be giving birth in the middle of her own trial. And two weeks after that, Tipple's own child was due, and it looked as though he might miss the birth.

On Monday, the jury – nine men and three women – were empanelled before Justice James Muirhead. The Defence team knew very little about the potential jurors whose names appeared in the list given them, with the exception of one, Yvonne Cain (who later identified herself), whom they felt would give a good hearing because her child had been bitten by a dingo. The trial venue had been shifted, in the hope of getting a jury less tainted by the publicity. There was fat chance of that. On the day the trial began, two women appeared in front of the court wearing t-shirts, one proclaiming "Darwin's Theory" and depicting Lindy Chamberlain climbing out of a dingo suit. The other had the word "Azaria" dripping blood and being cut by a pair of scissors. Police spoke to them and told them that if they did it again, they would be prosecuted. When the t-shirts were brought to his attention, Muirhead described the women as "fools" and left it at that. But it was a worrying sign. If that attitude was out on the streets, had it not infected any potential jury? The prosecution tendered exhibits. One was described as a photo of a dingo. It was followed by a photo of a dingo "blown up", and at the double meaning, the jury burst into fits of laughter. That in itself was a grim portent. If they were going to laugh at that, were they not going to laugh at the whole dingo story?

Barker in his opening address to the jury demonstrated from the outset his mastery of language when he described the dingo story as "a calculated, fanciful lie designed to conceal the fact that the baby had died at her mother's hand".

The first primary witness was Sally Lowe, who was led through her evidence by Tom Pauling. Tipple mused that this was a clever ploy – the junior normally taking less critical evidence – and would send a message to the jury that Barker did not think her evidence was very important. Sally said she and her husband, Greg, had been with Lindy and the baby at the barbecue area. Lindy had had the baby with her. Then she had taken the baby away, with Aidan, and had come back with Aidan. Phillips' cross-examination was exacting. If Sally Lowe had seen spots of blood in the tent, how many were there? In a later letter to Tipple, she said: "I know there were several spots & I saw them in front of me & to the right. This being the general area I looked in. This is why when asked again about the spots at the trial – the exact number and area – I felt it best to say I didn't remember. Meaning from the answer I didn't remember the exact number or area. But as usual I had failed to express myself properly."

Greg Lowe in his initial statements to police said he had seen Lindy go to the tent with the baby. He had then seen her come back to the barbecue area with Aidan. He did not say, though he could have, that after he saw Lindy go into the tent with Azaria and Aidan, he saw her crawl out on all fours a few minutes later and stand up. He saw that she was not holding the baby and went to the car with Aidan. It was potentially vital evidence supporting Lindy Chamberlain's. But when he stepped into the witness box again, he believed he was obliged to stick to his original statement and had he added anything more it would have smacked of "recent invention" and been open to attack. He could still have said it, and whether it was or was not recent invention would have been up to the jury. But the opportunity passed. There was no problem with the evidence of Bill and Judith West. They had heard the dingo growl. Judith said she heard the growl "five to 10 minutes" before Lindy raised the alarm, and Bill supported her. These two couples were, as Phillips said, "salt of the earth" people, honest and responsible, whose evidence could not be seriously attacked.

There was ample circumstantial evidence about the increasing intrusiveness and boldness of the dingoes at Ayers Rock. Wallace Victor Goodwin, who found Azaria's clothing a week after the baby disappeared, said that when he visited Ayers Rock in 1976, dingoes had not scuttled away from humans. They had stood their ground. But when he visited in 1980, "they would come right into the camping area, sniff around and lick right out of the frypan". Derek Roff said he had become so concerned about the behaviour of dingoes at Ayers Rock that he had written to his superiors, asking for permission to carry out a cull and the ammunition to do it. The natural reserve of dingoes to humans been broken down, partly because tourists were feeding them. John Phillips asked: "It was your opinion, wasn't it, that this contact was bringing about a change in the habits of dingoes towards humans?" Roff replied: "In the Ayers Rock region, that is right." Phillips asked: "Now, as a result of your observations at Ayers Rock, you have not the slightest doubt that a dingo would enter a tent if the opportunity arose?" Roff replied: "No, sir."

That evidence, combined with evidence of dingo tracks, the drag marks and the fabric pattern on the sand, should have been enough. It had been enough to convince Denis Barritt. On its own, it was a good circumstantial case. The dingo on that scenario had gone in quickly, seized the infant and dashed out in a few seconds, not long enough to have deposited much blood, saliva, dingo hairs or anything else.

From the outset, the scientific evidence cast doubt on the dingo hypothesis. Even in the incompetent search of the tent and belongings, hairs had been found and were examined by Dr Harry Harding, a forensic biologist from Adelaide. He said he had examined hairs taken from the Chamberlains' belongings when they had been at the campsite at Ayers Rock. He said he had examined the hairs and compared them with dingo hairs and had concluded they had probably come from a cat. He thought the hairs taken from the jumpsuit were inconsistent with dingo hairs. Under cross-examination from Andrew Kirkham, he conceded that the hairs could be dingo hairs but it was unlikely. Dr Andrew Scott said the blood staining on the jumpsuit indicated a significant blood flow and he expected to find more blood in the bassinet and items in the tent if the injuries had been sustained there. None of the blood drops had been very large and some had been pinhead size. There had been no saliva on Azaria's clothing when he examined it. He conceded to Kirkham that if the dingo had picked up the child by the matinee jacket, then the saliva could have been deposited on that garment.

With this evidence, the concessions were the important thing. Harding in his evidence on the type of hairs was only expressing probability. How did the guilt theorists explain why there was any blood in the tent at all? On their reasoning, it must have been transferred there by a bloodied Lindy. Scott was conceding that there was blood in the tent and the only question in his mind was how much he *expected* to see. Leaving aside the question of why the blood was there in the first place, the question of quantity came down to an opinion. And that brings in all sorts of factors, including the speed in which the baby was removed, how freely the blood was flowing. Scott's major concession about the saliva was that it might have been deposited on the matinee jacket Lindy said the baby was wearing, but which had not been found.

Detective Jim Metcalf gave evidence about his discovery of the under-dash spray in the Chamberlains' car. It might well have been "sticky to the touch". Phillips asked: "Doesn't it strike you that 13-1/2 months after Azaria's disappearance, it is astonishing that it is in a sticky state?" Metcalf replied: "I cannot really comment on that." Metcalf was not in a position to make a judgement on what he had found. But Joy Kuhl, who was scientifically qualified, could. She claimed she found blood not just under the dashboard but various parts of the car, including the front of the car, on both the driver's and passenger's sides. She had also found it contained foetal haemoglobin. She had obtained positive reactions for the presence of foetal haemoglobin on the floor at the front, also on a towel, on a chamois and chamois container and on a small pair of curved nail scissors found in the car. After extensive testing of 230 bloodstains from adults and children, she claimed that "not one" sample of adult blood had reacted with the serum. She had concluded that the positive reactions she obtained from the stains extracted from the Chamberlain car and possessions meant it came from a baby under three months of age. And if that evidence stood up in the jury's eyes, concessions gained by the defence and the common-sense objections as might have arisen that the spray was sticky, came to very little.

The identification of the blood became the battleground of the case – not whether there were dingo tracks, or why Lindy would have wanted to kill the baby – but whether the blood supposedly found in the Chamberlains' car, and on their possessions, was baby's blood. Michael and Lindy Chamberlain maintained that if blood was found in their car, it must have come from Keyth Lenehan, the accident victim. If only DNA technology had been available then! It could have shortcutted the whole process and brought about a resolution. But that was yet to come. The battle now had to be over the identification of blood as being of foetal or adult origin. When the jury was taken to Ayers Rock for a view, Tipple and Boettcher stayed in Darwin to prepare for the cross-examination of Joy Kuhl. They looked closely at the photographs of the tests Joy Kuhl had done on bloodstains after the second coroner's inquest, which she relied on to confirm that the anti-serum she had used would only react with foetal haemoglobin. Tipple and Boettcher, who had not previously had a close look at the photographs of the test for infant's blood and saw two bands, confirming that the anti-serum in fact reacted to something else as well. Was the second band a reaction to adult haemoglobin? Boettcher said: "If it looks like a duck and quacks like a duck, you can say it is a duck."

Joy Kuhl said that in her original test plates, she only got one band, which (if specific to foetal haemoglobin) indicated that the sample contained foetal haemoglobin. The court had to take her word for it, because the test plates had not been photographed and had been destroyed. But the defence was saying that if Joy Kuhl had got just the one band, then what was it? Was it a reaction to foetal haemoglobin, or to adult haemoglobin? If it could be demonstrated that the anti-serum Joy Kuhl had used was not specific to foetal haemoglobin, then her conclusions were invalid. Boettcher and Tipple had to bring John Phillips up to speed on all this. Being the principal defence counsel, he had to cross-examine the principal scientific witness. But despite his many skills as counsel, Phillips was no scientist. When Boettcher and Tipple showed Phillips one of the photographs of Joy Kuhl's tests, he asked: "Why aren't there two bands in this test?" The test he was pointing to was of adult blood where there was only ever going to be one band. Two bands only showed up in the tests of infant blood because it contained adult and foetal haemoglobin. Tipple and Boettcher felt their jaws drop. Phillips was way behind. They had to work overtime to bring him up to speed.

In cross-examining Kuhl, Phillips asked Kuhl why the test slides had not been kept or photographed. Tipple thought the team was on a winner. "I think one of the most brilliant bits of court work I have ever seen was how he highlighted that the test plates had been destroyed," Tipple said later. "Kirkham held up to the jury a photo one of Kuhl's demonstration plate to the jury showing how easy it was to photograph and preserve the test plates. Phillips asked Kuhl where the real test plates were. She said they had been destroyed and there were no photographs. We thought we had really kicked a goal." When confronted with a double band depicted in her own demonstration photos, Joy Kuhl said the second band was not a true band at all but merely smudge or "artefact – an accidental feature of no significance".

"The scissors were a critical link in the Crown case providing the implication that they were the murder weapon and used by the Chamberlains to cut the clothing," Tipple said. "Kuhl admitted that her controls had failed but counted this as a positive result by saying there were 'indications' of the presence of foetal blood. No competent laboratory in the world would ever have allowed her report of 'indications of foetal blood'. I could not believe that Culliford and Baxter would back her up." And what did the jury make of "indications" as distinct from "confirmation"? Probably not much. And of course, overriding all that evidence were other questions. How efficient was a pair of small scissors in cutting a throat? Why could it ever have been assumed that the scissors were even in the car when Lindy went to Ayers Rock? And why, oh why, if Lindy had used the scissors to murder her baby, would she have left them in the car? It simply did not make sense.

All the time, there was the question of the spray pattern beneath the dashboard. If it was blood, and it could at least be argued that the presence of foetal haemoglobin had not been demonstrated, how had it got there anyway? It could not have come from Lenehan. "The only thing we could not explain was the spray," Tipple said. "That was the smoking gun. And the camera bag was given to Michael after Lenehan, so we could not blame Lenehan for that either." Tipple had noted that in these critical tests on the samples from the under-dash spray, Kuhl had not recorded using proper controls in the work notes she gave him at the second inquest. He said later: "We decided to soften her up with questions about the double bands before turning to the under-dash spray test results which we saw as the most damaging evidence. The work notes she had given me at the second Inquest showed that she had not used adequate controls and on that basis the results should have been discarded". Tipple wondered how she could explain her way out of what had been carefully recorded by her in her own work notes and were according to her an accurate record. Kuhl knew the question was coming and was prepared for it. When asked if she had used and recorded proper controls, she turned to a page in her work notes turned it over and pointed to a notation she had written on the back of the page:

"No reactions

*with animal anti-sera (pig, sheep)"

Then she looked up at Tipple and said, "I do not really know whether that came out on the Photostat."

There was an asterisk on the back page note but no corresponding asterisk on the front page (which had been photocopied by Kuhl in Alice Springs with Tipple standing at the copier and given to him) It meant the under-dash spray evidence remained but raised a number of questions in Tipple's mind which were only answered much later. Her quiet, unruffled, but confident manner was undermining the effect of the cross-examination. Tipple said later: "We had no notice that was going to be her explanation. We didn't have any evidence to allow us to put to her, 'You are lying'. We realised the full story wasn't being told and she was not as competent as everyone else thought she was. If we had challenged to her, Barker would have had a field day telling the jury that the defence is so desperate they challenged the integrity of a witness who was just doing her job."

Joy Kuhl did concede that an ortho-tolidine test could not normally be regarded as confirmation blood was present. She agreed that soap could produce a positive reaction to the ortho-tolidine test for the presence of blood, as could rust. However, she claimed that false reactions would never fool a competent experienced forensic scientist like her. Other substances like nasal secretions and human waste could produce positive reactions because they had blood or breakdown blood products in them. With some items, such as the camera bag, she had only obtained positive presumptive indications that there may have been blood and other tests had failed to confirm the presence of blood. The jury was invited to conclude that even where there were only positive presumptive results, it probably meant blood had been there but had been cleaned away, consistent with the scenario that Lindy, after slitting the baby's throat, had stuffed the body into the camera bag and later attempted to remove all traces of blood.

Dr Simon Baxter, who had supervised Joy Kuhl in his work in the NSW Division of Forensic Medicine, supported her evidence. He said he had tested Keyth Lenehan's blood and not obtained a positive reaction for the presence of foetal haemoglobin. He supported Kuhl's evidence that the second band Joy Kuhl had obtained in her testing was not a true band, as she said, but merely an artefact. Bryan Culliford, deputy director of the London Police Laboratory, was called by the Crown to support Joy Kuhl. He said she had used "perfectly normal techniques and appears to have used them well". He also agreed that the second band was an artefact. But the simple statement about her competence in performing the tests was one of those pivotal statements in evidence that can swing a court case. Who could challenge Culliford? He had had 29 years' experience in identifying blood and had invented one of the standard testing techniques. The technicalities of the scientific argument probably went over the jurors' heads, and they probably made their judgements on the impression the experts gave from the witness box.

The Crown's scientific juggernaut rolled on, trampling down the protests that might have come from the reservoir of common sense. Professor James Cameron in evidence repeated his view that there had been a murder and that the baby's throat and neck had been cut. He added that a dingo would have had difficulty fitting its jaws round the head of a baby that age. That might have left open the question of whether the dingo had gone for the neck instead. Like Culliford, he had vast experience. He claimed to have performed 50,000 autopsies, and had spent his professional life studying the results of injury and wounding. The 50,000- figure seemed incredible, given the time each autopsy would have taken, but there was no doubt he was well qualified. John Phillips in his cross-examination pinned Cameron down on the Confait case in Britain in 1972, where Cameron admitted not taking a rectal temperature of the murder victim at the critical time, which would have drastically altered his evidence as to when the man died. Three boys who were convicted each had had an alibi for the actual time of death. Cameron conceded that he had been wrong. Phillips questioned him vigorously. But when he had finished, Barker asked quietly in re-examination whether there was "anything you have heard" that would now cause him to alter his opinion the manner of Azaria's death, to which Cameron said: "No". It was a simple question-and-answer which in the atmosphere of the trial appeared to cut away much of the thrust of the cross-examination.

Dr Tony Jones, senior director of the regional laboratory at the Institute of Veterinary and Medical Science in Adelaide, said the spray pattern under the dashboard of the Chamberlains' car was consistent with the upwards spurt of a small artery. In answer to Barker, he said: "It comes from the depth of the passenger space upwards to where the passenger would have been sitting if there had been one there." The bleeding on the jumpsuit was "consistent with an injury to the neck and the blood vessels there", and "consistent with lacerations or incisions." It was evidence that had been supported by Cameron and backed Cameron's scenario to the hilt.

So here we have Lindy in the prosecution scenario, who for all the world was a loving mother just minutes earlier, cradling her beloved baby, now sitting in the front passenger's seat ripping a knife, or pair of scissors, through its throat, even cutting its head off, disposing of the body, cleaning herself up somehow, then returning to the barbecue site with her son. Who on earth, in a reasonable frame of mind, would accept that?

Then the evidence turned to the cuts, apparent evidence of a devilish plan to make it look as though a dingo had done it. That was leaving aside the question of whether someone who had killed the baby would have wanted the clothes found at all. But all that was overlooked by the guilt theorists, who were reinforced by the evidence of Malcolm Chaikin, now supported by Bernard Sims, who said the jumpsuit had been cut and not torn. The Australian public was enthralled. Even newspaper reporters, dictating their copy by phone to copytakers – in the days before emails – would be plagued by questions by copytakers saying: "Did she do it? Did she do it?" On one occasion, dictating a list of material items brought up in evidence, such as tent pegs, water bottles, towels and whatever, Malcolm Brown included "torches". The copy taker took down everything correctly, except the last-mentioned item, which she took to be "tortures", and that went into print.

On 13th October, a month after the start of the trial, Phillips brought out his defence line-up. From the mob perspective, if not the jury's, he was behind the eight-ball. He started with Lindy who, bloated with pregnancy, stated emotionally that she was innocent. "I did not kill my baby," she sobbed. When she was presented with evidence that a spray of blood had been found under the dashboard, she replied she did not know how it got there.

Barry Boettcher was the key defence witness and he started confidently enough. He said that in his own testing, he had obtained two bands, so if Joy Kuhl had only obtained one band she would not have been able to tell whether she was getting a reaction to foetal or adult haemoglobin. He stood by his opinion that any second bands Joy Kuhl had obtained in her confirmatory tests were not artefacts but real reactions. It proved, he said, that the anti-serum Joy Kuhl used was not specific to foetal haemoglobin at all. Boettcher went into a great deal of technical explanation, which sadly went above the jurors' heads. Barker at the start of his cross-examination asked whether Boettcher was "an academic", a theoretician and not a working forensic biologist. Boettcher conceded that, and agreed he was not a member of a forensic society. It was apparently a standard line of attack, to make out that a theoretician would be hard-put to displace the opinion of someone at the coalface. When reading reports of this, lawyers throughout Australia recognised that, with some wry amusement. Boettcher agreed that Joy Kuhl had more experience than he had with forensic samples. Barker put to him that he was in the Chamberlains' "camp", having breakfast with them and their lawyers and otherwise being in their company. It is quite normal for a principal expert witness to be in the company of those engaging him, but the questions created an impression that Boettcher had become too close to the defence and was just a hired gun. There was no evidence Boettcher was anything other than objective.

Boettcher's seemingly high-handed performance in the witness box – leaving aside the truthfulness of what he had to say – was disappointing to Tipple. "I can tell you that when you are dealing with him on a one-to-one basis, I never thought of him as being elitist," Tipple said. "We thought Boettcher would go through and just kill them. He was so impressive. I think his failure in the witness box was because he thought what he said weighed so heavily and was so important." It undoubtedly was, but juries tend to look to other things, such as style, manner and presentation. The jurors, some of whom had started yapping to friends all over Darwin – some of that getting back to Malcolm Brown – described Boettcher in a most disparaging way that said much more about the person who made it than the subject. Boettcher was no fool, and what he had to say did matter, but such is the nature of adversarial proceeding that the intrinsic value of the information is only one aspect of the evidence. Things would undoubtedly have been different had Boettcher given his evidence to a panel of experts.

Richard Nairn, Professor of Pathology and Immunology at Monash University, supported the Boettcher's opinion that a finding of foetal haemoglobin could not be determined from the tests Joy Kuhl had conducted. A veteran of 5,000 post-mortem examinations, he said he had read Mrs Kuhl's work and did not accept her finding of foetal haemoglobin. In answer to Barker, he said that though he had never been asked to give evidence on blood identification in a criminal trial, blood was just another body fluid and he had plenty of experience in identifying body fluids. He rejected that he was only "a teacher", he was a working biologist. He did not agree he was an academic with his head in the clouds. Nairn made some remarks critical of forensic laboratories in general and he did not easily dispel the image of the high-handed academic.

Professor Vern Pluekhahn, director of Pathology at Geelong Hospital, disagreed that the pattern of bleeding indicated a cut throat. He said it could have been produced a number of ways. He had studied photographs in black-and-white and in colour and ultra-violet fluorescence photographs of the jumpsuit and he could not see the impression of a human hand on the jumpsuit. The blood pattern on the jumpsuit was consistent with what would have come from puncture wounds to the head if the dingo had seized the baby in this way. He had seen similar circular patterns of bleeding from people who had sustained head injuries in motor accidents.

There was so much that was sensible, from a layman's point of view, about what Pleuckhahn said. How can anyone say with certainty how a blood pattern is formed? There could be a number of ways. Professor James Ferris, of the University of British Colombia, expressed a view equally at one with common sense that a dingo could have seized the child from the cot with minimal loss of blood and that more extensive injuries could have been caused later. There had been numerous instances, he said, of killing having been done without much loss of blood. And the stain on the jumpsuit? It was just a series of blotches. Pleuckhahn similarly could not make out any pattern. But Pleuckhahn became excitable and seemed on the verge of losing his temper. And again, that fitted the image that appeared to be forming in the jury's minds that the defence had trotted out a series of rather arrogant academics trying to brush aside the less academically qualified.

Professor Keith Bradly, Emeritus Professor of Anatomy at Melbourne University – initially an engineer, who had done an about-turn and qualified in Medicine – said that in his experience blood could flow from an incised head wound in a circumferential pattern around the neck and he had seen blood flow like that. But he agreed with Barker that he had seen this with a patient who was "anaesthetised, immobile and prone". That phrase by Barker probably destroyed a lot of the effect of his evidence in the minds of the jurors.

Dr Hector Orams, a reader in dental medicine and surgery at the University of Melbourne, said he had examined dingo skulls and determined that dingo teeth were longer and more cylindrical than dogs' teeth. He had looked at the holes in Azaria's singlet and thought that might be consistent with a single tooth penetrating the pinched-up singlet it had picked up in its jaws. If the singlet were held in a certain way, he said, it would not be necessary for holes of other teeth to be near the hole he had examined. But he conceded in cross-examination that he had not given evidence in criminal cases in Victoria on bite marks and had not examined the clothing of someone attacked by an animal, though he had occasionally been asked by police for an opinion on certain matters. He had thought the jumpsuit material had been "torn" rather than cut and he conceded that his opinion on tearing was a lay opinion only. When asked what sort of material it was, he said it was "cotton flannelette", one of the women jurors shook her head and that, again, seemed the critical question-and-answer that destroyed the effect of his evidence. The material had been described in detail in the Crown evidence as nylon/cotton fabric.

The defence scientific witnesses were all deservedly prominent in their fields but Barker at that stage of the trial was like Don Bradman on a roll, sending their arguments to the boundary, contrasting them as high-flyers daring to condescendingly attack the work of humble working pathologists and biologists who were carrying out the tests they described every day of their working lives. Tipple said of Barker: "He very much played the Territorian evaluation of them against us, with Phillips being an outsider with our experts being toffee-nosed outsiders."

Michael Chamberlain's turn came in the witness box. Unlike the procedure in the second coroner's inquest, he was at least being called after he had heard the evidence. Asked why he and Lindy had stayed around the campsite rather than gone out widely on the search, he said he and Lindy had stayed where they could get news from other searchers, though he had made some local sorties that night and the next day. Barker asked why he had made it such a priority to get black-and-white photographs for a news organisation the next day. Michael replied: "Because I wanted to warn people about the problems associated with us."

The common-sense view is that people in traumatic circumstances do and say all sorts of odd things, like the mother of a girl killed in a traffic accident, going into the morgue to identify the body and taking a coat so she does not get cold, or in William Dobell's painting, "The Dead Landlord", portraying a corpse stretched out on a bed while his wife mechanically combs her hair in the mirror. There is no rule that says people must react in any particular way to trauma. However, the combined behaviour of the Chamberlains – staying in the camping area, Michael organising photographs, and the decision to leave Ayers Rock on the Tuesday while people were still searching – did not do the Chamberlains any good at all. The question might well have been asked: "Did they behave in that way because they knew the baby was dead and how it had died?"

When Michael Chamberlain was cross-examined by Barker, he was minded, like Lindy, to tell the truth honestly and exactly, without ever trying to "gild the lily". Ian Barker asked him about the staining on hats found in the Chamberlains' home during the search of the Chamberlain home – stains which Lindy had claimed may have been Azaria's blood spilled in the tent where the hats had been. Michael conceded that he knew now it was not blood but some form of gum arabic, a sap from an acacia tree, but he denied he had always known it was not blood. Barker asked: "Is that staining not intended to simulate blood, Mr Chamberlain?" Michael replied: "I wouldn't know – I don't know how it got there." He said that when Lindy showed him the stains, he had been curious but had not asked her how it got there. He told Barker that the tent was clearly illuminated from the barbecue area some 20 metres away and it was sufficiently clear to see objects in front of it. Barker asked: "There would've been no difficulty in seeing a dog with a baby in its mouth – the baby being dressed in white - would there?" Michael replied: "I can't comment on that." He had not seen the dingo with the baby, but he believed his wife's account.

When Barker asked about the cuts in the jump suit, Michael said he did not know whether it had been done by scissors or a dingo. When asked whether Lindy had cut the sleeve and the collar, Michael said: "I don't think so." When Barker questioned Michael on his initial statement to Inspector Michael Gilroy, that he had seen a dingo at the base of Ayers Rock staring intently at his family, hours before Azaria disappeared and he thought it was the "same dog" that had taken Azaria, Michael said it had been a "silly statement" which he could not back up. Barker put to him that he had made that statement to implant the idea in Gilroy's mind and help his wife "deceive" the police and the coroner as to what had really happened. Michael denied that. He did not think Lindy had told him after Azaria disappeared that the base of the rock was where a search should be made. He did not remember telling Constable Morris or Derek Roff that they should search there. He had not gone himself because it was "too horrible". He did not think he ought to go himself because it was more important for him and Lindy to stay at a central place and receive any news of the search. When Barker asked Michael whether he buried the baby clothed in the jumpsuit, he said he had not. When Barker asked: "Did your wife?", he replied: "I don't think she did." When asked whether he had rubbed Azaria's jumpsuit in the vegetation he said he had not. When asked whether Lindy had done it, he said: "Not that I know of."

None of this condemned Michael Chamberlain. He was giving evidence under the strictness guidelines of truthfulness. He was of course giving evidence under extreme stress, but his seemingly equivocal answers to critical questions did him no good in the eyes of the jury. Stuart Tipple said: "We must remember how excruciating it was for Michael to give evidence. We had left him till near the end because we were presenting a case for him and Lindy. It was very frustrating. You sit there expecting him to rebut with, 'My wife was loving mother who would never have harmed any of our kids', instead you got what the transcript shows. I felt like screaming at him."

When John Phillips started his final submissions to the jury on 25th October 1982, he went straight for raw common sense. Why would Lindy have done it? What on earth would have been her motive? "Ladies and gentlemen, women do not usually kill their babies, because that would be contrary to nature," he said. "One of the most fundamental facts of nature is the love of mothers for their children and the love of a mother for her baby. That happens again and again." There was no evidence that Lindy had had any form of depression and the killing did not fit into the category of motiveless killings. The Crown had been "stone, motherless broke" when it came to proposing a motive for the killing and even Barker, one of the in the best in the business, could not come up with one. Even if Lindy had had a motive, whatever it was, how could she have done what was alleged, including collaborating with Michael to bury the body, dig it up again and dispose of it, in the time frame available with all those people around in the 3-1/2 hours between the time Lindy raised the alarm and the time they left the campsite? Phillips said the defence had answered the scientific case put up by the Crown, point by point, expert by expert, and it really left just the evidence of the primary witnesses, who all supported Lindy's story. There was evidence of the intrusiveness of the dingoes, he said, and their harassment of children. Traces of the baby might yet be found, possibly even in the dingo droppings. It was an excellent performance. After he had finished, a Western Australian journalist said to Tipple: "They cannot convict her after that!" Tipple said he remembered walking back to the Travelodge with Phillips that night and heard him break into an operatic song after he closed his door. "I was exhausted," he said, "I don't know how he had the energy he had displayed but could sense his relief that there was nothing more he could do".

Because the defence counsel had called witnesses, the Crown had the last turn in addressing the jury. Barker, beginning his final submission on 26th October 1982, said he and the defence at least had common ground on one point: either it was a dingo attack, or it was murder. In his submission, it could not have been a dingo attack. People at the coalface, in the forensic laboratories, had found evidence suggesting another explanation. They were being contradicted by people who fancied themselves for their culture and intellectual acumen. He put himself personally on the side of the downtrodden, humble front-line workers. "It's just as well, isn't it, that we wear wigs and gowns in courts?" he said. "I don't know why law reform societies and commissions seem to want to do away with them. It permits people like me to take one faltering step towards people like Mr Phillips in elegance if not in eloquence; and the gown, of course, enables me to cover up my old shirts. That's what distinguishes the Melbourne bar from the Sydney bar."

Barker's final address might well go down in Australian legal history as being one of the most brilliant ever delivered. He said that despite the intellectual challenge, the humble laboratory workers had successfully stood their ground, Barker said, adding: "Both Mrs Kuhl and Dr Baxter, particularly Mrs Kuhl, were subjected to a long and exacting cross-examination and never retreated from what they said in their evidence-in-chief, and there was no attack on their credit." He derailed the defence argument point-by-point. The dingo story, in the light of the scientific evidence, could not be sustained, if one were to try to explain the state of the baby's clothing. "It managed to cut the sleeve and collar with a pair of scissors, an unlikely circumstance you might think even if we are dealing with the most intelligent and perceptive of animals," he said. Then it would have had to walk at least five kilometres before dropping the clothing where it was found. And what about the droppings Phillips had mentioned? Barker said that even if 100 square kilometres had been cleaned of dingo droppings, "it would have made the land cleaner and the air purer, but Phillips would have claimed, 'You've missed a bit!'" Barker said the Crown case consisted of many strands, and together they constituted "a rope with many strands, some weak, some strong", but in combination very powerful. He said the dingo attack scenario was, as he had said from the outset, was "a calculated, fanciful lie", which in the light of the Crown scientific evidence, could not be sustained. On motive, he did not suggest any, but he did not have to. On Phillips' description of him as one of the best in the business, he said he would not elaborate on that, "It embarrasses me!" which caused amusement.

Phillips and his team were still confident even after Barker's address but Phillips kept warning: "You can never be sure of a jury." There was, however, ample reason to be satisfied once Justice James Muirhead began his summing-up. At the outset of his directions, Muirhead said there was no evidence that the mother suffered post-natal depression or that the baby was deformed or anything similar. "You may be satisfied that she is an intelligent and controlled person," he said. In his view, if not stated explicitly, the dingo attack scenario had not been destroyed, and was still available, and should be seriously considered. "When in a criminal trial the Crown case rests wholly or substantially on circumstantial evidence, you must not convict unless these circumstances are inconsistent with any alternative hypothesis," he said. "You must utilise your experience of life and people and that is why you are here."

In reviewing the evidence, Muirhead told the jury the under-dash spray on Webber Roberts' Torana, had little evidential value. Why he did that is not clear. Perhaps he thought there was no proof that it had always been there. Perhaps it was coincidental and therefore of no relevance. Michael Chamberlain's later view was that it could have amounted to a misdirection of the jury. Nobody at that stage knew its full significance. Muirhead's directions, however, remained extremely favourable to the Chamberlains. Sally Lowe, whose credibility had not been challenged, had said she had heard the baby cry out after Lindy had left with the barbecue area with her and returned, when on the Crown scenario the baby would have been dead. Muirhead said that if the jury was satisfied that she had heard the cry, that was not just a very strong element in their consideration, but a bar to finding her guilty at all. The evidence of the baby's cry was the last thing he said to the jury, something Barker said later he had left "ringing in their ears" when the jury retired to consider its verdict. When Muirhead asked the defence team whether they had any objections to the summing-up, Phillips could only shake his head.

The Crown lawyers were less than impressed; after all their hard work, the judge had virtually directed the jury to bring in a not guilty verdict. After the jury retired to consider its verdict on the afternoon of Friday, 29th October 1982, they went across to the Darwin Hotel and sat glumly: they had presented a good case, the judge had in their eyes done his very best from his privileged position to derail it. Tipple and Phillips went for a walk around the block. "We walked smack-bang into Charlwood," Tipple said. "He was grinning. We said, 'We are on the home stretch now'. I said, 'Who do you think will win?' He laughed and said, 'Us, of course!'" In the jury room, there was nothing definite at all, at least at the beginning. Initially, four were for a guilty verdict, four for acquittal and four were undecided. Then it evolved to five for a conviction and seven either undecided or going for acquittal. The jury foreman's notes revealed by the NT police after the Royal Commission confirmed he thought the defence case was just a smoke screen. As the hours passed, 11 were for conviction and one was holding out. There was no real comprehension of the scientific evidence. Some of the jurors' chatter about the case to friends in Darwin got back to Malcolm Brown. According to what Brown deduced from this, most of the jurors had decided at the conclusion of the Crown case that the Chamberlains were guilty, and were just interested to hear what the defence had to say. The defence case, and its arguments, were not lost on some of them. How the reservations of those were overcome in the 6-1/2 hours will probably never be known. A strong personality, a brilliant arguer? Who knows? When the one juror holding out was persuaded the join the others, the jury had its decision. The foreman said: "OK, let's get out and announce it!"

At 8.37 pm on Friday, 29th October, after a retirement of 6-1/2 hours, the jury pronounced Lindy guilty of murder, Michael for being an accessory after the fact. Lindy gasped as though she had been shot. One female was seen holding her face in her hands and crying. Muirhead had no option but to immediately impose a mandatory life sentence on Lindy, with hard labour. The court adjourned. Journalists rushed off to get the news out. Malcolm Brown turned towards the departing jurors and said: "You pack of bastards!" Hardly his best moment, and most unfair to the jurors. Jurors have to make tough decisions. At that moment, the great safeguard the Chamberlains had looked to — the jury system – had failed them.

Lindy was taken from the court to Darwin Gaol. Muirhead, who was not obliged to impose a mandatory sentence on Michael Chamberlain, adjourned the hearing till the following Monday. News went across the nation, to be greeted in many places by tumultuous applause. In New South Wales, the news went out to a dental convention. The dentists, who had been following the odontological evidence closely, and for the most part backing the Crown, clapped and some of them cheered. There was similar applause at the University of New South Wales, where many academics were backing one of their own, Professor Chaikin. The defence team had prepared for a victory celebration. Phillips had bought a crate of champagne which had been delivered to the Darwin legal aid office where a celebration party was to be held with the team and its supporters. Cavanagh had obtained a CD featuring Vangelis's *Chariots of Fire* which he planned to have triumphantly blasting from his car when he picked the Chamberlains up from their last victorious walk from the court.

A forlorn Tipple and Michael walked back to the Travelodge. "There was little comfort to give a man who rightly asked, 'So that is British Justice for you?', and expected to soon join his wife in gaol," Tipple said. Stuart and Michael talked well into the next morning. "There were many plans to make and Michael did not want to be alone," Tipple said. "Who would look after the children and how soon could a bail application and appeal be heard?" Tipple didn't give a toss about the champagne but that night he promised himself that one day the truth would be known and he could drive away with *Chariots of Fire* blasting away.

In the immediate aftermath, there was a cry of dissent, however faint. That night, Tipple received a telegram from Hobart, at about midnight Darwin time: "Distress at verdict on circumstantial evidence. Stop. Our prayers are with you. Stop. It was from Bonnie, Noel and Ian Roberts and Julie Allen." For many closer to the case, there was disbelief. Lawyer and author John Bryson, who was writing his book on the case, *Evil Angels*, was to say on ABC Radio years later: "Here we have a case in which before the verdict the defence lawyers were convinced that they'd won, the accused were preparing to return to their children, the two remaining Crown prosecutors thought their best chance was a hung jury, the trial judge had favoured the defence case in his charge to the jury and journalists who had followed the trial for a week had so swamped their bookmaker with wagers on acquittal that the betting closed."

Michael Chamberlain returned to his lodgings in Darwin that Friday night. For the remaining hours of the night he tossed and turned, calculating, then recalculating, all the possibilities. How long would he be locked up? What was going to happen to the children? Would he ever see Lindy again? Phillips, utterly crushed by the verdict, wanted to get out of town straight away. With Kirkham, he went to see Muirhead that evening. They were ushered into Justice Muirhead's chambers where he invited them to join him in a whiskey and observed: "Well, I didn't think I summed up for a conviction!" Muirhead agreed to hand down sentence the next day. In the morning, Michael appeared before him, stiff and tight-lipped, ready for the worst. Muirhead handed Michael a sentence of 18 months gaol, suspended with a bond for three years and $500 recognisance. He said: "You have suffered and will continue to suffer, intolerably. For a long time, your children will, also." He could have imposed a maximum sentence of two years gaol or a $40,000 fine but he declined to do that. "Evidence has been presented of a man who should stand up for his wife," he said. "I've no doubt he will continue to do so."

It appeared to take a few seconds for Michael to register that he was not going to gaol, then he stood in the dock and for the first time in the trial lost all control and sobbed. Greg Cavanagh, the Legal Aid solicitor, grimaced as he tried to blink away his own tears. Two lives had been wiped out and other lives severely affected over something which, on any clear-headed view of the facts, even then, they were innocent of. They had turned to Tipple, and despite his best efforts, this had happened. They were entirely innocent. Somewhere, somewhere in that wilderness, someone, somewhere, had to see that. And, of course, there were more safeguards, being the Federal Court, which could hear their appeal, and beyond that the lofty heights of the High Court. There were brilliant jurists who would take it up, away from the hothouse of Darwin. Surely, they would be able to peel away the superfluous nonsensical material and get to heart of the matter. It was now the turn of the Apellate system to come up to scratch and show its solidity and reliability as the next great safeguard. It had worked in the past.

CHAPTER SEVEN

CONVICTIONS?
IT AIN'T OVER YET!

> *In the adversarial system, trial by jury is often regarded as a touchstone of the democratic administration of justice providing a check against arbitrary or oppressive exercise of power by the state. However, alongside notions of the jury as a "protector of liberty", there is an uneasy ambivalence within the legal profession regarding the competence and comprehension of lay jurors.*
> — Australian Law Reform Commission

On Saturday night in Darwin, 30th October 1982, police and prosecutors, and most of the media, gathered for a party on the Saturday night. Michael and Lindy Chamberlain had been convicted and punished. Police were happy that they had solved a baffling crime. Lindy Chamberlain had been found guilty of murdering her baby and husband Michael of being an accessory after the fact. Graeme Charlwood said: "Well that's over. On to something else now."

For Stuart Tipple, it was one of the lowest points in his life. The Chamberlains had turned to him. The entire church, in a sense, had also turned to him. And what had he given them? All those hours he had put into the case, all that thought, all that anguish, and it had all come to this. Tipple was suffering the gloom that befalls any lawyer charged with the responsibility of defending a client who genuinely believes his client or clients are innocent and who has failed. "It is easier to get over when you think your client is a crook, much harder when you see there has been a travesty of justice," he said.

Tipple was by no means unhappy with the way the trial had gone or what he had done. "It actually went better than I thought it would," he said. "The main disappointment was the under-dash spray. I think we had established reasonable doubt [about my clients' guilt] and that is all you have to do. We certainly won the judge. As you know most of the journos were backing us and even the Crown thought they were going to lose. When the verdict came, it was not the agony of knowing what might have happened, it was the agony of having a system let you down. I don't mind being fairly beaten but I was robbed and the Chamberlains were robbed. As John Winneke [John Winneke QC whom he later engaged] was to say time and time again, it was a crook result. I play a lot of sport and I am a very competitive person. And for me to lose when I should have won is like being robbed and it's hard to take."

All this had a very personal impact on Tipple in another way. His wife Cherie was heavily pregnant, due to give birth in six weeks. The life and health of babies, and parental love, were very present in his mind. When his own baby arrived into the world, he wanted the baby to come into a household full of joy and happiness, not despair.

If it was any comfort to Stuart Tipple, he was not alone in his belief that the Chamberlains were innocent. But it appeared at that stage that the number of dissenters in the general public were quite limited. Those who ran the justice system were entitled to shrug their shoulders and say they relied on evidence and due process, not public sentiment. There was certainly no vindictiveness. Once it had been proved that Lindy had killed her baby, for whatever reason, and had fabricated the dingo attack story, more humanitarian concerns could come into play. There would not have been much concern had the judge – if the law had allowed it – given Lindy a suspended sentence. Barker was glad it was over, and despite his role as a prosecutor he did not relish what he had seen happen. He said he had not enjoyed the job, and if there were to be a retrial, another prosecutor would have to be found. He heard someone say that the experience would make Michael Chamberlain a better Christian. Barker said: "Well if I had to go through all that to be a better Christian, I'd be an atheist!"

The next morning, Sunday 31st October, Michael Chamberlain, a convicted criminal, flew with Stuart Tipple back to Sydney. When he returned to Gosford, Tipple found a letter waiting for him, written on 25th October by Barry Boettcher, in which Boettcher praised Tipple: "Although the jury has yet to consider the verdict in the Chamberlain trial, I am confident of the outcome. There is only one verdict that would be appropriate, and I am confident that the Chamberlains will not only be found not guilty, but that there will be a wealth of commentary at the time to dispel any consideration that Michael and Lindy had anything to do with Azaria's disappearance. I certainly hope so, because it would be appropriate and needed. I recognise that Andrew Kirkham and John Phillips are excellent in court, and that other members of your profession will give them the professional acclaim that their abilities deserve. However, the credit for assembling the material with which they could work goes to you. I applaud you for the tireless effort that you put into the case – in pursuing all sorts of leads – and for being a very effective interlocutor between witnesses such as myself and the barristers. You certainly developed a keen appreciation of some immunological concepts and techniques. I trust that you will always carry with you a feeling of personal satisfaction for the excellence with which you performed your tasks in the Chamberlain Affair. There is no doubt that you gave yourself and your talents fully to the defence of the Chamberlains. Sincere congratulations on the task performed excellently." It was just too much, Tipple said. "I got up shut my office door, sat down and cried. I wasn't just feeling sorry for myself. I cried for the Chamberlains and how our system which I thought till then was the best in the world, had failed them."

The primary witnesses – people who had been at the campsite, who had seen and heard what had happened – and whose evidence had supported Lindy and Michael's account, felt much the same. "The case changed the lives of everyone who gave evidence," Tipple said. "Those who gave the primary evidence thought they had let the Chamberlains down. They felt that had they given their evidence differently, there would have been a different result. In fact, they had done a darn good job!" Sally Lowe told Tipple in a letter of her own: "I'm afraid I was nearly off my brain when I appeared in court. I was so surprised by the prosecution pre-court interview being so light, I was a bit frightened what they would say to me in court (or I would say – how they would try to twist the truth)." She said that before she went to put the baby down in the tent, Lindy had been wearing a parka, dress, socks and sandshoes. When Lindy returned from the tent with Aidan, she had the same clothes on. There were no tracksuit trousers. But when Lindy was at the barbecue area, she was looking at her from "hands up". When Barker asked her at the trial what she was wearing at the barbecue site, she had told him what she saw from the hands up. "I'm afraid my tendency to rave on and failure to express myself makes it hard for people to understand what I am saying," she said. Sally said she stood by her evidence that Lindy had been away from the barbecue area only a short time, that she had not changed her clothes and that when Sally had gone to the tent, she had seen spots of blood. She was quite convinced of the innocence of the Chamberlains. She said: "I know you share our hurt at seeing an innocent woman in jail. Please do your best with an appeal. Our hopes of true justice be with you."

Derek Roff contacted Tipple because he felt he had not had the opportunity of giving important evidence at the trial. He said that in the area where the baby's clothing was found, at the base of Ayers Rock, he had seen flattened vegetation consistent with a dingo having lain there, but he had not been asked any questions that allowed him to give that evidence. "It is rather an unusual situation, in any criminal case, when all the primary witnesses supported the innocence of the accused and even after the convictions come out and protest," Tipple said. Even to those who had followed the Chamberlain case from a distance, there was consternation. Nothing added up. So much of it simply defied common sense.

Greg Lowe wrote directly to James Muirhead, on behalf of himself and his wife, repeating his evidence that had favoured the Chamberlains, and seeking His Honour's advice. "Our main individual statements were made more than 13 months after the disappearance of the Chamberlain child, yet the essence of our statements demonstrate the fact that the child was seen alive in the BBQ site, the Chamberlains were a pleasant couple, another person was in the company of the Chamberlains for the short time that she was away from the BBQ site, that her composure had not changed on her return, that a dingo unwary of human presence was in the immediate vicinity, my wife did hear the baby's cry while Mr & Mrs Chamberlain and their sons were in my presence, the alarm was made in desperate earnest, a considerable amount of blood was seen in the tent by my wife, that the search was actively carried out and that both parents were obviously distraught over the disappearance of their child. These facts are inconsistent with the Crown allegations, and I humbly seek your advice on any action we can take, in light of the documented evidence." Muirhead might well have agreed, privately, with what Lowe said, but he was not in a position to advise Lowe. He sent the letter on to Tipple.

Tipple had very little time to brood or search his soul. "I returned to my practice after being away for over six weeks," he said. "There was a pile of work waiting on my desk to be done but as always the Chamberlain work took precedence. From being the junior, it was now just me. I had to brief new counsel and prepare for the appeal and get them up to speed. I had to prepare the bail application for Lindy's release. And on the personal front prepare for my first child who was born in December. But being the only identifiable member of the legal team left, I was bombarded with people who wanted my time to hear their theories. I had to listen to everyone. I was the one who copped the abuse and the allegations of having failed. In particular when people heard the eye witness evidence they formed an erroneous belief that I had concentrated too much on the blood evidence and not enough on the eye witness accounts." Tipple said he had not called the shots. That had been up to John Phillips, to decide what to do and what strategies to follow. "I ended up with the blood evidence and Phillips, Kirkham and Dean proofed the camp witnesses and the trackers ... The critics didn't care they just wanted someone to blame. In preparing for the appeal I now had to take control of everything." Sometimes the stress was released in a flash of irritation. Malcolm Brown later met him in a court lift and commented on a rather outlandish report in a tabloid newspaper. Tipple snapped back and said: "You're probably put out because you did not think of it first!' Brown said: "I think I'd be more ethical than that!" To which Tipple replied: "Ethics? No!"

Of course, questions of how the defence might have been handled were only one thing. Even if she was in fact guilty, look at the punishment! If Lindy had in fact killed Azaria, what on earth justified this reaction, and the punishment? A woman who would kill her baby, in some if not most circumstances, did deserve sympathy. This sort of thing had happened in the past. Malcolm Brown had been assigned years before to report on a case in Nowra, on the NSW south coast, where a woman had claimed hysterically that a man had knocked at her front door, snatched her baby from her, declared it was "not fit to live" and made off. It was a most unlikely story, greeted by police with natural scepticism. The police broke her down the next day. The baby had been sickly and the stress of it had driven her to desperation. She had taken the baby and thrown if over a cliff onto the banks of the Shoalhaven River. The police searched and found the body, half-eaten by rats. The last news of her was that she was an in-patient at the Northside psychiatric clinic in Sydney.

With regards to Lindy, the police and the Crown lawyers were, after all, husbands and fathers themselves. Bill Hitchings, who had reported on the case for the Melbourne *Sun* had a report published in his newspaper on Monday, 1st November 1982, quoting a senior police officer: "We are in a difficult position. The Northern Territory Police have been vindicated and that is the end of the matter as far as we are concerned. After two years of intense investigation we have provided, to the unanimous satisfaction of the jury, that Mrs Chamberlain murdered her child. We are not vindictive and we would not want this couple – and particularly Mrs Chamberlain – to suffer unnecessarily." He said that if Lindy Chamberlain were released too soon, there would be uproar. "She has been found guilty of a crime and she must pay the penalty account to the law. But women who have done such a thing are rarely imprisoned for long time.

We would not oppose a short sentence." According to Hitchings, lawyers, police and other authorities in Darwin said the most likely outcome of Lindy's conviction would be that she would serve another six months before being released.

From a professional point of view, congratulations went all round, including praise for the performance of Ian Barker. The *Australian Law News* was soon to publish an article headlined: "Ian Barker, Azaria Prosecutor," and "The Man who won the Azaria trial". It said: "Barker will probably go down in history as the lawyer who won Australia's most publicised and most difficult murder trial. With no body, no motive, no witness, he established a very strong circumstantial case which the defence was unable to answer and which most lawyers assumed would result in a hung jury. After an extremely well-balanced summing-up by Mr Justice Muirhead, the jury, despite 300 exhibits, overwhelming scientific and technical evidence, and disagreements by expert witnesses, took only a few hours to reach its verdict. Observers at the trial have accredited this to Barker's prosecution tactics and brilliant address to the jury at the end." The article outraged members of the legal profession and the *Australian Law News* saw fit to publish a strident letter of protest in its following edition. Praise of Barker had gone too far.

A prosecutor neither wins nor loses cases. A prosecutor's job is to ensure that the Crown evidence is properly presented and justice is done. In the United States in the Patty Hearst trial in in 1976, the high-flying defence lawyer, F. Lee Bailey, attracted all the headlines. Patty, a newspaper heiress, had been kidnapped by members of the self-styled Symbionese Liberation Army and after a period in custody, had participated in a bank robbery with them. Bailey's argument was that had Patty Hearst not been kidnapped, she would not have been committing that bank robbery. Reports of that submission swept the country. But prosecutor James L. Browning Jr plodded on. Yes, Patty Hearst would not have been committing a bank robbery had she not been kidnapped, he said. But a point had been reached where she made a conscious decision. At some point, she had to be held responsible for her actions. Browning prevailed, and Hearst was convicted of armed robbery and using a firearm to commit a felony. There had been no histronics from Browning.

In the Chamberlain case, Phillips approach had been strait-laced and conservative. The basic thrust of his argument appealed to common sense. Mothers do not normally kill their babies, was one of his principal arguments. There was no motive in this case and the prosecution could not come up with one. Barker's submission, delivered with his normal flourish, was based on the simple argument: "Either the dingo did it, or it was murder." The murder case was anchored on the alleged presence of baby's blood in the car, which could not be explained in any other way than foul play. It was open to Barker to ridicule the dingo story, in particular how it could be sustained in the light of alleged scissor cuts in the baby's clothes and how the clothing was found. It must also be stated that Barker was not putting on an act. His performance in court was his natural style. He had a brilliant intellect, a bubbling personality and a courtroom manner that could not have been more tailor-made to sway juries. Barker had an impish sense of humour, on one occasion broadcasting to media listening via closed-circuit television in another room: "Attention media, this is your captain speaking!"

The manner and style of counsel can make a difference. Retired NSW District Court judge Harry Bell recalls in his autobiography, *Bachelor, Barrister, Benedict - Recollections*, a time when as a solicitor he was instructing for a plaintiff in a defamation case. The counsel he had retained had to go off to a part-heard case. "We briefed instead Percy (later Sir Percy) Spender and we lost the case," Bell said. His firm, K.W. Gunn & Co, maintained that this was because Percy was "too good", which Bell took to have been a euphemism for "not in tune with ... working men". The defendant's counsel, R.L. Taylor, was able to 'speak the language better'," Bell said. Barker was to demonstrate this down-to-earth style over and over again, for example in the defence of Lionel Murphy, who was being retried on a charge of attempting to pervert the course of justice. Barker's unconventional approach – declining to put Murphy into the witness box and instead attacking the credibility of the chief witness, Chief Magistrate Clarrie Briese – won the day.

But let us return to the Chamberlains and their reaction to the verdict. In the immediate aftermath, there were howls of outrage from the defence experts. On 1st November 1982, Richard Nairn wrote to Tipple expressing his dismay at the verdict which he said was "tragic, barbaric and a travesty". He said that if the facts of the case were taken away from a tiny corner – being the jury room of the NT Supreme Court – and presented to the world at large, there would be outrage. He asked: "What is our legal position about publishing any or all of Mrs Kuhl's worksheets and trial demonstrations in Australian and international biomedical journals or privately? I might be able to arrange for you to send representative samples for the Medical Council of Australia, which would ensure world-wide coverage. It would be a bombshell in view of the international interest in the trial and the verdict. Could you mount a discreetly organised campaign, on the basis of: Why spend several million dollars to justify the

Northern Territory Police after the first Coroner's verdict, only to result in the sentencing to life imprisonment of an inoffensive woman of impeccable character in a case where there was no body, no weapon, no motive, no opportunity except for a highly trained magician, no evidence that was not refuted by the Defence's experts, incapacity by Darwin jury or judiciary to understand modern science?" Nairn offered further informal assistance without fee.

Les Harris, president of the Dingo Foundation of Australia, wrote to Tipple on 2nd November saying he felt "a deep sense of unfairness" at the verdict. He said: "I am sure that no one could say that you did anything less than your best." He was not at all unpersuaded that a dingo had taken the baby. "I have said from the outset that Lindy Chamberlain's only claim, that a dingo took her baby, has never been investigated by anyone who knew how to make such an investigation and, further to that, the only thing that could have been investigated after the disappearance was wilfully destroyed – the dingoes that wilfully foraged in the Ayers Rock camping ground," he said. "What constitutes grounds for appeal in the Northern Territory, I do not know, but surely investigation by people not competent to make such investigation and the destruction of evidence has some bearing on it. I am acutely conscious of the fact that I was not asked (at the trial) to pass any opinion on the probability of the matter, or on a host of matters which we know to be relevant. If an appeal is made and if the Foundation is asked to furnish information, it will be my recommendation to the committee that the matter of what is relevant and what is not is something that we will decide".

The same day, Ken White, a journalist with the *NT News*, who had covered the Chamberlain trial, said in the newspaper that the sentence was extraordinary when compared with punishments meted out for lesser crimes such as manslaughter. He repeated Nairn's point that there had been no motive, no eye witnesses, no weapon and no body. He questioned the credibility of Professor Cameron. He finished with: "I was told that the verdict last Friday night had restored the Attorney-General's faith in the jury system in the Territory. It was an all-up $4 million gamble and it paid off. Had it been a hung jury, there would have been no retrial. It is sadly ironic that it had to be a person like Lindy Chamberlain, who up to two years and three months ago was an obscure housewife, to restore the Attorney-General's faith. But millions of words have been written since that fateful August night. I won't bore you with any more. Except to say Paul Everingham got his pound of flesh."

White's article stung Everingham and provoked widespread criticism.

Everingham was like anyone else entitled to respect a jury's verdict and to allow for the appeal process and need not be deemed to have any personal interest in it at all. In a note to Tipple soon afterwards, White said: "Enclosed is an article which, I gather, has rather upset our Chief Minister. He has demanded $10,000 for defamation and a public apology. In turn, he has been told to go whistle Dixie. The response to the article has been overwhelming. My phone hasn't stopped ringing for two days. Also enclosed is a photostat of the anonymous letter I mentioned." That anonymous letter said: "I heard two weeks ago that many big heads would roll if a guilty verdict was not found. That was said in Govt Depts. I cannot sign my name as I may get the sack. Please keep up the good work – your article was spot on – congratulations, please keep up honest reporting. If only people knew the truth, the verdict was certainly unjust."

Dr Eric Magnusson, a former principal of Avondale College, Cooranbong, and later on the staff of the Australian National University, said in a note to Tipple: "The shock result can only be put down to the strength of the initial decision made by so many ordinary people in Australia under the impact of the evidence at the 2nd inquest." In a letter to the *Sydney Morning Herald* on 3rd November, P. Stevens of North Bondi made some very perceptive comments about juries: "Publicity surrounding the Azaria case has at last exposed the shortcomings of our jury system. Whenever evidence for the prosecution and defence are about equally balanced, the outcome must depend on opposing counsel's rhetoric and legal tricks to turn jurors' minds that way. The verdict more reflects attorneys' skills than a cool consideration of the available evidence. The phrase, 'get yourself a good lawyer', proves the courts quite openly reject responsibility to find out actual guilt or innocence."

An anonymous correspondent wrote to Tipple telling him that one of the jurors in the trial had gone to Adelaide after it was over, become drunk and then told his audience that that the jurors knew the Chamberlains were guilty before they even went into court and that they had all talked it over and it was "cut and dried". Well, maybe. It might have happened, but people shoot their mouth off in pubs. The one recorded incident of jury indiscipline was when a juror had accosted Tom Pauling, representing the Crown, at a night spot in Darwin and wanted to talk. Pauling had quite properly pushed him away.

In a letter to Dr Jim Cox, president of Avondale College, Jess Duthrie, of Burwood, Victoria, asked: "Have the Chamberlain family asked that a 'time and motion' study be considered for the time it would have taken to clean up fresh blood, remove bloodied clothing, dispose of a bleeding infant (*all with a six-year-old standing nearby and a four-year-old sleeping nearby*) all in campsite conditions?

No re-enactment of the alleged killing has been done with a dummy child spurting sticky blood, in a similar car. Where were the flies which would have been buzzing around the smell of blood when the passenger got into their car that night? Flies can't be deceived. Blood can't be cleaned off easily in the best of conditions – let along a campsite! If Mrs Chamberlain killed her baby, she not only needs an Oscar for acting, but she should be entered into the Olympics for speed and dexterity in changing mood, changing clothes in a small tent in a caravan park, with a couple of boys nearby, performed the alleged murder, cleaning up the blood in a hand towel, and returned to the bar BQ area to open a can of beans, with Aidan! In a caravan Park or camping ground, one can be disturbed by anyone. I'm only a normal housewife and mother of two, who also goes camping in small tents. Frankly even if I'd been the murderous kind, I would have found it impossible to perform in those circumstances. Could you please pass on my suggestion of a re-enactment of the alleged crime to Michael and Lindy? It could prove their innocence."

That was, of course, pure common sense, which kept breaking through spasmodically but ineffectively during the saga.

And what of Lindy? Malcolm Brown went to see her with permission from the prison authorities soon after she was incarcerated. She was in what was essentially a cage, inside a fenced compound, outside the main gaol, with razor-wire at the top of the fence. Lindy presented herself as cheerful and resigned, and with two prison officers standing over them, Brown could hardly question her about the way she really felt. The prison authorities had allowed the interview because they wanted an article showing the world that she was being looked after. Brown reported her laughing comments, even at one point said she had "giggled". He had thought he might be writing a soulful article conveying the devastation of a woman locked up for life, separated from husband and family, in circumstances which Brown believed were at least contentious. He thought such an article, an "exclusive" as it was, might have won him an award. However, the material was not there. He could not fabricate, so he simply reported, like any good reporter, what he saw and heard. His report upset Tipple and Phillips, but he replied that he could only report what he had seen and heard. An anonymous writer was apparently provoked by what Brown reported and said he had "left the church" because of its "hypocritical support" for her. Addressing Michael and Lindy, the writer said: "Both of you should be in gaol, not to giggle as you do but to pray for your soul in your spare time".

Gene Janes, writing for News Ltd publications, presented a gloomy picture of what confronted Lindy. He said: "Like so much connected to and with

Berrimah Prison, the female section is a foul-up. This is mainly because it was never intended to house female prisoners, was not designed or built for it. It was originally planned as a work-release section, a block outside the walls of the jail itself housing prisoners close to the end of their sentences who were to be permitted to work at an outside job, returning to prison after work. Only a work-release scheme was never implemented, was never even so much as attempted. Neither, it must be pointed out, is any other kind of rehabilitation program operating at the prison. Also, totally lacking is any attempt at organised sport, except, that is, for very spasmodic basketball practice for the male prisoners. The females have no sport avenues whatever. This lack of opportunity for physical exercise is particularly harsh because the female section of the prison lacks any sort of outdoor exercise yard – since the building was intended for a work release section, a dormitory to house prisoners working outside the jail all day, there was no real necessity for an exercise yard …. Eighty percent of the female prisoners' out-of-cell time is spent in the recreational area, a room measuring around six to 12 metres. Lindy's fellow prisoners include a woman who killed her *de facto* husband with a knife, three Aboriginal women who battered a pensioner to death with an iron bar in the grounds of a Darwin pub, and women serving time for drug offences, mostly imported heroin from Asia."

Immediately after being sentenced Lindy offered Michael a divorce.

In the meantime, there was concern in the professional community as to what was to happen with the baby Lindy was to bear. A consultant physician and psychiatrist on the Queensland Gold Coast wrote to John Phillips on 1st November 1982 expressing serious reservations about Lindy being allowed to keep the baby. He said: "Let us assume, for a moment, for the sake of argument, that while in a disturbed state of mind, perhaps even of disassociation and amnesia, reduced awareness and reduced responsibility, Mrs Chamberlain killed the baby. Then, whether she is guilty or not of murder depends on her intent and if it was '*mens rea*'. In a woman a few weeks after child-birth, puerperal psychosis would be the likely cause of infanticide. As is well-known, after child birth, vital hormones and chemical substances are, at that time, undergoing tremendous upheaval and re-adjustment. The disturbances in these chemical hormones can, and very often do, produce marked changes in feeling, thinking, bizarre behaviour and behaviour completely out of character." Puerperal psychosis is defined by *Wilkipedia* as: "A psychiatric emergency in which symptoms of high mood and racing thoughts (mania), depression, severe confusion, loss of inhibition, paranoia, hallucinations and delusions set in, beginning suddenly in the first two weeks after delivery. The symptoms vary and can change quickly. The most severe symptoms last from 2 to 12 weeks, and recovery takes 6 months to a year." The doctor told Tipple: "If Mrs Chamberlain suffered from puerperal psychosis after the birth of Azaria, there is a danger of recurrence after the birth of her new baby and the possibility of her attempting to damage it. And any suggestion of psychosis after the coming birth might strengthen the suggestion of psychosis after her last childbirth."

That was, at least, a sensible and properly considered opinion. The big flaw in it was that there was never at any point prior to the disappearance of Azaria the slightest suggestion of these symptoms in Lindy.

The other point is that, learned as they are, experts can be wrong. In England, Professor James Cameron, the man whose report had triggered the second investigation into Azaria's disappearance, and whose evidence had held such sway in the trial, was under fire. On Friday, 5th November 1982, a mere week after the Chamberlains were convicted, Cameron and his colleague, a consultant paediatrician, Dr Graeme Snodgrass, were severely criticised in the Chelmsford Crown Court in Britain over their evidence in a case in which a baby, Jason, had died. It was obviously significant because of ongoing questions about Cameron's credibility. Graeme Snodgrass had given written evidence supporting Cameron in the Chamberlain case and might at one stage have been called as an expert witness. In Jason's case, the child had been found dead in his cot in 1981. Cameron had done a post-mortem on the baby and had concluded that the baby had died from malnutrition and hypothermia. The parents had been charged with wilful neglect.

The baby's weight was critical evidence but Cameron had adopted a very casual approach. According to the judge, Gerald Butler, the weight had been "jotted down on a piece of blotting paper". Cameron's evidence was that the baby weighed about 4-1/2 kilograms, compared with the average weight of a child that age of 6-1/2 kilos. Butler, said: "When one looks at Jason's birth weight and normal development, one sees his anticipated weight would have been just over 5-1/2 kilos, not 6-1/2 kilos as appears to have been suggested by Prof Cameron." Butler said Snodgrass had given a damning piece of evidence which cross-examination had showed to be "rubbish". Snodgrass had given evidence about the child's height which tended to confirm malnutrition and said the baby had not put on weight since it was five weeks old. When shown growth charts, he admitted he was badly wrong. Snodgrass had been wrong when he said in his report that Jason "definitely" did not suffer from a rare disease called ectodermal dysplasia, which affected a child's growth, and in the trial the prosecution had to concede that Jason did suffer from that disease. Jason's parents were acquitted of wilfully neglecting their child.

The mother, Susan Madison, unlike Lindy, did not project the image of being a loving mother. She admitted having ill-treated the child, having broken his arm, leg and ribs, and she was gaoled for four months. But the question for the Chamberlain supporters was that if Cameron had taken such a casual approach in investigating Jason's death, had he been as casual when making his assessment of the evidence in the Chamberlain case?

All this was brought to Tipple's attention by the wife of a prisoner in Britain, James Godfried, who was serving a sentence for rape, a crime Godfried said he had not committed, and who had been convicted mainly as a result of Cameron's evidence. The natural question arose: If Cameron was found to be wrong in Jason's case, and some of the criticism was directed at his methodology, could these faults also have manifested themselves in his approach to the Chamberlain inquiry?

Of course, the nutter letters kept coming, and sometimes provided comic relief. On 9th November, an anonymous correspondent sent a letter to Tipple, saying: "Dear Sirs, my view on the Chamberlains case is that it could be a conspiracy concocted by the Vatican. As the 7th Day Adventists are not afraid to denounce the Catholic faith and the People and the Vatican as the Anti-Christ. There could well be a plot to make the Christian churches look bad especially the 7th Day Adventists. We Christians are praying that the light will be shed and the truth shall set them free. If you read The Godfathers, Double Cross and Big Betrayal by Chiniquy, printed by Evangelical Literature Enterprises, of Geebung, Queensland, you'll see the cunning ways that the Vatican destroys churches world-wide, using Jesuit priests, the confessional and the people at large to carry out their evil desire."

The SDA Church remained in support of the Chamberlains, and of Stuart Tipple. On 11th November, Ron Craig, secretary-treasurer of the Trans-Tasman Union Conference of the Seventh-day Adventist Church – a quiet man but strong and steadfast – wrote a letter to Tipple enclosing a cheque for his work on the case. He said: "May I take this opportunity, Stuart, of saying again how much we appreciate all the hours you have put into the Chamberlain case. I know you have worked tirelessly, and spent many, many hours with John and Andrew in preparing evidence for the court case. Certainly, everything that could be done was done, and you left no stone unturned in your efforts to secure a 'not guilty' verdict the trial. I want to thank you for the way you have stood by Michael and Lindy, and particularly the way you supported them during the trial. I am sure that both Michael and Lindy very much appreciated your being with them in Darwin." He asked that his appreciation be passed onto the barristers.

For Lindy, she had no option but to look forward. She gave birth to a girl, Kahlia, on 17th November 1982. On her account she resisted giving birth, knowing the baby would be taken away from her. When she was able to hold the baby in her arms, she desperately wanted to keep her. She applied for bail so that she could look after Kahlia. In the bail hearing next day, affidavits were tendered from a psychiatrist and a psychologist who said they could see nothing abnormal about Lindy Chamberlain or anything contradicting the proposition she would be a loving, caring mother. Dr Louise Metcalf, a Macquarie Street specialist, said she considered Lindy Chamberlin to be just that. Dr Frederick Smith, a Northern Territory psychologist, also said he could detect nothing abnormal about Lindy Chamberlain. The three judges were at odds. Justice Fox said there was need for a mother to bond with a child, irrespective of whether she was serving a life sentence. Justice Lockhart, dissenting, said it was "somewhat odd and incongruous" for a woman who had been convicted of a crime of that nature to be given custody of "another baby daughter". The court decided two-to-one to grant bail, pending the outcome of the appeal to the Federal Court's decision. Lindy had to enter a $3000 surety and strict bail conditions were set. Lindy returned to Cooranbong and was reunited with her family.

There was to be no peace for the Chamberlains. A t-shirt found its way to the streets: "Watch out Kahlia – Mummy's coming home!" On 20th December, a letter arrived at the Chamberlain household in Cooranbong, addressed to Reagan Chamberlain. It said: "Your mother and father murdered your sister Azaria. Ask them where they put the body." The writer signed himself/herself off as, "One Who Was At The Scene", and added: "Your mother was the dingo." Another, written to "Miss K. Chamberlain", said: "Poor little Kahlia. Parents a Failure. Murdered Your Sister. Deep Sympathy for a poor little child." A letter to Michael Chamberlain, referring to a German Shepherd he had acquired as protection against intruders, said: "I suppose you will give your baby a toy dingo to play with for Xmas, you will want to watch out your guard dog doesn't get your baby and bury the clothes in your garden, and as for your sons I suppose you will give them each a photo of the jail to hang on the wall of their bedroom and a tin of baked beans, and you will get the red carpet treatment from everyone around you."

Within the outer reaches of the Seventh-day Adventist laity, rumbles of dissent became apparent. The SDA hierarchy, which had always been quietly supportive of the Chamberlains, had been at pains not to take up a public position on innocence or guilt. This was an issue, quite properly, to be left to the secular authorities. But others within the SDA laity felt not only had Michael and Lindy Chamberlain been wrongly convicted, but if they had had a better defence they would not have been. Phil Ward, who had made an earlier appearance in this narrative, entered the fray as publisher of his *Adventist News*. A feisty, energetic layman, based in Epping in Sydney's north-west, Ward ran a very successful business turning out business newsletters. In some instances, he was quoted in mainstream business journals. In March 1981, the *Sydney Morning Herald* quoted him giving advice on tax, when he said that inflation was a tax in itself and it was wise to arrange investment to avoid the unfairness.

Ward knew Michael and Lindy Chamberlain. Ward had trained in theology at Avondale College in the 1960s while Michael was there and had attended Michael and Lindy's wedding. But Ward had given up the prospect of a clerical life and become a publisher. He decided, through *Adventist News*, to take his own look at the Chamberlain case. Into his investigation he brought Don McNicol, who claimed to have met Lindy as a teenager at an SDA camp in Melbourne. McNicol was concerned about the convictions, and agreed to work for Ward without fee, though Ward would pay his expenses. Ward and McNicol consulted Arthur Hawken, a former builder, who, following an injury to his back, had gone gem-hunting in the Northern Territory and had built up an extraordinary rapport with the Aborigines. Hawken had spoken to Nipper Winmatti, an elder of the Pitjuntjutjara people, and who had done tracking when Azaria disappeared. According to Hawken, the Aborigines had told him things about the incident at Ayers Rock in 1980 that other researchers had not discovered. Ward called for support among the SDA laity, and the laity responded. But they were only part of the vanguard. Elsewhere forces were moving.

In Darwin, the custodians of the justice system bunkered down. The Chamberlains had had the benefit of a jury trial. They had had advantage of a defence. They had the appellate system open to them. But for some members of the public, the Chamberlains had been condemned forever. A letter sent by air mail, addressed to Lindy Chamberlain at Avondale College and postmarked 29th December 1982, contained newspaper pictures of Lindy Chamberlain with her eyes cut out. A note in the envelope said Lindy was a "brutal killer" and said: "Beware killer bitch. I am on mine [sic] way to Cooranbong, to cut your throat before New Year. I'll cut her throat the exact way she cut Azaria's, ear to ear." One letter showed a picture of Lindy with eyes narrowed and said: "Hi Mrs Lucifer. Get a load of those eyes! I need say no more. A lot of us are ~~wake up~~ awake." Also arriving in the Chamberlains' letter box was a letter from Mt Lawley Western Australia, claiming to be from "Murdered Azaria". It said: "I did not have a chance to do on Earth the work of God. I am in Heaven now and do not fear anyone here. Think of what you did for the rest of your life and further my belief you are innocent but not heavenly people." Another person sent a photo of "Azaria's grave", saying it was "40 miles from Ayers Rock at a placed called Crystal Springs". Yet another told Lindy: "You are a Murderer and a Liar." Tipple said: "Lindy never got those letters. I guess that is one of the advantages of being in gaol."

It was not only the Chamberlain parents who received such mail. Reagan got a letter telling him it was "very easy for your mother to get out of jail. All she needs is to tell the truth to the very experienced police officers that questioned her. It was very obvious that she was lying (Even a novice could tell). So just tell her to tell the truth." One addressed to Aidan was so repugnant that it does not bear repeating in any form. Such letters would hardly have been passed on to the children, but there had been stress on Aidan and Reagan from the outset. Part of the frenzied speculation had been that one of them had killed the baby and that the mother had taken the blame to cover up for them. There was not the slightest evidence that either of them was involved. But the suggestion that "one of the kids did it" was, sadly, to be brought up later even by a Federal Appeals Court judge, Kenneth Jenkinson. Jenkinson, quite rightly, slapped his own idea down, but why bring it up in the first place? The two boys, haplessly caught up in things beyond their control, were to suffer horribly and it was to affect them for rest of their lives.

CHAPTER EIGHT

RESEARCHING A DISASTER

"

Sherlock Holmes and Dr Watson went on a camping trip. After a good meal and a bottle of wine, they lay down for the night and went to sleep. Some hours later, Watson woke and nudged his faithful friend. "Holmes, look up and tell me what you see," he said. Holmes said: "I see millions and millions of stars. Astronomically, it tells me that there are millions of galaxies and potentially billions of planets. Astrologically, I observe that Saturn is in Leo. Horologically, I deduce that time is about a quarter past three. Theologically, I can see that God is all powerful and that we are small and insignificant. Meteorologically, I suspect that we will have a beautiful day tomorrow. Why, what does it tell you?" Watson replied: "Well, Holmes, seeing you ask, I deduce that someone has stolen our tent!"

— *A joke, altered from the original, told by Sydney playwright and Dylan Thomas aficionado, Clive Woosnam*

Very few of the appeal judges saw that the Emperor of Crown Evidence was wearing no clothes, especially if you consider the prime exhibit – Azaria's jumpsuit.

— *Charles Waterstreet*

As 1983 dawned, Stuart Tipple's focus was naturally intent on winning the appeal before the Federal Court. There would be three judges and surely outside the Darwin hothouse three highly educated and rational minds would be able to see things differently. Tipple decided that the key to winning the appeal was to attack the scientific evidence. It was the scientific evidence that had convicted them. If evidence continued to stand up that baby's blood had been found in the Chamberlains' car, then the only rational conclusion would be that there had been foul play. If there were no baby's blood in the car, then the Crown case could not be sustained.

The lack of convincing primary evidence was always a fundamental weakness in the Crown case against the Chamberlains. In a normal criminal prosecution, primary evidence comes first and the scientific evidence is used as confirmation. When Sef Gonzales, a disaffected youth of Filipino extraction, murdered his parents and his sister at Ryde in Sydney's north-west in 2001, he was unable to cover his tracks. He tried to establish an alibi but there was plenty of primary evidence against him. What forensic examination could do was point to a smear of blue paint on his shirt. This was deposited when he had painted the words, "fuck Off Asians KKK", on the side of the family home to suggest the murders had been the result of a racist attack. The primary and scientific evidence then locked together. But if a prosecution case relies solely, or principally, on scientific evidence, then it is vulnerable. Already in the Chamberlain case, the primary evidence did not back up the Crown case and questions had been raised in the evidence of Joy Kuhl. and in her recorded notes and confirmatory tests.

Tipple wanted to find those answers but he had many things on his mind. He was juggling several balls. He had his wife and baby to look after and the pressure of other work. While battle continued over their future, the Chamberlain family remained virtually marooned at Avondale College, Cooranbong. Tipple had to depend on the college to continue with a protective and supportive barricade around them. When he wrote to the college on 17th January 1983 confirming they would continue that protection, Alex Currie, Dean of Students, replied: "Avondale College, its staff and students have been only too happy to care for the Chamberlains as best we could. It has been a difficult time for the Chamberlains and I do trust that we have been able to provide the nurture and care that has been necessary during the crisis they have endured. We have appreciated the support, encouragement and guidance you have given them throughout this difficult period."

Having received a satisfactory answer there, Tipple returned to forensics. On 23rd January, he wrote to the NSW Ombudsman arguing that Kuhl's performance, and by implication that of Dr Simon Baxter who had supervised and supported her, had prejudiced the Chamberlains' defence. He said that the test where Joy Kuhl had allegedly found baby's blood on the pair of scissors should not have been reported let alone accepted because the controls she had used had failed. The test had used a control of baby's blood so that its reaction could be compared with the reaction against the material taken from the scissors. The control of baby's blood did not give any reaction. The control had "failed" and any reaction from the tested sample could not be properly interpreted. Instead she reported the result as a positive reaction confirming there was baby's blood on the scissors.

There was no way of directly checking Joy Kuhl's other tests of samples from the Chamberlains' car and possessions. The test slides had been destroyed and no photographs had been taken of them. The only thing available was Joy Kuhl's work notes. The Division of Forensic Medicine had not kept any samples for independent testing. There had also been no routine practice of testing test sera before using them. Tipple's complaint was referred to the secretary of the NSW Department of Health, which ran the Division of Forensic Medicine. The Ombudsman received an indignant reply from the department that the complaint was unjustified.

On 3rd February 1983, Vern Pleuckhahn joined Richard Nairn in condemning the verdict. He told Tipple: "I have never been surer that an accused person would be acquitted and consider the unanimous decision of the jury as one of the greatest travesties of justice that has ever occurred in Australian legal history. It also dents my faith in the jury system. In retrospect, I think that the peculiar confidence and attitude of the average Territorian and educational standard of the stratum of society from which many of the jury came may have had some effect on their consideration and acceptance of evidence which could have conflicted with their own preconceived ideas and knowledge of the habits of the various predators of the Territory. I remain completely convinced of the part the dingo could have played in the tragedy and the correctness of what I have said about Cameron's evidence. My only regret is that I did not have the jumpsuit to examine more critically and at length over a few days, but I doubt whether any evidence would have altered the opinion of the jury."

Pleuckhahn offered his continuing support and work on the case without fee. He said: "I know I could rally additional help from at least two other senior Australian forensic pathologists in other States whose training and experience I respect. One of those rang me yesterday from Perth to offer help if required and to tell me of the overwhelming amazement among professional circles in

Western Australia concerning the decision of the jury and following your presentation and weight of expert evidence." He said that from the pattern of bleeding which was more prominent on the back part of the collar, "There was more trauma and bleeding to the back of the neck and skull and ... this could possibly have been from the dingo 'biting and crushing' the lower part of the skull or nape of the neck." It was possible, he said, that the baby was lying on its back when the subsequent 'oozing' took place.

In an extraordinarily prescient remark, Pleuckhahn said: "On Wednesday 20th October 1982, [Les] Harris said that from his knowledge of the habits of a dingo, he thought, if given a chance, that he may be able to 'find' the matinee jacket in the area where the other clothes were found. While this new possibility may be very remote, such a find would be substantial new evidence and could very likely put a seal on many of the hypotheses of Cameron and provide very substantial grounds for appeal."

Aspects of the scientific evidence did not escape lay scrutiny, in particular the extraordinary so-called blood spray discovered by Jim Metcalf when he examined the car. Diane Lapsley, from Mooring Rock, Western Australia, said in a letter to Tipple: "Constable Metcalf is quoted as saying he noticed a dark stain under the car's dashboard which was sticky to the touch and he thought it could have been a spray from a soft drink like Coco-Cola. I am assuming this refers to the spray which was later said to be baby's blood. Is it not strange that after such a long time it was still sticky to the touch?" That was more common sense.

Some who did have scientific knowledge but had not been involved in the case believed that fundamental principles had been flouted. Eric Magnusson wrote to Tipple saying: "The point should be made, if appropriate, that forensic science is not a branch of science but a branch of *applied* science. Expertise in it consists of proper selection of scientific tests, proper collection of samples and proper recording of results. Where there is a question as to the significance of the results, an expert in the specific branch of science should be called in for an opinion, not an applied scientist. Prof Boettcher is such an expert and his inexperience in forensic work is irrelevant. To allow the jury to be misled on this point is an error because he was not called to give forensic evidence but to comment on it." Magnusson said Joy Kuhl was not an expert in immunology. He said: "Her MSc is in plant biochemistry; she is probably familiar with the standard immunological testing procedure but not with the basic science of immunology on which the significance of her results rests."

Tipple made contact with an internationally renowned blood expert, Professor Robin Carrell, who headed the Molecular Pathology Research

Program for the New Zealand Medical Research Council. Tipple was particularly interested in Joy Kuhl's claim that foetal haemoglobin was more stable than adult haemoglobin and she was therefore able to detect it in a severely denatured sample of blood, that is, blood that had been exposed to the elements for some time and had lost some or many of its qualities. Tipple sent the trial transcript to Carrell. Carrell read it and became seriously concerned. In an affidavit, he said the tests used by Kuhl were suitable for relatively fresh samples but was not rigorous enough to give unequivocal results on the severely denatured samples. Carrell said there had been insufficient testing done on the serum Joy Kuhl had used. In the Crown case against there had been "undue reliance was placed on the immunological testing which was not satisfactorily corroborated". Carrell said: "It is my opinion that for the reasons stated above the presence of foetal haemoglobin was not demonstrated beyond reasonable doubt in any of the tested samples."

On 7th February, the Federal Court of Appeal sat to consider the Chamberlain case. Presiding were the Chief Justice of the Federal Court, Sir Nigel Bowen, Sir William Forster, Chief Justice of the Northern Territory, and Justice Kenneth Jenkinson, a Victorian. They were worldly-wise and experienced. Bowen had been adjutant of the 2/43rd Water Transport Company that had Australian commandos in New Guinea in 1945. He had gone on to become the Attorney-General of Australia. Sir William had been an airman in World War 11 and he had been a magistrate in the Adelaide Police Court, the same part of the world Denis Barritt came from. Surely these, together with a very "activist" judge, Jenkinson, often intervening to ask questions, would get it right.

The Chamberlains were represented by Michael McHugh, a queen's counsel for 10 years, who was then president of the NSW Bar Council, and later to become a judge of the High Court of Australia. His junior was Glen Miller, formerly Australian Government representative to the Inaugural Australasian Conference of Forensic Scientists. Ian Barker QC represented the Crown.

In his submission to the Federal Court on 15th February, HcHugh tendered Carrell's affidavit. He said the fact that there had been such strong disagreement between scientists was significant because that itself raised a reasonable doubt. But straight away he ran into the obstacle of the sanctity of the jury decision. Sir Nigel said that the trial jury had had the advantages of seeing the witnesses in the witness box and being able to choose between them. McHugh said: "In a civil case, that may be so. But not, in our opinion, when it is reputable evidence and when the quality of the people who put forward the evidence is considered.

The best Mr Barker could say in reply was that [the expert witnesses called by the defence] were academics who had spent their lives in universities instead of being people who were found in forensic laboratories."

McHugh said that in Kuhl's notes of the tests she had done on the Chamberlain samples, she had said only a single band had been produced, but in the confirmatory tests she had conducted there had been double bands, and on this, he said, the entire validity of her evidence foundered. If the anti-serum reacted to something other than foetal haemoglobin, who could say whether the single bands Joy Kuhl said she had obtained in her testing had been reactions to the presence of foetal haemoglobin? McHugh said there was a reasonable explanation for so much that had been held against the Chamberlains. What of the damage to the jumpsuit? It was only assumed that if a dingo had not made those cuts that the cutting must have been for some nefarious purpose, such as fabricating evidence of a dingo attack. Why should that be so? The presence of tufts had been held up as incontrovertible evidence that the jumpsuit had been cut by a bladed instrument. McHugh conceded that there were tufts of material in the Chamberlain car. Lindy had cut other jump suits as the boys had grown out of them, and this was the explanation for the tufts of material found in the Chamberlains' car.

The Chamberlains, attending every day, were on tenterhooks. The trend of the hearing was not going their way. Pastor George Rollo, a seasoned and highly respected SDA pastor who had been assigned to accompany and mentor the Chamberlains, said later: "During the Federal hearing, I often escorted Lindy from the Court to the city shops and was embarrassed by the inordinate attention of the public to the movements of the accused as she did the normal things connected with walking the street or shopping. Some shop assistants would lose track of what they were doing as they gazed after the 'criminal'. Others made derisive comments. The constant presence of these factors steeled Lindy into aggressive reaction. Michael tended to [avoid] offensive people."

Because of another commitment, McHugh had to leave the hearing before it was finished and Glen Miller took over. He said that because the prosecution in the Chamberlain case had relied so much on opinion, there was an inherent danger that it had become "trial by expert opinion". For this reason, he felt that it was most important for the Federal court in this appeal to critically appraise the opinions and reasoning of those experts.

Barker submitted that the Chamberlains had had a fair trial, and the benefit of a summing-up which was "not only fair but manifestly favourable" to them. He said the points being brought up by the defence now should have been brought up at the trial. Reserving these points for the appeal was "not how the system was intended to work or what was meant to work here," he said. The Chamberlain lawyers were quibbling over points that had been available at the trial, subjected to exacting cross-examination and considered by the jury. The Chamberlain lawyers, he said, were "kicking goals by moonlight".

Given the favourable summing up Tipple believed the most viable ground of appeal was that the verdict was unsafe and unsatisfactory but the majority of the judges decided they were bound by an earlier decision and this ground was not available. Bound by strict rules of evidence, the judges refused to admit the evidence of Professor Carrell and Ranger Derek Roff, ruling that it was not fresh evidence in the legal sense and lacked "cogency in the relevant sense". Bowen and Forster said that scientists, like any other people, were capable of being mistaken. "If two are in disagreement, plainly one must be wrong," they said. "It is for the jury, if they can, to determine the facts and the appeal court is not usually in a good position to say they were wrong." They said it was for the jury, though they appeared to hedge their bets a little more when it came to the handprints on the jumpsuit. "Whether Cameron was right to say that there was an impression of a hand was peculiarly a question of fact for the jury acting as jurors, we agree with Cameron without being able to say that those who thought otherwise were clearly wrong." The judges were persuaded by the same sort of argument Barker had put to the jury: how could a dingo have been expected to have done all attributed to it. Bowen and Forster said: "The fact that the singlet was found inside the jumpsuit but *inside out* is unexplained. Even if a dingo was capable of removing the child from the jumpsuit it is hardly likely that it could have removed the singlet from the child's body and replaced it in the jumpsuit inside out?" On 29th April 1983, the Federal Court unanimously dismissed the appeal, and the penultimate safeguard was gone.

Tipple was appalled by the decision and was later to write in a prize winning essay that the reason the judges gave were "fundamentally flawed". "If a panel of judges with access to the evidence and further submissions, no pressure on them and curial experience, could not make a decision as to who was right or who was wrong, what hope had a jury?" he said.

Common sense would say that materials, whatever they are, can end up in all sorts of places and in all sorts of arrangements, once left to the whims of the elements, birds, mammals or just about anything else. Who knows how a wild animal might scratch and pull and tug clothing from a deceased person? Lindy's mother, Avis Murchison, said that in highlighting the improbability of a dingo laying the clothes out in the way they were found, they were being sarcastic.

She later claimed that the singlet, as shown in the photo, was not inside out and she felt that the judges knew this. She was perhaps being too harsh on the learned judges. Whether the singlet was inside out or not did not amount to anything much. What was far more to the point as far as Malcolm Brown, reporting the case, was concerned was the impossibly convoluted legalist language they sometimes used. Kenneth Jenkinson said in his finding: "But in my opinion no juror could reasonably have failed to acknowledge that, reason as he might, he was not in a position to assure himself of the correctness of a conclusion against the opinions of the two professors to the degree which would eliminate reasonable doubt as to that conclusion". Work that out as you will.

Lindy Chamberlain was held briefly at Mulawa women's prison in Silverwater, in Sydney's western suburbs. The media was of course desperate for news of her. One journalist, Paola Totaro, a livewire and very accomplished journalist on the *Sydney Morning Herald,* rang the police and said she had some unpaid traffic fines in order to try to get into Mulawa to interview Lindy, but the police would not buy it. "We know what you are trying to do, Paola!" they said. On 3rd May 1983, a correspondent in Buderim, Queensland, wrote to Tipple saying she believed that depriving Kahlia of access to her mother was one of the most tragic outcomes of the case. "I wish to draw your attention to the fact that this child has committed no crime and that she is a member of our society in her own right and yet her basic moral rights are being deprived, her mental, physical and emotional well-being neglected," the correspondent said. "I also feel that the family is subjected to further unnecessary distress by the transposition of Mrs Chamberlain away from New South Wales, where her family is in the more secure environment of their church centre."

On 2nd May, Justice Brennan in the High Court refused Lindy's application for bail. He said it was unlikely the Federal Court's decision would be set aside by the High Court and the prosecution of the Chamberlains had already survived an attack on it in the Federal Court. He said: "The poignancy of her return to custody and the traumatic disruption to family life needs no elaboration. It needs no psychiatric evidence to establish the tragic nature of those events." Tipple said: "With his observations about the sanctity and finality of the jury verdict ringing in my ears, I left the High Court hoping Justice Brennan would not be one of the Justices to decide the substantive appeal."

On 4th May Lindy was taken to Berrimah Gaol. The Chamberlains sought special leave to appeal to the High Court on the grounds: the case raised fundamental issues for the administration of justice in Australia; the issue of the jurisdiction of the Federal Court in criminal appeals; the proper principles of law which should be applied by the Federal Court in hearing and determining criminal appeals. In the meantime Lindy, having looked after Kahlia every day for months, applied to have her with her in gaol. Michael Chamberlain, left at Avondale College with his two bewildered boys, could only hope for help. He was not in a position to look after baby Kahlia as well. She went to foster parents at Avondale College, Wayne and Jenny Miller. The church was paying Michael a sustentation salary, normally available to retired SDA pastors, and he was working in the college's archives section.

In a letter to Tipple dated 18th May, Barry Boettcher said: "I recognise (most probably) that the only way we can contribute assistance to the Chamberlains in the future is through public channels, such as the media. In order to be willing to do this, I wanted to be certain that you consider that the goals I would be striving for would be worthwhile, and right now, more than ever, I am firm in my resolve that I will continue to work until it is accepted by the people of Australia that the forensic evidence related to the conclusion of HbF [foetal haemoglobin] on the items of the Chamberlains' car were unsound, and incorrect – and that the Chamberlains should never have been found guilty."

There were plenty of members of the public ready with a view as to what happened. Tipple received many letters. One said that there were lions at Ayers Rock, another, written from Wollongong on 21st May 1983, said that what really happened was that someone desperately wanting a baby had seized the baby after the dingo took it from the tent. The dingo had dropped the baby and the baby-starved individual had grabbed it. "Azaria was stolen by some person," the correspondent said. "This person folds the baby's clothes up and departs Ayers Rock, as soon as it is convenient and dumps the baby's clothes on the way, and was well on the way by the time the police get around looking for clues, and there were none, and they were baffled as to what happened."

Another man told Tipple that the baby had been taken by Aborigines and brought up as one of them, and he was going to go find this white child living among them and retrieve her. He told Malcolm Brown that there were white children in Aboriginal camps and he was sure Azaria was one of them. In fact, he had seen a white child in Aboriginal company and thought she might have been Azaria. Tipple told him he was "a brave man" to go on his mission and wished him luck. Another gentleman rang Malcolm Brown at the *Sydney Morning Herald* and said what had really happened was that Azaria had been "spear-tackled" by her mother at the Mt Isa supermarket before the Chamberlains left for Ayers Rock, that the baby was badly injured and needed a blood transfusion, that the

Chamberlains had refused because blood transfusion was against their religion, that the baby had died and that the parents had gone to Ayers Rock and staged a dingo attack, with Seventh-day Adventists colluding with them to go to Ayers Rock to be witnesses. What capped it all, Tipple said, was when a man from Potts Point visited him at his office and said that Azaria had been snatched by "a giant bat", and that Lindy had not seen it because she had been "blinded by the downdraft of its giant wings". It had then taken the child out to sea. Tipple pointed out that the sea was a long way away and it would have to be a long flight. The man rang back later with a modified theory. Soon after that he went to the Northern Territory to get Lindy released "on the grounds that she had been taken by a bat". He contacted Tipple seeking approval to see Lindy and claiming compensation for his expenses.

More worryingly, Michael Chamberlain received a letter from someone calling himself or themselves The Avengers". It said: "Your wife is dead if she is let out of jail. Leave her where she is and she will live."

The Northern Territory officialdom had no intention that Lindy Chamberlain should suffer any harm in gaol. Naturally enough, they were careful about anyone who might visit her. But they were concerned about Lindy having a baby in gaol. Lindy Chamberlain's application to have Kahlia with her in gaol met with a frosty response. Mr R.F. Donnelly, NT Director of Community Development, Corrective Services Division wrote in a letter to Lindy dated 25th May: "You recently wrote to me requesting permission to have your daughter, Kahlia, with you at Darwin Prison whilst you are serving your sentence. Before making a decision on the matter, I have sought the advice of Child Welfare and Health Authorities. After due consideration of all the factors involved, I have to advise you, your request has been refused." Tipple thought a media campaign might persuade the NT authorities to relent. He contacted Malcolm Brown at the *Sydney Morning Herald* with that in mind. Brown said it would not be possible for officialdom to allow that. If Kahlia went in with Lindy, there would be controversy over a convicted child murderer being given another baby, there would be endless queries as to how the baby was, and if something did happen, such as the child having an accident, getting sick or dying, there would be uproar. Tipple replied: "Yes, I agree with some of that but I can't... I can't be objective!"

There was now civil war within the broad framework of the Chamberlain "camp". One side, which Tipple championed, was to reach out to scientific experts. The other, championed by Phil Ward, held that the mystery was not a scientific one but one relating to hard factual evidence of what actually happened at Ayers Rock.

Barry Boettcher took the first approach. He decided that the really promising option for him was to turn to his professional peers. On 26th May 1983 he wrote to Tipple telling him that he had attended the annual meeting of the Genetics Society of Australia and presented his case that foetal haemoglobin had not been found in the Chamberlains' car. "At the conclusion of the talk I requested that interested people might sign a sheet indicating that they agreed with my opinion," he said. "At that stage, there was some discussion and it was felt that it would be undesirable to have the name of the Society on the sheeting bearing the signatures. Consequently, sheets with an alternative working had to be prepared. As well, there was an expression by members that the Society should take a definite interest, simply as a scientific society. Eventually, I prepared a hand-written sheet and obtained six signatures from senior geneticists."

The signatures Boettcher obtained were significant enough. They included Professor J.A. Thompson, Professor of Genetics at Sydney University; Dr Max Whitten, chief of the Division of Entomology with the CSIRO and Dr M.J. Mayo from the Department of Genetics at Adelaide University. All were serving or past presidents of the society. Boettcher said it was suggested that the society might take an official interest and he was making an official approach to the secretary to bring this about. "Since I have forwarded the manuscript on my ideas to the *Medical Journal of Australia*, and since I have presented oral reports to senior immunologists and senior geneticists of Australia, I believe that I can be accepted as having been willing to subject my ideas to the scrutiny of my scientific peers," he said. "I think this is important for public credibility of my ideas when the situation becomes public. Consequently, I think the groundwork for ultimately having the opinion on the forensic evidence reversed, is going very satisfactorily."

Phil Ward and Don McNicol felt the primary evidence was still vital and they claimed that Tipple had not handled the case competently. They claimed that Tipple had given Phillips incomplete instructions and had not briefed him on all the relevant material that was involved in the case. The relevant material they considered had been overlooked was more extensive primary evidence. If a dingo had taken the baby, what dingo was it? Who knew about it? Was there intervention in relation to disposal of the body and the clothing? McNicol contacted Phillips directly about the possible involvement of an Aboriginal man. McNicol said investigations had been made by Queensland police concerning that man, but nothing had ever come of it. Arthur Hawken, who had liaised on behalf of Ward and McNicol with the Aborigines at Ayers Rock, represented something far more substantial. He had a tape-recording of a conversation with Nipper Winmatti which strongly supported the dingo attack scenario. According to McNicol, Phillips had no objection about him carrying on further investigations.

Tipple wrote to Phillips on 22nd June and asked him what he thought about all that. Phillips responded on 28th June by issuing a formal statement: "It has been brought to my attention that certain persons are alleging that Mr Tipple of the firm Brennan and Blair, Solicitors, who instructed me and Mr Kirkham of Counsel in the above matter carried out his duties in relation to the Chamberlains' defence in an incompetent fashion. I state categorically there is no foundation whatsoever for such allegation. As a result of our association I formed a most favourable view of Mr Tipple's competence and dedication. I am further informed that it is alleged that, during the course of a telephone conversation after the conclusion of the Chamberlains' trial, I gave support to the above allegations by discussing certain aspects of my instructions from Mr Tipple. I had never met the other party to the call and although I was given to understand that he was legally qualified, I knew that he was not engaged as a solicitor for either Mr or Mrs Chamberlain. Any use made of this telephone conversation for the purpose of lending support to the allegation made against Mr Tipple is quite unwarranted." In a private note to Tipple, Phillips said that he had no objection to McNicol continuing his inquiries but that was because, even if he did object, he had no power to direct him to stop them. But that was irrelevant to questions of Tipple's competence.

Andrew Kirkham also rejected the allegations against Tipple. In a letter to Tipple, he said: "I have no hesitation in categorising such criticism as being baseless and unfair. I confirm my earlier advice given to you shortly subsequent to the conclusion of the subject trial that in my 17 years practice at the bar I have not had a better instructing solicitor nor a solicitor who worked harder or contributed more by way of instruction, preparation and invaluable advice towards the presentation of my case. I do not consider any solicitor could have done more than you did in attempting to secure an acquittal for Mr and Mrs Chamberlain." But Ward and McNicol believed their material was very important and, leaving aside what Tipple thought of it, it should go directly to the Northern Territory.

Tipple retained the services of a private investigator, Les Lundie, of Wagga Wagga in the state's south to look at what Ward and McNicol claimed to have uncovered. Tipple said later: "We did not just concentrate on the scientific evidence. I was not involved in the interviewing of primary witnesses before the

THE DINGO TOOK OVER MY LIFE

trial so I also retained Jim Redmond, a private investigator, who was recommended to me by Glen Miller. Unbeknown to Ward and McNicol, Redmond reinterviewed all the critical witnesses and got further statements just to make sure nothing had been missed.

The "Dingo Baby Case" had by now made news around the world. Professor Cameron addressed the British Academy of Forensic Sciences on the case and took questions. He invited Ian Barker to attend a "Summer Friends Dinner" at the Ballroom Suite in the Dorchester Hotel, London, on 5th July 1983. It was advertised that after the dinner Barker would take part in a discussion on the case. Two weeks later, Tipple and Boettcher travelled to Germany to continue the research into the Behringwereke antisera that had been used by Joy Kuhl to identify foetal haemoglobin.

At home, Avis Murchison worked away at the primary evidence. On 8th July, she wrote to Tipple: "Regarding the footprints on the space blanket – how do you get hold of that blanket at all and if so, would a forensic expert of your choice be able to find anything on it, I wonder? They were not just light dusty paw prints that could have been blown off. Do you think there might be traces of sandy dry clay substance that could be detectable or if they had rubbed or washed them off? Could the patch be different in any way from the rest of the blanket unless they were cunning and dunked the lot in water? I couldn't say *exactly* where the paw prints were now but I know that when the blanket held with the little nicks running upwards to the light the prints were in the lower right-hand corner. If I saw the blanket, I might be able to come close to it. After three years it is hard to say exactly. They were absolutely distinct and indisputable as to their origin and the policeman that picked the blanket up only took one glance and was totally convinced the marks did not disappear by themselves nor by the handling in transit. Of that I am absolutely convinced."

While this was going on, the Chamberlain family suffered further misfortune. On 17th July, Reagan went to a neighbour's home to call Aidan to come to dinner. Some boys were playing in the front yard and one of them apparently threw a bottle into the fire. The bottle exploded just as Reagan arrived, sending a fragment of glass lacerating Reagan's left eye and nose. The eye injury was serious and would leave Reagan with only 10 percent light vision in it. The news had a shattering effect on Lindy, in gaol and helpless to do anything. "The incident was the lowest point for Lindy," Tipple said. "It really knocked her. She felt totally powerless." Tipple asked the NT prisons department for temporary release by Lindy to attend to Reagan. That was refused. The word she got was that she would have got it had a child been killed or a psychiatrist would certify there would be irreparable psychological damage to Reagan. A second appeal 10 days later for her temporary release was refused.

In the Northern Territory, Superintendent Plumb interviewed Ward and McNicol. Their material was then handed to Graeme Charlwood, who travelled to Ayers Rock on 20th July to investigate. That day, the *Sydney Morning Herald* reported that the NT Police had reopened their inquiry into the disappearance of Azaria Chamberlain after having received information from Ward and McNicol.

On 21st July 1983, Behringwerke sent a letter to Stuart Tipple saying that the anti-serum on its own could not be relied on to confirm the presence of foetal blood and that back-up tests were needed. The company confirmed that Boettcher had tested the same anti-serum as Joy Kuhl had used, batch 2456. Here was material that could potentially destroy Kuhl's evidence for good. And it looked more and more that everything was going to depend on the scientific attack. Graeme Charlwood finished his inquiries at Ayers Rock and said there was no substance in what Ward and McNicol claimed had happened.

Les Smith, a humble, smiling, very genial employee of the Sanitarium Health Food Company at Cooranbong, who sported only a Diploma in Science, had come in on Tipple's side. After the trial, he approached Tipple and said: "Can I help?" Tipple said he could. "The first thing I wanted to do was to solve the under-dash spray," Tipple said. Lenehan's bleeding could explain so much of the blood in the car but not the spray on the under-dash. "So, I asked him to look at that," Tipple said. Smith then examined other Holden Toranas, and what did he find? Under-dash spray patterns in some of them, similar to what had been found in the Chamberlains' and Webber's cars. And what did that spray consist of? Smith set out to investigate. He asked one of the Torana owners, whose car sported the spray pattern, whether he could buy the car. The owner replied: "I didn't kill nobody in this car!"

Smith persisted and found that the spray pattern, found in the Holden Torana was DUFIX HN1081. It was a sound-deadening compound, sprayed under the Torana's during manufacture. "Using simple geometric calculations, from the direction of the spray, Smith established that the material had been sprayed by chance through the plenum drain hole," Tipple said. "Simply by chance this sound-deadening compound could be sprayed through this hole and on to the under-dash area. It didn't happen to every car but it had happened to the Webber's car and four of the other vehicles Mr Smith inspected. After travelling to the High Court in Canberra, I watched him examine the underdash plate before he handed it to me. Using his 10x magnifying glass I could see that the spray material was covered in yellow over spray paint. Whatever the spray matter was, it had been deposited there before the car was painted and left the GMH factory."

Smith then turned to another contentious issue, the damage to the jumpsuit. With a colleague, Ken Chapman, he conducted experiments. These were simple experiments – not making deductions from such things as the presence of tufts, as Chaikin had – but seeing what damage canine teeth could do. Ken Chapman asked Taronga Zoo for permission to conduct some tests on the biting capabilities of dingoes. The zoo director said it was "not felt in the best interests of the zoo or the dingo to comply with your request". So, Smith and Chapman resorted to Smith's kelpie/border-collie cross, Suzie, no longer a great runner, with only three legs, but a happy chewer. The result? Scissor-like cuts and tufts. There was quite marked similarity to the damage to Azaria's jumpsuit. In some cases, it was indistinguishable. So much for Chaikin's contention that tufts could only have been produced by a bladed instrument. It was a vitally important finding, given the importance the Crown had placed on his evidence, saying it was "unassailed and unassailable" and "the clearest evidence of human intervention".

Beyond the realm of the backyard experiment, there was now a throng of people not prepared to entertain such nice objections. On 24th August 1983, a group claiming to represent "many thousands of concerned Australians" started a petition requesting a judicial review of the case. It published an advertisement in the *Australian* inviting thousands to join. The address was "A Pleas for Mercy" c/o Guy Boyd, a member of the Boyd artistic family, who lived in Melbourne and had started a popular movement for the Chamberlains. The petition read: "To his Excellency the Governor General of Australia. The petition of the undersigned citizens of Australia respectfully shows that we strongly object to the verdict of guilty and the sentence of life with hard labour given to Alice Lynne Chamberlain in Darwin on the 29th October 1982 on evidence that was overwhelmingly circumstantial. Your petitioners therefore urgently request that a judicial review of the Chamberlain case be conducted, the quality of mercy be shown, and that she be released on licence so that she can re-join her family."

Betty Hocking, a member of the ACT Legislative Assembly and very supportive of the Chamberlains, had looked closely at the Splatt case in South Australia. Edward Charles Splatt had been convicted purely on the basis of scientific evidence – without a shred of primary evidence – and which was the subject of a royal commission, conducted by Commissioner Carl Shannon. The royal commission, largely brought about by the investigative work of a journalist, Stewart Cockburn, sat for the first time on 24th January 1983 and was continuing. Vast slabs of scientific evidence that had been brought against Splatt were being unravelled and people like Sergeant Cocks and Rex Kuchel, who had been involved in the Chamberlain inquiry, were being critically questioned.

Hocking wrote to Tipple in August 1983 giving him information passed onto her by Cockburn. The Splatt case, she said, had had no confession, no fingerprints, no weapon, no motive and no previous association with the murdered woman. Psychiatric assessment of Splatt had detected no tendency towards such brutality. She said: "Cockburn tackled a transcript of the trial and found it so complex that even with some knowledge of Physics and Chemistry, the forensic evidence was impossible to unravel. He was able to interview 11 of the 12 jurors and found that like himself, with one exception, they were people who did not have even the basic education in the language of science, yet 90 percent of the evidence involved complex scientific factors." She went on to say: "We cannot expect juries or judges who are not educated in science but in the humanities to cope with cases like this." There were alternative approaches. One, adopted overseas, was to empanel expert assessors to sit with a judge or magistrate. The other was to empanel special juries educated in the type of disciplines under discussion.

Ward and McNicol continued their own line of inquiries. They were convinced that they could prove a conspiracy and they wanted to mount a private prosecution. They contacted Peter Dean in Alice Springs and asked him to act for them. Dean wrote to Lindy asking for her consent that he act for Ward and said that unless he got that support from both her and Michael, he would not act on Ward's behalf, as his earlier association with the case would have meant he was acting with the Chamberlains' blessing. Tipple discussed the proposed action with Michael Chamberlain and with the Darwin lawyer, Greg Cavanagh. On 15th September, he wrote to Dean telling him that the Chamberlains did not want in any way to be associated with the private prosecution. He said the Chamberlains were concerned that such an action might have an impact on the High Court case. They were also concerned that because Dean had acted for them in the past, they might be associated with Ward's action. Tipple said the proper path for communication would be through himself.

The Ward and McNicol material had been examined by Kirkham and Miller and it was their opinion that the material could not be used in ongoing court proceedings. Tipple wrote to Lindy: "We are now very concerned that Ward and McNicol plan not only to launch prosecutions against people they believe are involved in the disappearance of Azaria but now appear to be planning a prosecution against high-level politicians and government employees. We have not seen any evidence to suggest that this latter action has any foundation at all and believe that even the suggestions of such action can only harm your cause. In accordance with your instructions to date, we have continued to deny that you in any way have supported the Ward and McNicol endeavours."

In the meantime, Tipple pushed on with the High Court appeal. Though the High Court was not permitted to consider new evidence – ruling out all that had been discovered about the specificity of the anti-serum, the under-dash spray and the cutting – he hoped that surely in the minds of these learned gentlemen there would be a spark of common sense that would cut through all the legalism and see the facts for what they were. He was annoyed that rumours were being circulated that he had filed no grounds of appeal to the High Court. Correct procedures had to be followed to get a High Court appeal on foot and he followed them. Tipple said to the Chamberlains: "Thank you for your continuing support and without that support our job would have become impossible. We can assure you that all that can be done will be done and you have the support of thousands of people."

Ward, continuing to publish *Adventist News*, was attracting his own legion of supporters. He published an article: "The Azaria Case, Get the True Facts", and called for more subscribers to his publication. His supporters included some prominent Adventist laypeople, Jim and Cavell Driscoll, from Murwillumbah in northern New South Wales, honest people, well-meaning to the Chamberlains, who believed that Tipple and the counsel he had engaged were pursuing the wrong rabbits down the wrong burrows. In a letter to Tipple, Lindy said Michael had been "hassled" a few times by Jim Driscoll who was wanting to "report on the lawyers' work".

Tipple believed that the campaign led by Ward was muddying things with the Northern Territory. On 6th October, Ward sent a telegram to Tipple: "I understand you are concerned that my proposed private prosecution may affect your High Court case. I would give due consideration to your concerns should you be prepared to share them with me. I will put any matters you raise before my lawyers and request that they give due consideration to any legitimate concerns." Lindy said she fully supported what her retained lawyers were doing. "I hope the 'opposition' doesn't put too much of a strain on you," she said. "You'll never know how much your support means to me as I find words too inadequate to express it. You are like family members to me in a lot of ways yet I hardly know you in others ... the indelible tie is there. The support your family gives wafts across the miles. I hope the support can swing just as heavily in the opposite direction whenever you need my support too."

On 16th October 1983, Lindy wrote to Paul Everingham distancing herself from the Ward-McNicol campaign. She said she knew both men but was in no way involved in their actions and in no way condoned them. She said: "Numerous recent mail has made me distressed to realise people think I condone, and indeed am involved in, the private actions of Mr Phil and Mr D. McNicol. Although I know both these gentlemen to some extent, I do not support their actions in any way whatever, indeed I have asked both gentlemen in separate instances to desist from their activities, and also instructed their lawyers for the same reasons. I wish you and your government to know I will have no part in their actions, and that they are not supported by myself, husband or family. I have seen first-hand of what malicious gossip and fabricated hypothesis has done to me, and do not wish to see another similar situation which I fear may be the case."

Michael Chamberlain was a lost soul. His whole world had collapsed around his ears. He sought solace among other things in photography, which was his passion. Some of the pictures he took might have been considered risqué, and some got into police hands. The police thought they could be used against him and kept them on file. The real battle was elsewhere. It was in barbed-wire prison compounds and in the rarefied atmosphere of Australia's highest court.

In gaol, Lindy was aware of most of what was going on. She had had a visit from Michael and their children. Kahlia, who had been removed from her as a tiny baby, was now, as she said in a letter to Tipple, "quite relaxed with me this time – well, comparatively – and calling me 'mummy' with the boys. Think it is really starting to register that this is 'mum' from the pictures at home". She also revealed some glimpses of the life she was leading in gaol. She said: "It is after midnight, and I'm the cook tomorrow. So, it's up at 6 am to cook porridge of all things. Well there is worse, but no one is wrapped in that stuff but must do anyway so a bit of sleep would help." To console herself, she turned back to her religious faith, even when it acquired a mystical aspect. God was with her and would not let her down. In her letter to Tipple on 17th December, she said she saw some uncanny coincidences. Azaria was born on a Wednesday and died on the 17th day of a month. Kahlia had been born on a Wednesday and it happened to be the 17th. She said the trial verdict had been on a Friday, 29th, and the Federal Court dismissal of her appeal had been on a Friday 29th. She thought all this might have been orchestrated by God. God gives and God takes. He took Azaria and gave me Kahlia. He has me here for a purpose of his own. He can take me out. Strange, isn't it? Maybe we put too many things down to coincidence at times."

If the truth was ever to be brought out, and Tipple believed it had not been, it would require sheer cold hard reasoning, not mysticism. He and his clients had to look forward to their encounter with the ultimate safeguard, being the five learned gentlemen of the High Court who would consider the case anew. If that failed, there was nothing beyond it, at least, not in the system so painstaking developed over centuries to give people like Michael and Lindy the best chance of getting justice.

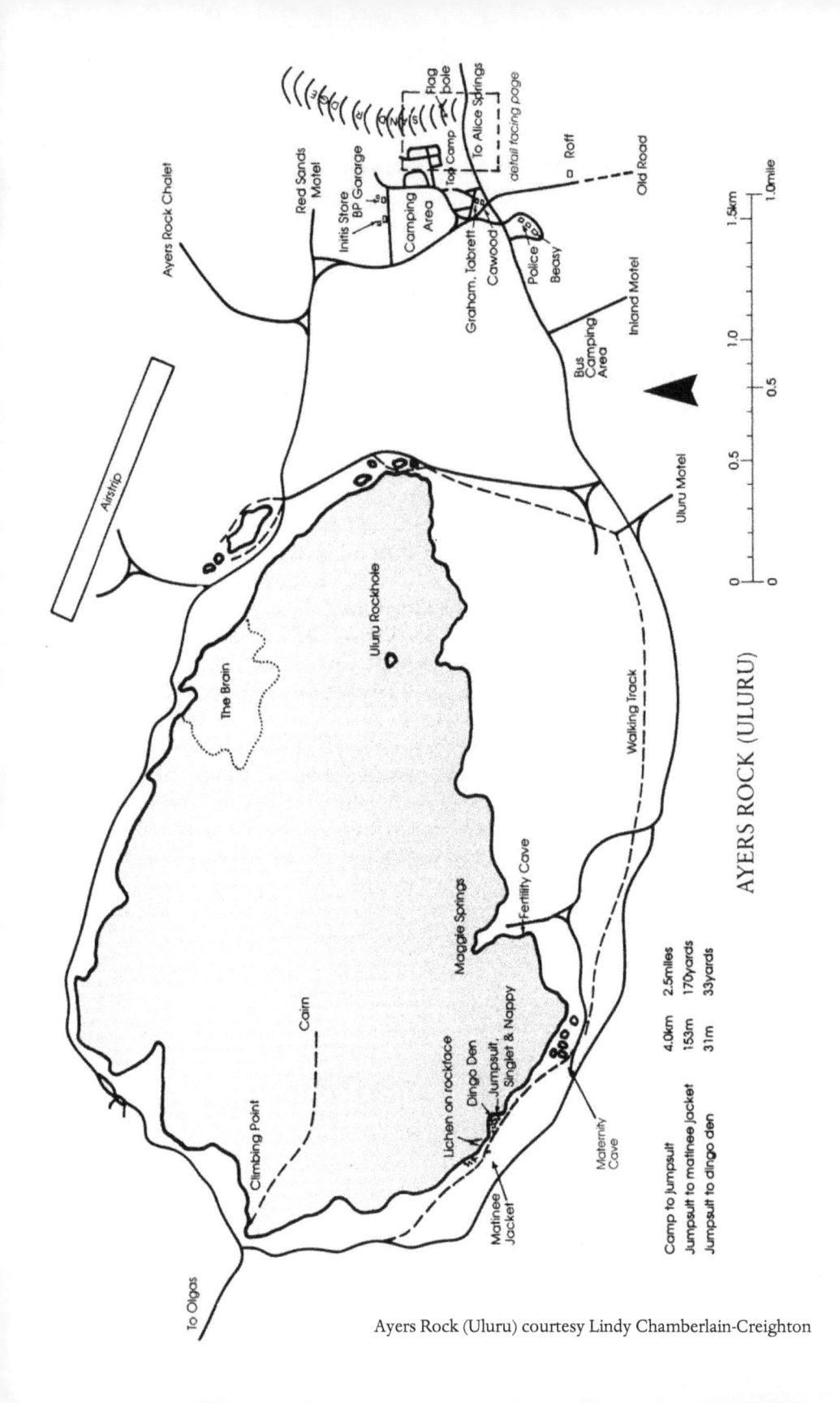

Ayers Rock (Uluru) courtesy Lindy Chamberlain-Creighton

Uluru standing 348metres (1141') tall with a circumference of 9400 metres (5.8 miles) in 2002 (*Stuart Tipple*)

Michael Chamberlain on the way to Uluru with the family Torana car. (*Lindy Chamberlain-Creighton*)

Michael Chamberlain holding Azaria on Uluru (*Lindy Chamberlain-Creighton*)

Lindy with Reagan and Aidan on Uluru
(Michael Chamberlain)

Michael Chamberlain with Reagan and Aidan on Uluru
(Lindy Chamberlain-Creighton)

Murray Haby took this photo of a dingo at the door of his camper van close to the Chamberlains' tent just before Azaria was taken.
(Murray Haby)

The Aboriginal Trackers with Head Ranger Derek Roff *(Michael Chamberlain)*

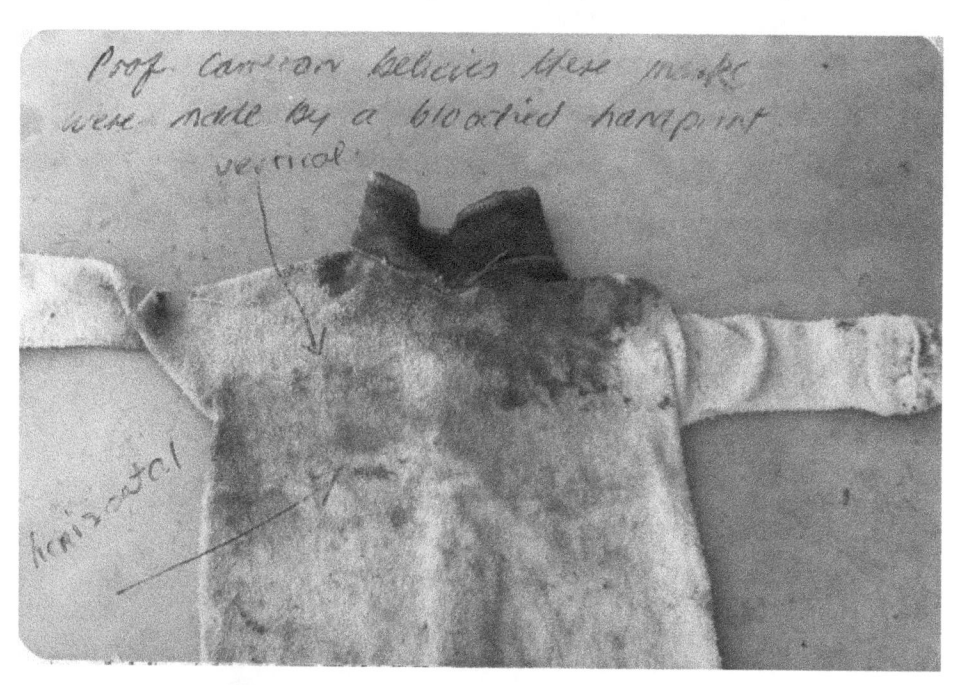

Azaria's jumpsuit showing alleged handprints *(Stuart Tipple)*

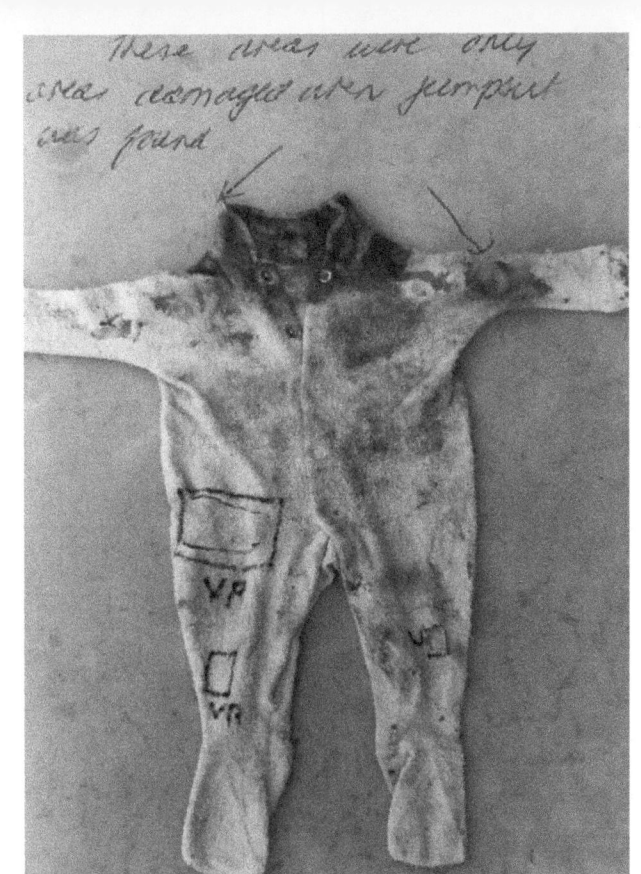

Right:
Azaria's Jumpsuit showing area's of damage
(Stuart Tipple)

Below:
The camera bag alleged by the Crown case as where the Chamberlains' placed Azaria's body before burying her
(Stuart Tipple)

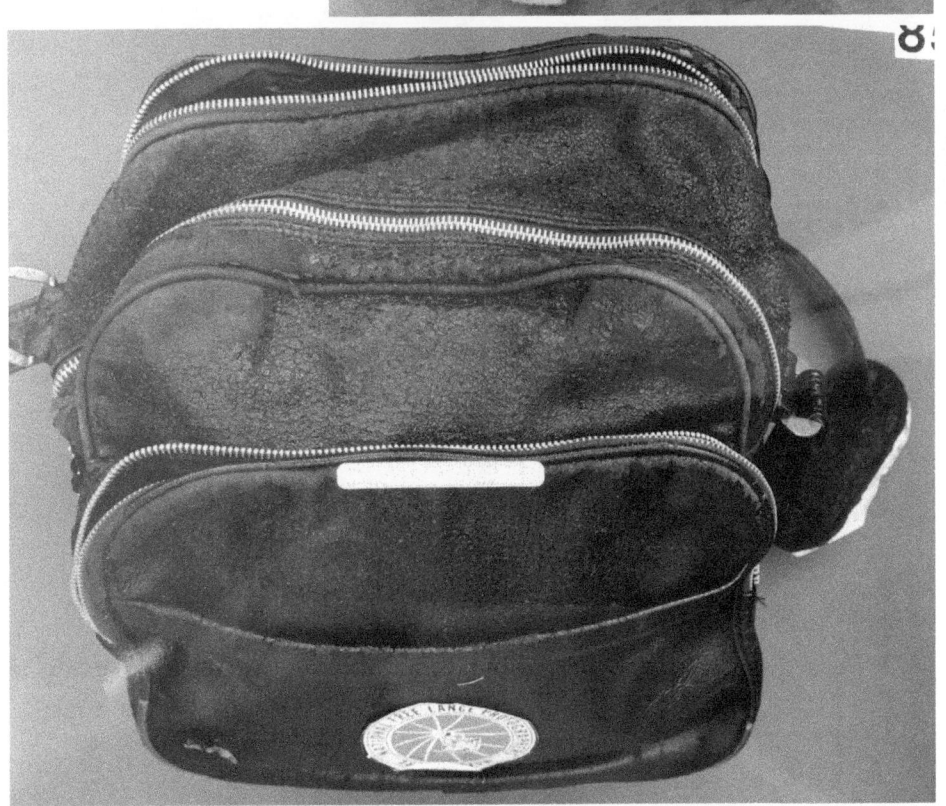

Legal Team arriving at Darwin Supreme Court *(Stuart Tipple)*

Defence Legal Team, Andrew Kirkham, John Phillips and Stuart Tipple

An identical matinee jacket fitted over the jumpsuit
(*Stuart Tipple*)

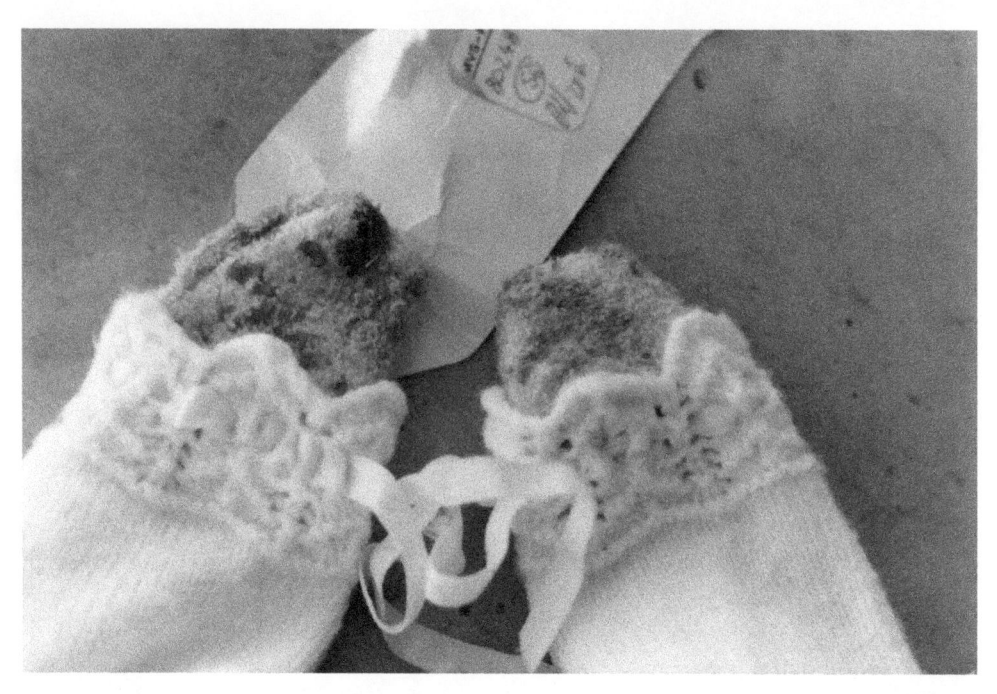

The matinee jacket sleeves fitted perfectly around the sculptured blood staining on the sleeves (*Stuart Tipple*)

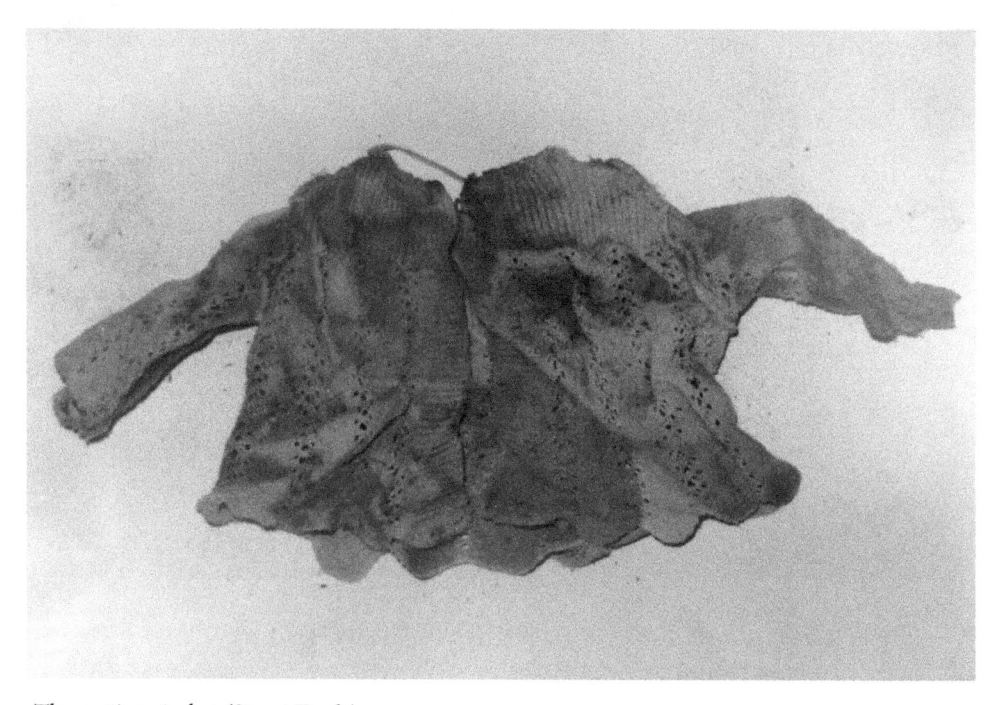

The matinee jacket (*Stuart Tipple*)

I never lit a candle. I never made a birthday wish. Why didn't you come and look for me. I was so cold and so frightened

Have a *very* Happy Birthday

Two of many cards sent by anonymous senders. *(Stuart Tipple)*

With love on *MY* ~~your~~ Birthday
DEAR MUMMY,
from me
I hope you'll be *happy*
As happy can be.

ATTORNEY-GENERAL

DARWIN

12 NOV 1985

Mr. S. Tipple,
Messrs Brennan Blair & Tipple,
Solicitors & Attorneys,
P.O. Box 1117,
GOSFORD SOUTH   NSW   2250

Dear Sir,

I refer to your submission and material in support of it seeking a judicial inquiry concerning the verdict and subsequent conviction of your clients Mr and Mrs Chamberlain.

I enclose a copy of a report prepared by the Solicitor-General. After careful and detailed consideration of the submission, the material in support and the report I have concluded that there is nothing raised by you which is cogent, or of such substance, whether new or otherwise, as to warrant the holding of the inquiry sought.

Given media speculation, it is proposed that a copy of the submission and the material in support and the Solicitor-General's report will be tabled in and authorised to be printed by the Legislative Assembly today.

Yours sincerely,

MARSHALL PERRON

The letter rejecting the application for a Royal Commission from the NT Attorney General. *(Stuart Tipple)*

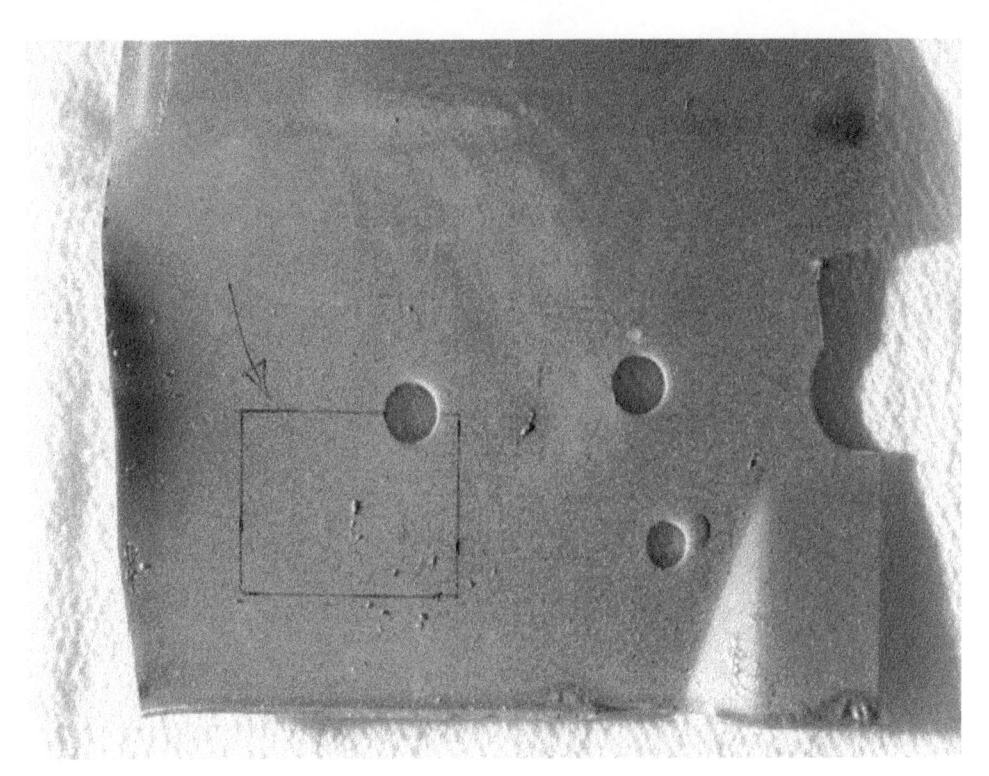

The plate cut from the car showing the alleged arterial blood spray *(Stuart Tipple)*

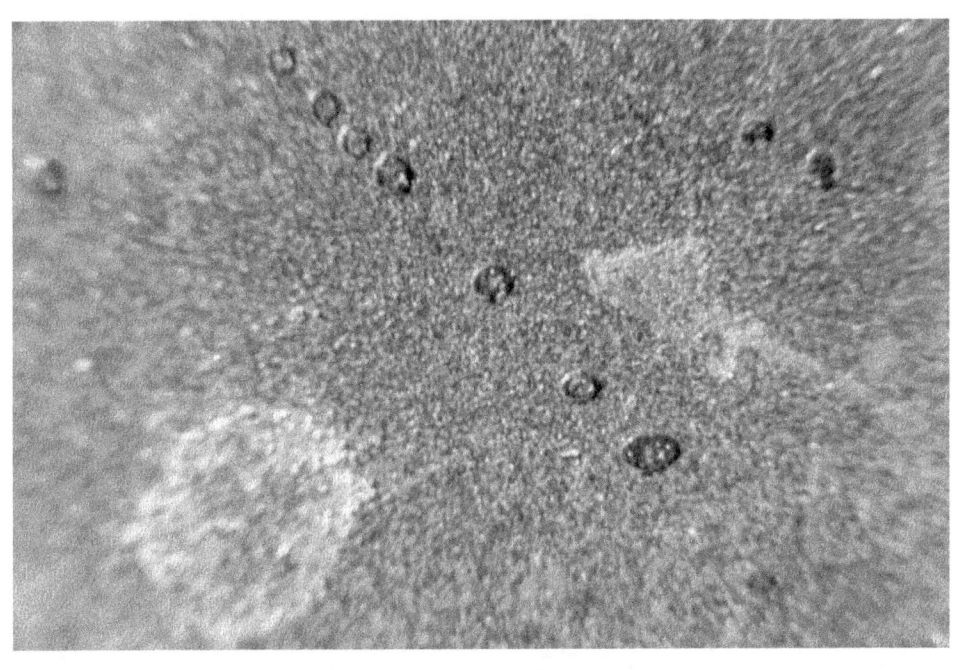

What a real blood spray looks like on a similar car plate *(Les Smith)*

A magnified view of the spray material on the car plate showing the yellow paint overspray over the spray material (*Les Smith*)

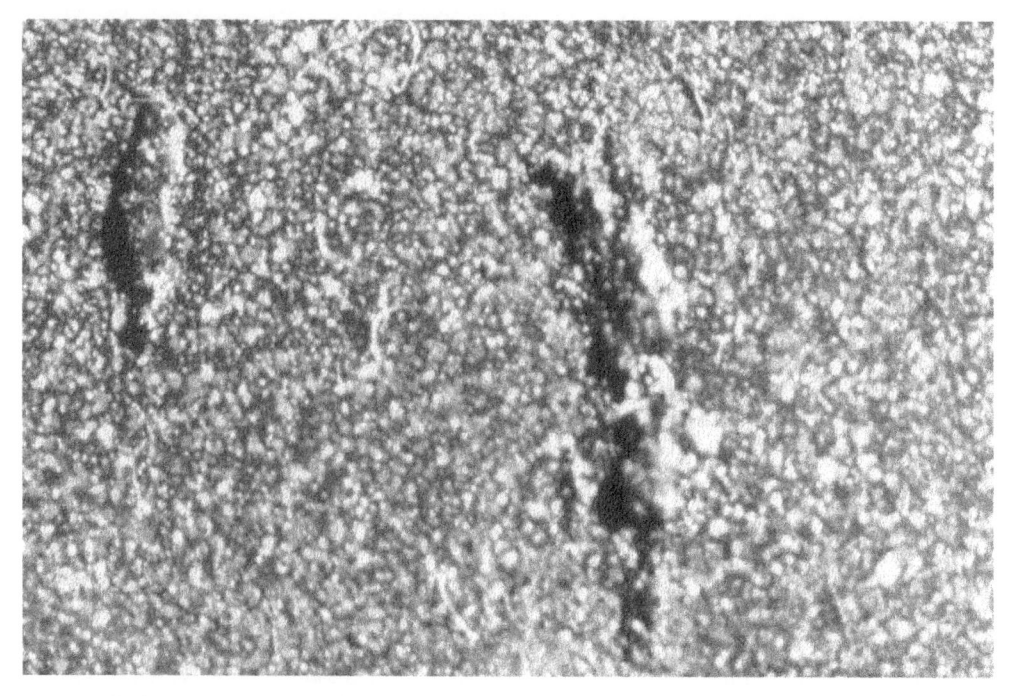

A magnified view of the alleged arterial spray on the car plate. (*Les Smith*)

A cotton tuft from jumpsuit material which Professor Chaiken claimed could not have been caused by a canine and probably made by scissors found in the Chamberlain car.

A cotton tuft caused by Les Smith's dog Suzie. *(Les Smith)*

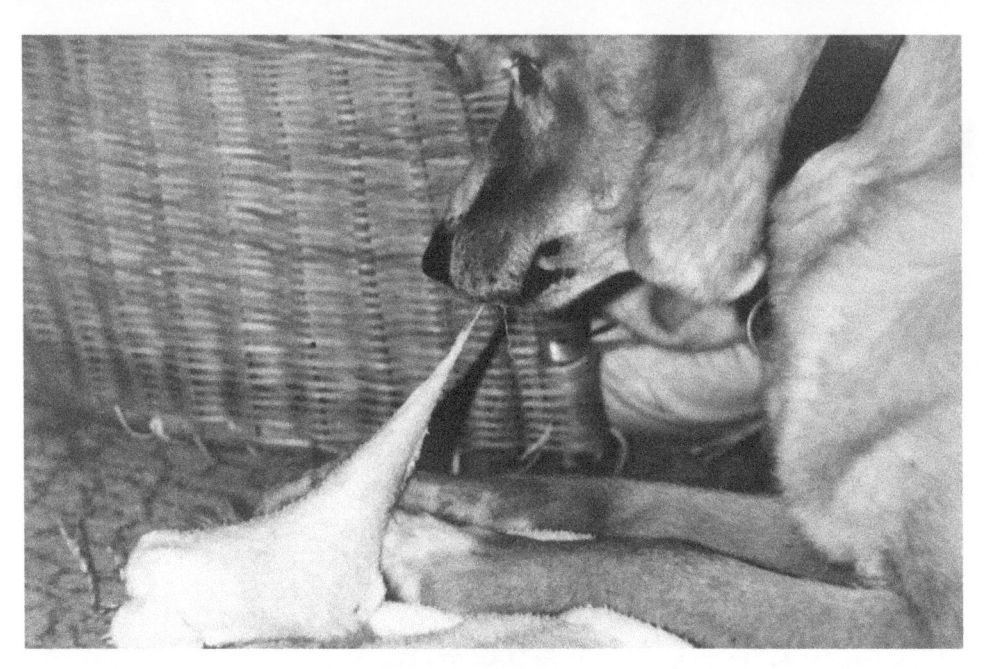

Suzie extracting food from a jumpsuit. *(Les Smith)*

Lindy and Stuart in Darwin after Lindy's release and about to return home.

Professor Barry Boettcher and Stuart Tipple at Azaria's Celebration of Life *(Cherie Tipple)*

Lindy and Stuart Tipple in 2014 *(Cherie Tipple)*

Stuart Tipple and Malcom Brown at the Fourth Inquest *(Cherie Tipple)*

Stewart Tipple and Lindy Chamberlain-Creighton addressing media after the Fourth Inquest *(Cherie Tipple)*

Michael Chamberlain holding the death certificate after the Fourth Inquest
(Cherie Tipple)

Patricia Flemming
(Stuart Tipple)

Les Smith
(Stuart Tipple)

Ken Chapman

CHAPTER NINE

THE POLITICAL STRUGGLE

"

The law is the anchor of our feelings. If the law holds our feelings well, it directs our feeling well. If, however, the law fails to hold our feelings well, our feelings become free enough for us to do what we feel freely.

— Ernest Agyemang Yeboah

With Lindy Chamberlain, back in gaol and the Federal Court appeal dismissed, the world at the beginning of 1984 was inclined to move on. It was not shaping up to be the nightmare world that George Orwell depicted, but there was a lot happening. Australians had voted in the Federal Labor Government under the charismatic Bob Hawke. The Government was making moves to lift Australia from the economic downturn of the previous year. Ronald Reagan held sway in the United States and terrible trouble was bubbling in the Middle East. A coal mine exploded in Japan, Brazil had a massive oil fire, more space walks were planned, the computer revolution was continuing and the first baby was about to be conceived by embryo transplant. As one journalist said of the Chamberlain case: "It's finished. Too much else happening now."

There was, of course, the question of the Chamberlains' appeal to the High Court, but given the unanimous verdict of the Federal Court, many people considered a tilt at the High Court to be a mere formality with little prospect of success. Legal Aid refused to fund it.

For those involved in the action, memories nevertheless ran long and deep. After the dismissal of the Federal Court appeal, Joy Kuhl, the forensic biologist whose evidence contributed so much to their conviction, continued to work in the NSW Division of Forensic Medicine, but she was in an increasingly wretched situation. Though the convictions had been upheld, the wholesale assault on her work by eminent scientists had been nationally publicised and naturally caught the attention of her superiors in the NSW Department of Health. When she was transferred from the forensic section to one dealing with disputed paternity, the question naturally arose as to whether she had been pushed. A spokesman for the director of her division said the transfer was routine and in accordance with normal procedure, but Kuhl, apparently taking umbrage, resigned. She went to the Northern Territory to take up position there in forensic science. The Northern Territory, closed ranks around her and treated her as one of their own. From one point of view the reputations of the police, the politicians and the bureaucrats were now linked with hers. She took up a position heading and upgrading the NT Government forensic laboratory and from later reports she did a very good job. When she was required to attend an inquest in Sydney over a matter in which she was involved in her previous position in New South Wales, the Northern Territory paid for her to come to Sydney to give evidence.

In the meantime, the legal system grappled with what the forensic scientists had left behind. Professor Barry Boettcher decided to send his material directly to the Chief Justice of the High Court, Sir Harry Gibbs, who returned it unopened saying it would be improper for him to consider anything that might be before the court. The High Court comprised Sir Harry, and Justices Anthony Mason, Sir Gerard Brennan, Lionel Murphy and Sir William Deane. At the hearing, Michael McHugh QC represented the Chamberlains. McHugh argued that there were huge flaws in the Crown case. However, he was hamstrung by the rules of jurisdiction, which prevented the court from considering new evidence. Ian Barker QC representing the Crown said, in his core submission, that once it had been proved there was foetal blood in the car, the dingo theory could be dispensed with because dingoes did not kill babies in cars. The jury was entitled, he said, to conclude that a human being had carried out the killing and it was Lindy Chamberlain.

As Tipple and McHugh got onto the plane, McHugh was optimistic. Tipple said we discussed how two judges were for us and two against, and the "swinger" was the Chief Justice, Sir Harry. According to Tipple, McHugh said: "The CJ will never down us three-to-two." Word got out that the High Court might uphold the appeal. A group of journalists quickly got up to Darwin on 21st February 1984 in anticipation of that, and the possible release of Lindy. Malcolm Brown was one of them. On 22nd February, the day the High Court finding was due, he had lunch with journalist Bill Hitchings and a police officer closely associated with the case. The police officer spent the whole meal avoiding eye contact with Brown, apparently antagonised by the line Brown had taken in his reporting. Word came in mid-afternoon that the High Court had dismissed the appeal, and Brown caught a plane back to Sydney. He heard later that the police officer had told the other reporters he was going to get Brown that night, beat him up and throw him into gaol. The police officer might not have meant it, and certainly would have been circumspect about publicly stating such intentions, but there was considerable resentment of anyone stirring the pot in the media. Brown made some inquiries and was told by a reliable source that "half the police force" wanted to get him into an alley. He rang the media officer in the NT Chief Minister's office and asked that the police be told to lay off. Brown pleaded he was just doing his job.

Gibbs, contrary to McHugh's expectations, came down on the side of Mason and Brennan in rejecting the appeal. In their finding, Gibbs and Mason said the jury verdicts could not be regarded as unsafe or unsatisfactory. Brennan concluded that the evidence against the Chamberlains was sufficiently strong as to have supported the verdicts. "An appellate court cannot speculate on what facts were found," he said. "It cannot interfere with a verdict if an inference could have been safely drawn from the primary facts which the jury were entitled to find beyond reasonable doubt ... The question for the court of criminal appeal is whether it is open to the jury to be satisfied by the appellant's guilt, not whether the court is satisfied."

Significantly, the High Court rejected the Crown evidence on the finding of foetal blood by a four-to-one majority. The one judge in the minority, Gerard Brennan, who said the jury were "entitled to accept the evidence of the prosecution experts on this issue and to find that the samples from the car which gave positive results contained in fact foetal haemoglobin." Gibbs and Mason rejected the Crown evidence on the identification of foetal haemoglobin and held that there was reasonable doubt on it, but that if the other evidence were taken into account, the verdicts were not unsafe or unsatisfactory.

The majority took particular exception to Professor James Cameron's claim that he had seen bloodied hand-prints on the baby's jumpsuit. Gibbs and Mason said: "No other witnesses saw this imprint and we confess that it was not visible when we examined the jumpsuit and the fluorescent photographs of the jumpsuit." Brennan said: "It is difficult to detect a hand print on that which was tendered to show the distribution of blood on the garments. However, unless there is some reasonable possibility that might explain the presence of smeared blood consistent with the dingo hypothesis, the existence of those marks betokens a human handling of the baby when her life blood was flowing away or shortly after she died." Murphy said: "This court examined the jumpsuit and the photographs. The jury should have been directed that this evidence was not 'scientific' but highly imaginative and directed to disregard it."

Murphy was not prepared to stop with just dismissing the evidence on the supposed hand imprints. Of all the judges, if any was to try to cut through the strict legal formalities and try to get to the heart of the matter, it was Murphy. Murphy had a long and colourful history. Appointed a High Court judge, he had dispensed with wearing a wig. A radical with First-Class Honours in Law from Sydney University, he had long tended to dispense with conventional wisdom and follow an independent line of reasoning. His lack of convention was to get him into serious trouble, but that was another matter. In the Chamberlain case, he said the defence case that a dingo had taken Azaria was quite reasonable. Evidence concerning a dingo's involvement was "strikingly consistent with the hypothesis of innocence". Cameron's evidence was not scientific, he said. "It was highly imaginative. The jury should have been instructed to disregard it." The jury should not have been left to decide between Joy Kuhl's evidence and that of the defence scientists. As it turned out in this case, he said, the Chamberlains were "required to prove their innocence". Sir William Deane, an esteemed if quieter individual, who was to become the Governor-General, supported Murphy in finding that the Chamberlains had been unjustly convicted. Both would have upheld the appeal and quashed the convictions.

Murphy and Deane were not enough. The convictions were upheld by a three-to-two majority. In strict legal terms, that was it. There was no avenue for further appeal. The last safeguard to arrest the progress of this horrible injustice had failed. In Darwin, there was, if not dancing in the streets, a nod of the head and a feeling: now let's forget about it. As a receptionist at a Darwin hotel said: "Oh, I'm so thrilled they're not getting off. I knew they wouldn't get away with it." At Alice Springs, a businessman said: "Look, everyone up here is sick of it. Everyone knew they did it and it was just being drawn out."

On 8th March 1984, Steve Brien published a book, *Trial of the Century*, in which he supported the guilty verdict, and added details which the police had not considered cogent. One was that Azaria had been dressed in black when she was taken to the doctor for what would have been her last medical check-up. Another was that a bible found in the Chamberlains' home had a passage underlined referring to a death of a man named Sisera who was killed in a tent, having had a tent spike rammed through his skull and then beheaded. Police had also found a small coffin in the Chamberlains' home. None of this had been used as evidence against the Chamberlains, and rightly so. The colour black in itself meant nothing. The small coffin was what had been used during anti-smoking campaigns and carried around to encourage people to dispose of their cigarettes. Tipple told Malcolm Brown that the bible was not marked at all, that police opened it at that particular place. The passage on one of the pages might have looked suspicious to a person whose mind was orientated that way.

The way the defamation law works in Australia, once someone has been convicted of such a heinous offence, they are deemed to have no reputation, or so little of it that people can virtually say what they like. In this case, what Brien said implied that there had in fact been an element of satanic ritual. A reviewer described the book as "raunchy". The book appeared to have done Brien no harm in police eyes. It was very much pro-police and soon after it was published, he was appointed the Director of Public Relations for the NSW Police. Policing is a hard job and like anybody else police like good press. When someone goes berserk, it is always the police who are called upon. Sometimes police are killed. At the time of writing, a police officer was shot dead in the Lockyer Valley in Queensland. The annals of police history are pockmarked with such tragedies. The police must tackle the most dangerous and cunning criminals, their work is underrated and when they get it wrong, lawyers, politicians and civil libertarians are quick to pounce. In the investigation of Azaria's disappearance, the police were quite within their rights to rely on expert scientific evidence. Brien was one who sympathised. At that point in the Chamberlain saga, he was also within his rights to endorse the verdicts.

Upon the release of the book, Brien said his own personal verdict on the Chamberlains was: "They're guilty." Writing in the *Sydney Morning Herald* on 11th March, he said the police were simply doing their duty. "The case is not, and never has been, a crusade on the part of the Northern Territory Police against a husband and wife," he said. "Once police were satisfied that Azaria had been murdered it was their duty to apprehend the only person who could have committed that crime. Time and again I have hoped that the full ramifications of the allegations against Mrs Lindy Chamberlain would simply fade away. Even today, I don't believe Mrs Chamberlain should be in Darwin's Berrimah gaol. She should be having therapy and counselling from those who may be able to help her." Brien then went into details about Azaria wearing a black dress, the marked bible and the coffin, matters which were not used by the Crown because they lacked cogency. That begs the question as to whether those facts should be used in any context.

A lawyer and tennis-playing friend of Tipple, Patrick Donnellan, concerned about the continuing stress on Tipple, seemingly beating his head against a wall of granite, wrote a compassionate letter to him. He said: "I am deeply concerned about the pain that this latest turn in the Chamberlain case must have caused you. I am concerned about the future for you because I have a sense of this thing using up your precious and excellent life that [has] had enough, but it must be the case that it is starting to use up the lives of your wife and son. Can you surely say that since you ceased our tennis which I enjoyed so much for your company that they have had as much of *you* as they are entitled to? I am talking about the period of time that has elapsed. I know the degree of your love for your family but I would still seek reassurance from you. I also know [how] determined you are and how you hate to lose (even a game of tennis against me for Chissakes!). Understand dear friend that I am only voicing – that that determination will keep you going at what cost it is fearful to speculate on. I know how you feel. I really do – your sense of outrage at this injustice and your powerlessness in which the face of red-necked narrow-mindedness and your concern for this poor woman. I know all that, but, if your determination is leading you to continue, I say to you that the truly courageous and charitable thing to do is to stop – now. Let somebody else set her free and you go about setting yourself free. I am not meaning to lecture you. I am putting this to you as a possibility. If it means nothing, it means nothing, but I want to say it to you because I want you back!"

Tipple's response to the High Court decision was neither aggressive nor despairing. But he was not inclined to give up. He had not been surprised by the High Court's decision. From previous appeal work in New South Wales, he knew how hard it was to win an appeal against a jury decision. This was particularly so because of Muirhead's very favourable summing-up to the jury and the fact that it did not contain any errors in law. "Once convicted, the appellant has the onus to prove there was an error serious enough to have the appellate court quash a conviction," he said later. "Winning a criminal appeal is rare event and only happens on average in two cases each year in New South Wales." He knew that getting his clients out of this mess meant relying on further scientific investigation.

Was any of this really satisfying? If two highly qualified and gifted individuals who had made it to the High Court would have set Michael and Lindy free on the spot, how could anyone be sure they were guilty? It would have taken one, just one of the other three to agree with them and that would have been that: Chamberlains acquitted and it was all over. So, the entire case then centred on what was really the view of life of that one individual who, of three dismissing the appeal, might have gone the other way. Tipple was later to write: "As it was, a three/two majority can hardly be regarded as a satisfying result for the community." The judges' four-to-one rejection of the evidence on identification of the blood was particularly disturbing. Barker himself had said that the Crown case rested on that. It was the battleground over which the case had been fought. Greg Lowe, who had been a principal primary witness, said: "On the basis of our knowledge and understanding on that night, we know that any purported blood found in the car could simply have not got there in the manner suggested by the Crown." If the court could not be satisfied that baby's blood was in the car, what else was left?

Be that as it may, in practical terms, it appeared to be all over. At Cooranbong Michael Chamberlain had been assigned to pastor the Dora Creek Church while studying in the Master's Program at Avondale College. When the case was reopened, he had felt he could not continue in his pastoral duties until his name his name was cleared, and he later resigned from the SDA ministry. The church hierarchy also took into account certain "moral" aspects of Michael's behaviour. When Malcolm Brown tried to find out more, a church official said: "The church can't have him back because things have got to be right." That is all he would say. Michael conceded that the church had reasons for "de-credentialing" him, as he himself expressed it. He took it very hard. Michael Chamberlain continued his job in the Avondale College archives and felt other stings that afflict convicted persons. He received a note from the Electoral Office that because of his conviction, he was unable to vote for the time being. He was visiting Lindy in prison, but the circumstances were awkward and trust was draining from their relationship.

Tipple was certainly not prepared to give up. He decided that he would have to persist with investigating the scientific evidence. There was obvious ground to be explored with the blood, but there was other material as well. Hans Brunner, an expert on animal hairs, had attended the High Court with Tipple and had examined the hair samples taken from the clothing that had been mounted in glass slides. He told Tipple he was in doubt that the hairs were canine. Tipple told Barry Boettcher to retain all the materials relating to the foetal antiserum from Behringwerke. Boettcher did so but thought the only way forward now was the public arena.

Phil Ward and Don McNicol, who had already taken to the public arena, were not travelling well. In the NT Legislative Assembly, Attorney-General Jim Robertson tabled a letter from Lindy Chamberlain saying she did not want to have anything to do with their inquiries or their statements. Robertson said the claims made by the pair were an "incredible and a scurrilous attack on the NT Government and the Territory's system of justice." Robertson said the material had been examined by the Solicitor-General, Brian Martin, who had said it was confusing, unclear and equivocal. In his report, Martin had said the two had had misinformation about the dingo and that the matters they had drawn on were either unsubstantiated or were capable of innocent explanations.

There was always a question of whether the Federal Government could become involved, given that it was only a territory involved and not a fully-fledged state. On 1st March, the Attorney-General, Senator Gareth Evans, put paid to that by saying that neither he nor the Federal Government had any authority to become involved the case. It was a matter for the Northern Territory. But nobody else was shutting up. Greg Lowe went public the same day saying that Lindy had taken the baby away from the barbecue area, entered the tent and come out without the baby in her arms, and he had not said that at the trial because it was not in his original statement and he would have been accused of fabrication. On 2nd March, the *Sydney Morning Herald* published a summary of Ward and McNicol's "Ding Theory". Ward, interviewed by the *Herald*, said he and McNicol were standing by what they said. Ward and McNicol were now briefing their own legal team. They had retained the services of a well-known criminal lawyer, Trevor Nyman, who was briefing John Lloyd-Jones QC and his junior counsel, Clive Steirn. To pay their fees, running at $2,500 a day, Ward was appealing to his many followers through *Adventist News* and money was coming in.

On 2nd March 1984, Les Smith sent material to Professor Chaikin, relating to what appeared to be the real ability of canine dentition to make scissor-like cuts in jumpsuit fabric and produce tufts. A week later, on 9th March, Chaikin replied: "Thank you for your letter of the 2nd March with enclosures which I am returning herewith. I do not believe that I should enter into any correspondence on this matter." Why did Chaikin not meet with them? Chaikin told Malcolm Brown years later that the experimental work by Smith and Chapman was "all rubbish" and he was not going to waste time on it. But the real reason might be that he would be forced into a position where he conceded that he was wrong, and all his much-heralded and publicised evidence would be shown up. Later, instead of entertaining the possibility that he really was wrong, Chaikin dived into deeper science, instructing a junior colleague to examine the jumpsuit material with a scanning electron microscope, which he said showed the ends of the fibres in "planar array". This, he said, showed that the cuts could only have been produced by a bladed instrument.

The only other avenue left for Smith and his group was to appeal to the media. Dr Norman Young, a theologian at Avondale College, gave some of Smith's material to Malcolm Brown for publication in the *Sydney Morning Herald*. Brown reacted with a degree of scepticism. Like many other lay people, he could not imagine that someone of the eminence of Chaikin could have his findings overturned by a simple backyard experiment. Smith, the backyard scientist, had the habit of providing persuasive answers. He later pointed out to Tipple that in the experiment that had been carried out in Adelaide Zoo, where a dingo had been fed a carcass dressed in baby's clothes. Dingo saliva had been found on the jumpsuit and singlet, but not on the nappy, even though the nappy had been ripped. The simple fact that no saliva had been found on the nappy, though a dingo had obviously damaged it, demonstrated how dangerous it was to conclude that no dingo was involved in the disappearance of Azaria.

On 13th March, Barry Boettcher wrote to Jim Robertson saying that Joy Kuhl's evidence was wrong and that the anti-serum she had used was not specific to foetal haemoglobin, it could also react with adult haemoglobin. He sent copies of the submission to the NT Opposition leader, Neil Bell, the Federal Attorney-General, Senator Gareth Evans, and the Federal Shadow Attorney-General, Senator Peter Durack. In Darwin, Robertson replied that Boettcher's submission and accompanying material would be examined "from a scientific point of view". But he said that irrespective of the merits of this material, he did not think it merited reconsideration of the Chamberlain case. A ministerial officer told Tipple the material would be sent to the Department of Law without delay.

Neil Bell took up the issue of Graeme Charlwood having been assigned to inquire into the Ward-McNicol allegations when the finding had the potential to reflect on his own investigation. When he asked in the NT Legislative Assembly whether this was proper, the Chief Minister, Paul Everingham, said angrily that the NT police worked under difficulties. Boettcher went on a national tour. He spoke to meetings of Chamberlain supporters in Newcastle, Sydney, Melbourne, Adelaide, Ballarat and Albury, the Latrobe Valley, Cooranbong, Brisbane, Hobart and Darwin. In Darwin, Joy Kuhl joined the audience and there were some angry words between them.

In all this furore, Lindy Chamberlain was serving her time at Berrimah. On any reasonable view of her and the penal sanctions and counselling available to her, she should have been out. Even the senior police had said after her conviction that a long prison sentence was not going to help anything. On 26th

March, Tipple took that up. He submitted to the Northern Territory in relating to infanticide and other grounds, which he considered to be "cogent enough to justify Mrs Chamberlain's early release". He said that in no other state or territory in Australia would infanticide be punishable by imprisonment. The NT administration was entirely fed up and, after they had made their point about allowing the justice system to work, they wanted Lindy off their hands. It was tacitly agreed that there was nothing evil about Lindy, and her act of infanticide was inexplicable. It was decided that if everyone would shut up, then a release on licence would be considered.

Brian Martin met with Stuart Tipple on 29th March. Tipple informed the SDA church hierarchy, and the church's communications unit sent a confidential letter to the church's five divisions saying what happened. It said: "Mr Martin made it clear that as long as the support groups maintained their pressure, and there was likelihood of legal action of a private nature – and as long as Michael and others appeared on TV, no consideration whatever would be given to assisting Lindy Chamberlain." However, the thought was conveyed that if the Chamberlains accepted guilt and undertook not to pursue their justification any further, something like a release on licence might be a possibility. Stuart as good as replied that such a course was totally unacceptable – and that was that. Nothing but the clearing of his clients' names would do. Sadly, that communication itself was leaked to the media, in particular to Malcolm Brown who published it, causing the Northern Territory to clam up completely and infuriating Stuart Tipple. The leak had created "a mess", one of the church boffins told Brown.

But the juggernaut kept moving on. By the end of March, signatures were being collected for a petition, at the rate of 3,000 a day, calling for an inquiry into the case. Of these, some 2,000 signatures a day were being gathered by the Save Lindy Chamberlain Group, led by Guy Boyd. Another thousand were being collected by a "Plea for Justice" group in Canberra, headed by Betty Hocking, who formed an ambitiously-named National Freedom Council. To this point, there were 94,000 signatures and it was planned that another 6,000 would be collected. On 4th April, TEN Channel 10 screened a documentary, *Azaria Chamberlain, A Question of Evidence*, produced by Kevin Hitchcock, a journalist who had become very favourably disposed to the Chamberlains. Hitchcock focused on the primary evidence supporting the dingo attack at Ayers Rock and included in the documentary, evidence from the Aborigines themselves.

In the Hitchcock documentary, a retired Victorian Supreme Court judge, Sir Reginald Sholl, took the matter up. The opinion of Sholl, who had spent 16 years on the bench and 20 years practising at the bars of New South Wales, Victoria and Tasmania, could not be easily dismissed. He said that had he been the trial judge he would have directed the jury that it was quite unsafe to convict on conflicting scientific and circumstantial evidence of that nature. He said: "I feel, on the probabilities, that there has been a very grave miscarriage of justice." Hitchcock said he received many calls after the screening, and they ran "five-to-one" in favour of innocence. Darwin television station NTD8 was under pressure to run the documentary as it had been shown in the states. The board obliged. Columnist Jacqueline Lee Lewes said in the *Sun-Herald*: "To my mind, [it is] one of the most interesting (and disturbing) documentaries shown so far this year."

On 5th April, Malcolm Brown reporting for *Sydney Morning Herald* published an interview with Max Cranwell, who said his three-year-old daughter, Amanda, had been attacked by a dingo at Ayers Rock on 23rd June 1980, some six weeks before Azaria died. John Phillips had heard about the incident and had desperately wanted to pin it down at the trial. At that stage the Cranwells had not been identified. Interviewed by Brown, Cranwell said he had heard Amanda cry out and had gone over to see her lying as "a heap on the ground" with the dingo standing over her. She had told him the dingo had dragged her out of the car. She had been bitten round the neck and shoulders and one ear. There were puncture wounds to the neck and ear and blood was oozing out. When he had reported it to Cawood, Cawood had said: "Oh yes, that is Ding," and, "Oh well, we will have to destroy it." He said something the next day to the effect that he had shot the dingo. The response of Jim Robertson in Darwin was that the information was "old and irrelevant".

The *NT News* published an editorial saying that the statement by 31 Australian scientists attacking the blood evidence in the trial was "an assault on the Australian legal system" and that "renewed agitation about the Chamberlain case needs to be watched and analysed very carefully". It said: "No matter how eminent the scientists are who now lead this assault on the Australian legal system – and make no mistake, it is an assault against the system – the fact is that Lindy and Michael Chamberlain have been found guilty by the due process of law. The principle at stake here is that if the scientists, supported by great sections of the media, the jury system and the tried and true legal system will stand endangered." The paper said Lindy Chamberlain should serve her sentence unless "there is a concealed truth that is unequivocally demonstrable". The paper concluded: "And there must certainly not be Federal intervention either by the Government or the Governor-General because the Territory is still subject to some colonial powers, which, if exercised, would destroy the very foundations of self-government."

In Darwin Prison, Lindy Chamberlain knew that this dreadful controversy was keeping her in gaol longer. She wanted her name and that of Michael cleared. She was steadfast on that. She believed, despite a number of suggestions to her otherwise, that Tipple was the man to stay with. In a letter to Phil Ward on 7th April, she rebuked him for what she said was inaccurate reporting on the case, and told him his reporting in *Adventist News* was doing more harm than good. She had gone along with the joint representation – Tipple on the one hand and the Nyman group on the other. She had consulted the Nyman group for almost six months but felt frustrated and remained in favour of Tipple. Lindy told Ward that reports of "a split between Michael and I" were mere "propaganda" and said: "How about putting all that energy into supporting my real legal team who are working solidly". She added: "Your knowledge of the legal system is sadly lacking to claim Mr Tipple or any of the rest of my team have been lax in their job. Yes, I mention team because Mr Tipple is not my only lawyer... Are you man enough to admit you were wrong, Phil, and print this in your letters section without inferring I am sick, cracking up or so isolated that I don't know what's happening? You can also forget the line that my lawyers dictate my public output (or private for that matter). Stop making sandcastles." Lindy said there was another body of new evidence but it would be publicly revealed at the appropriate time.

Lindy's continuing incarceration and Tipple's argument that the sentence was now unjust was not lost on the NT Authorities. On 9th April, Roberson and Martin discussed Tipple's application for release of Lindy on licence. A spokesman for Robertson said later that no decision was imminent but any decision would first be communicated to the Chamberlains' lawyers. The Administrator of the Territory, Commodore Eric Johnston, would have to make a decision following a recommendation from Robertson and based on advice from the Executive Council.

Three days later, a juror from the trial gave an exclusive interview to the Australian Associated Press correspondent in Darwin, Brian Johnstone. The unnamed juror was a 36-year-old man who said he was a senior public servant. He said evidence as to whether there was baby blood in the Chamberlains' family car had not played a significant role in the verdict. He said the jury's decision came down to whether the jurors believed it was a dingo that took the child. Tipple's response was: "The Police and the Northern Territory Government had used the media to good effect." Malcolm Brown rang Johnstone, who was a friend and a very good reporter, and asked whether this was a "put up job", a plant to quell the controversy Boettcher was stirring. It had been on record from Brian Martin that any reporter approaching a former juror would be put before the courts. Johnstone laughed at the suggestion he was being used as a stooge. And to be fair to him, a reporter cannot approach a juror but is not obliged to turn a deaf ear should a juror volunteer to speak. An interview with a former juror was a good story.

Boettcher wrote to Robertson on 17th April complaining of the dismissive attitude Robertson had taken to the new material. "I am surprised and disappointed with your view that the new material does not warrant any reconsideration of the Chamberlain case," he said. "Mr Ian Barker QC in his opening address to the court in the Chamberlains' trial said, 'the discovery of foetal haemoglobin in the car is critical to the prosecution case'. If the claim that there was foetal blood in the car is now established as being wrong, I cannot see why anyone should fail to entertain the possibility that the jury's verdict was wrong. As Justices Gibbs and Mason considered in their High Court judgement, that evidence may have made a great impression on the jury. Your comments about the judgements of the Federal Court and High Court are, of course, correct. However, the basis for the judgements from these courts was clearly summarised by Mr Justice Brennan in these words, 'The question for the court of criminal appeal is whether it was open to the jury to be satisfied of the appellant's guilt, not whether the court is satisfied'. These courts considered not whether the jury's verdict was, in your opinion, wrong, but whether the trial had been conducted in such a way that it was safe to leave the decision to the jury. In coming to their decisions, the jury of the Northern Territory Supreme Court, the Federal Court and the High Court did not have the material I have sent to you available to them. If they had, I am content the present situation would not have eventuated." He said bluntly: "I certainly believe that a serious miscarriage of justice has occurred, and that the incorrect forensic evidence about the presence of infant blood in the Chamberlains' car and the other items has been the factor which has led to this unfortunate situation."

So where was it possible to go from here? Reinstate trial by combat? Trial by ordeal? Or revert to the inquisitorial system in practice in Europe? Was the jury system, time-honoured though it was, the best system? Would a conclave of experts have been better to consider the scientific evidence, and then let their assessment of it be a factor in the jury deliberations? The only real prospect was a judicial review of some description by a judge having access to all the available facts. But the only hope the Chamberlains had of getting that was if the NT

Attorney-General was convinced it was warranted. And that, Tipple knew, was no easy task, seeing how much the Northern Territory had invested in the investigation and prosecution. The Attorney-General held all the aces. From Tipple's view, the only way the Northern Territory would grant an inquiry would be if it was forced. As far as he was concerned, it was time for the gloves to come off. He engaged a public relations firm, Charlton and Charlton, and invited a number of prominent people who had spoken out about the case to join a Chamberlain Innocence Committee.

Boettcher's other recourse was his fellow professionals. Among the group he appealed to was the distinguished Australian research biologist, Sir Gustav Nossal, famous for his contributions to the fields of antibody formation and immunological tolerance. Boettcher had obtained 31 signatures from the scientists endorsing what Boettcher had said about the non-specificity of the anti-serum. That was given to the media and publicised nationally. It brought a scornful response from the NT News. But the NT News was hardly the final authority. On 18th April, the NSW Ombudsman wrote to the Department of Health telling them that he had decided to conduct an investigation under section 19 of the Ombudsman Act into practices at the Division of Forensic Medicine. He referred in particular to Simon Baxter's evidence at the trial. Baxter had refused to take any responsibility for the destruction of the test plates and claimed that responsibility rested with the Health Commissioner of New South Wales. The Ombudsman began a comprehensive inquiry and sought advice and visited other laboratories to determine the best practice.

On 3rd May, Betty Hocking and Guy Boyd presented a petition containing 131,450 signatures to the Governor-General, Sir Ninian Stephen, asking him to exercise his prerogative of mercy and appoint a royal commission. Sir Ninian, who had served in a Water Transport Company in the Aitape-Wewak Campaign in World War 11, serving under the then Captain Nigel Bowen, was no pushover. He had a worldly-wise view of life. But like just about everyone else in the system, his hands were tied. The Commonwealth Crown Law Department advised Senator Evans that the Governor-General did not have a prerogative over the Northern Territory. On 6th May, Sir Ninian replied publicly that he could do nothing himself other than hand the petition and the accompanying letter to the Attorney-General.

In the meantime, Barry Boettcher continued to beaver away at Kuhl's evidence. And on 14th May, he received a letter from Behringwerke's Sydney agent confirming that the factory had conducted tests and it appeared that the serum would react with adult blood in some circumstances. If this were true, then Joy Kuhl's tests would have to be thrown out. But now of course, the wheels of justice had turned considerably. The world was moving on, he was indeed "kicking goals by moonlight", as far as the NT Government and legal establishment was concerned.

On 24th May, Phil Ward, whose hands were not tied and had ventured into areas where the stuffed shirts of officialdom were impotent, withdrew from his campaign. The campaign was taken up by Jim Driscoll, a Murwillumbah businessman who led the self-styled "Northern Pro-Chamberlain Committee". Driscoll retained the services of the Nyman team and pursued Ward's line, though he was not interested in a private prosecution. There were powerful forces massing. That month the "Chamberlain Innocence Committee" was formed, chaired by Sir Reginald Sholl. Other committee members were a retired deputy president of the Commonwealth Conciliation and Arbitration Commission, Frank Gallagher, together with Betty Hocking, Senators Malcolm Colston and Colin Mason, a renowned Melbourne sculptor, Guy Boyd, Drs Wes Allen and Fred Smith, a Darwin general practitioner, Dr Tony Noonan, and Adelaide chiropractor, Dr Tomlinson and the artist, Pro Hart.

On 14th June 1984, Senator Colin Mason introduced into the Senate a Private Member's Bill which, if passed by the Federal Parliament, would require the Commonwealth to appoint a Commission of Inquiry to consider new evidence relevant to the convictions of the Chamberlains. Part of his material comprised affidavits put together by John Lloyd-Jones QC and Clive Steirn, who were focusing on the dingo theory. Also in Mason's possession was scientific material compiled by Stuart Tipple. Boettcher pointed out that the Northern Territory had no mechanism for a judge to hold an inquiry if doubt arose as to a conviction, so the initiative should come from the Commonwealth.

Shortly after Mason presented his bill, Tipple joined Boettcher and Les Smith to meet interested senators in the Commonwealth Parliament House. They spoke about the new evidence, and about serious doubts it had cast on the verdict. Several Senators, Tipple said, were keenly interested and spoke with the group for some time. The next day, Boettcher wrote to Robertson, telling him some senators had real doubt as to the verdict. He offered to discuss the matter with Robertson. Robertson replied that the matters he had raised in his submission and on public comment were on scientific grounds and he did not think there was anything to be gained through discussion with him. Michael, through the facilitation of Betty Hocking, also went to Federal Parliament and spoke to "every Member of Parliament in the Upper and Lower house who would listen to me" as he expressed it. He spoke to 47 parliamentarians in nine days.

But there were constitutional problems. The Commonwealth was very aware of the sensitivities of the Northern Territory which as far as humanly possible should be left to manage is own affairs. The territory was not like a local government, which could be sacked by a state government and have an administrator installed. But it was not up with the states in terms of status and clout. Senator Evans said Mason's bill was not necessary because the Northern Territory could commission an inquiry if it considered there were compelling reasons to do so. He said that if the Northern Territory required assistance, the Federal Parliament could enact legislation necessary to ensure that the Federal Court could hear a further appeal based on new evidence.

Senator Mason called Lindy Chamberlain in gaol. She was quite chuffed by his call. Here the real heavyweights were coming in to her cause. She wrote to Tipple saying: "He talks more than me – how about that!! It will be interesting to see what comes out of it." But the senators were only one of a number of groups now competing for Lindy's attention. The other group were the Nyman team, now instructed by Jim Driscoll. On 18th June, Lindy wrote to Tipple saying: "Those working with Nyman and Lloyd-Jones seem anxious to cooperate at the moment and I think it is time I met them. It's time they learned from me who my lawyers are, and where I stand and who works for whom. I don't wish to have every man and his dog instructing 'my' lawyers on my behalf and employing whom they wish and dumping you on my behalf thank you very much!" The Nyman group and their supporters could work through Tipple or "go jump", she said. Ward himself decided to make a quantum leap and stand as an Independent against Paul Everingham for the seat of the Northern Territory in the Federal Parliament. With his normal irrepressible enthusiasm, he moved to Darwin and started campaigning.

On 28th June, Tipple had a meeting with Nyman, Lloyd-Jones and Steirn, who were complying with Lindy's demand that they work through him. Lindy had sent a letter giving working guidelines and instructions. The meeting agreed on areas of work they should concentrate on. Tipple would continue with the scientific aspects and the Nyman team would pursue the primary evidence. The Nyman team then visited Lindy in gaol and she spoke to them for three hours. But even though there was cooperation between the two legal teams, in the widespread Chamberlain support community there were feelings that Tipple should be replaced by the Nyman team. On 21st July, a Victorian man (claiming having an MSc), wrote to Michael Chamberlain, saying that the bill being put forward by Senator Mason was almost certain to be defeated. The official view, he said, was that the Northern Territory would prevail and only the Democrats would vote for it. He went on to say: "If Stuart Tipple remains in any way connected with the case, we are all finished. We may as well give up. Can you get rid of him?"

Indirectly, the Chamberlain cause was getting help coming from other quarters. On 1st August, Carl Shannon, the royal commissioner charged with investigating the conviction of Edward Charles Splatt in South Australia, brought down his findings. He began sitting on 24th January 1983, and concluded 196 days of hearing on 1st March 1984. Shannon found that it would be "unjust and dangerous" to allow Splatt's conviction for murder to stand. The scientific evidence presented to him "properly casts doubt" on the validity of what was presented to the Supreme Court at the trial. Splatt had served more than six years of a life sentence for the murder of Rosa Amelia Simper in Adelaide suburbia in December 1977. There had been no primary evidence or evidence of motive and the entire prosecution had been based on matching trace particles at his home with those at the murder scene. Piece by piece, that evidence had been dissected before Shannon and found to have been flawed. There was an alternative explanation for everything that had been found at Splatt's home. But it had taken the media, especially journalist Stewart Cockburn writing in the Adelaide *Advertiser*, to bring on the royal commission. What the Splatt case demonstrated was that apparently solid and persuasive scientific evidence presented in the hurly-burley of a trial could, under patient examination, be unravelled.

It was obvious, Shannon said, that a reformation of the system and a change of culture was required. He said a forensic scientist was first and foremost a scientist, and that his or her word should be subject to all the rigorous discipline of any scientific work, especially important when the liberty of an individual was at stake. An example of a properly run system was the forensic services of the Home Office in England. Senator Mason, campaigning in the Chamberlain case, wanted a similar reform by his Private Member's Bill seeking a royal commission into the Chamberlain case.

On the day Shannon's report was published, Mason told Tipple he had booked the Senate Committee Rooms for a meeting on the case in three weeks' time. "I understand that many more members are becoming sympathetic, so if we can make this one particularly professional and hard-hitting, we should have a good chance of at least having the Bill passed through the Senate in the Budget Session if the NT government takes no further action," he said. On 24th August, Boettcher rang Behringwerke to check what it had told Martin and Baxter during their visit. Baudner, one of the scientists, told him: "My information has not changed since you were here in the factory. What they did was not suitable [for the identification of infant blood]." Boettcher had it in one. If that was accepted, the Chamberlain convictions could not stand! He had to get the word out. Malcolm Brown helped him, but there was now a push to present the case in a broader context still. Several authors were now in print, trying to follow the outstanding success of Stewart Cockburn. Malcolm Brown had a chapter on the Chamberlain case in his book, *Justice and Nightmares: Successes and Failures in Forensic Science*, co-authored with criminologist Paul Wilson, published in 1992. In Melbourne, Guy Boyd had his book, *Justice in Jeopardy*, published the same year and in Melbourne John Bryson was completing his book on the case, *Evil Angels*, due to be published later that year.

In August 1984 Phil Ward published a book of his own, *Azaria, What the Jury Were Not Told*, outlining what he, assisted by McNicol, believed had really happened at Ayers Rock. It was distributed nationally, including Darwin. Comprising 192 pages, it had been printed in Adelaide by Griffin Press. The *Sydney Morning Herald* reported on 27th August that Ward was "chomping at the bit firmly by direct-mail advertisements to every household from Darwin to Alice Springs". According to Ward, replies from Darwin were running "3/1 in the book's favour" and about 400 residents so far had placed orders. It was a daring move. Seven people Ward named launched defamation proceedings. Leaving that aside, many people were getting upset with the case. Most were defending different positions, and nobody was satisfied. If they were to achieve nothing else, Ward and McNicol were out to break the stalemate.

CHAPTER TEN

THE BITTER STALEMATE

> *This administration is doing everything we can to end the stalemate in an efficient way. We're making the right decisions to bring the solution to an end.*
> — George W. Bush

The case did not go away. The High Court decision was meant to be final. Even in that it was unsatisfactory. Two judges would have thrown the whole thing out. Instead, as 1984 progressed the battle over the convictions of Michael and Lindy Chamberlain flared up across Australia. Local committees were formed. Groups championing the Chamberlains started holding meetings. When the reality of the whole case settled in, people were left shaking their heads. Journalists who covered the case and had looked favourably on the prosecution evidence were having second thoughts. In Darwin, Dr Tony Noonan, his wife Liz and a small group went against the tide of popular feeling in that part of the world and actively supported the Chamberlains.

After the trial and both appeals were lost, Tipple was under intense pressure to step aside. Many of the SDA laity accepted "the Ding scenario" pressed by Ward and McNicoll and saw this as the way forward and supported the legal team retained by Ward consisting of solicitor, Trevor Nyman, John Lloyd-Jones QC and Clive Steirn. Trevor Nyman wrote to Lindy enclosing some preliminary advice from Lloyd-Jones..

The Nyman team concentrated on the primary evidence. And in a case where scientific evidence had decided the issue, the primary evidence was never going to be enough, despite how good it was. Lawyer Dr Paul Gerber confirmed this in an advice he gave to a supporter. Writing from Brisbane on 11th September 1984, he said Lloyd-Jones' advice was a useful summary of the jurisdictional obstacles facing a second appeal to the Federal Court but he did not think that the additional evidence was strong enough to get that second appeal or to have the conviction squashed. It was not, in Gerber's opinion, "fresh" in a legal sense and would not be entertained by the court as the grounds for a new appeal. Evidence had emerged like the testimony of Greg Lowe, who was now putting it on record that he had seen Lindy go to the tent with the baby in her arms and come out without it. Potentially, that evidence had always been critical, but such were the rigidities and restraints of the legal system that there was limited scope for amendments to initial statements. Gerber said: "In short, he would be slaughtered in cross-examination, even supposing the ground got to the stage of hearing the evidence. If Lowe purported to act on legal advice, I doubt whether this could be corroborated. Who was the lawyer who advised him to deliberately conceal vital evidence from the court, evidence which it is now argued would make the difference between conviction and acquittal? I am sorry to be such a wet blanket, but I am sure you would want an honest opinion rather than paying lip-service to an opinion I cannot support."

On 21st September 1984, with very little having been achieved in the months that had passed since the High Court appeal, Tipple and the Nyman team met again, to discuss further advice from Lloyd-Jones. Tipple told Nyman he was officially on the team, answerable to Lindy Chamberlain and asked him to start immediately to prepare affidavits for the Northern Territory.

Elsewhere, other prominent people were joining the campaign for an official inquiry into the Chamberlain case. They included criminologist, Dr Paul Wilson, the NSW Public Defender, Dr Greg Woods and a senior Federal MP, William Charles Wentworth. Wentworth, a former Federal Minister in Charge of Aboriginal Affairs, with a long record of bucking the system and challenging officialdom, believed that Azaria's body would have been eaten but the one part of her that would have gone through the digestive system was an unexploded tooth, which was apparently indigestible and could be found. The prospects of getting anyone to dig around or under Ayers Rock where dingoes might have had their dens and left their droppings was daunting. Wentworth set about trying to get an inquiry into the case. Tipple received a telephone call from Greg Woods, with whom he had previously worked at Sydney University Law School. Tipple agreed that Woods would dictate to his secretary proposed negotiating points that would be typed up and sent to Wentworth, Nyman and

Lloyd-Jones. But the matter lapsed.

Tipple had one victory. A draft report by the NSW Ombudsman, George Masterman QC upheld complaints by Tipple into the procedures in the NSW Department of Health, Forensic Medicine Division, and in particular some laboratory practices. The Ombudsman's draft report had been delayed by the department. The departmental secretary had not wanted him to refer to the Chamberlain case. But the draft report had plenty of criticism of the laboratory procedures. Simon Baxter had had enough. He resigned from his position and said that whatever else he did, it was not going to have anything more to do with forensic medicine.

The Division of Forensic Medicine argued that it was very busy, conducting anything between 20,000 and 50,000 tests a year, and restricted in manpower and money. It had been criticised for rejecting the test slides on which Joy Kuhl had based her conclusions. To preserve slides, it would have had to have been done for every test, to avoid being accused of selectivity of one case over another, and that would have required additional staff, space, and money. The decision not to preserve the test slides made it impossible to review findings and thereby put the defence at a disadvantage. As Royal Commissioner Carl Shannon said in his royal report on the Splatt case, findings from forensic laboratories affect the lives and futures of individuals. If Simon Baxter complained about the forensic scientist being the "poor bunny" in the middle, attacked from all sides, the accused were hardly on Easy Street either. In South Australia, the findings of a review of the state's forensic science system were published in September, following the Splatt Royal Commission, and it was announced that the system was to be reorganised.

On 27th September 1984, Senator Mason sent a telegram to Paul Everingham, telling him that unless Lindy were released on licence and an inquiry ordered, he would throw the whole issue before the Senate the following Tuesday. "I seek your urgent and favourable consideration to granting an application to release Mrs Chamberlain on licence pending an inquiry into many areas of new evidence in this matter," he said. "Suggest this would take attention from this situation and facilitate constructive cooperation between your legal authorities and the Chamberlain defence. Stress my view that any initiatives ought not to criticise any previous hearings but concentrate on new material which is now emerging and which strongly appears to suggest a new view of the case." John Lloyd-Jones had prepared a 1,700-page opinion that the Chamberlains were innocent and was sending that to Everingham. But Mason's bill was facing difficulties. A spokesman for Gareth Evans said Evans had not shifted in his position: that it was a matter for the Northern Territory Government to resolve. There was other political support for Mason, in the form of Bob Collins, leader of the NT Opposition, who called on the NT Government to hold an inquiry into the case. Collins said that if that did not happen, he would call on the Federal Government to act. A furious Everingham called on the Labor Party to censor Collins. But the attacks kept coming.

After Greg Woods visited Lindy in prison, she wrote to Tipple asking him to give material from the Nyman team to Woods. She told Tipple in a letter: "He agreed that the eyewitness material was too shaky on its own from what he'd seen. (If you are talking to him tell him it's a bad habit to bite his nails like he does and I hope none of it is my fault. Boy are they short!). You may announce any evidence you see fit now, before Phil [Ward] scoops any more … suppose you know he is opposing Porky? [Paul Everingham] He is resident up here at the moment so you won't be able to sneak in and out I guess with Michael." She also said: "Writing on your lap in the dark is disastrous but the only time I have peace and privacy. Hope you can read it."

Paul Everingham, interviewed on Channel 0 in Brisbane on 15th October, was asked about the campaign to pardon and free Lindy and claims reported in southern media that new evidence had been discovered by Ward and McNicol. He replied: "My recollection is that the Attorney-General tabled in the Northern Territory Parliament a letter which I received from Mrs Chamberlain expressly disassociating herself from this group." The following day, Lindy wrote to Nyman officially retaining him and authorising him to brief John Lloyd-Jones and Clive Steirn to prepare material to affidavit stage, subject to the material being passed to Tipple, or direct to her if they were not happy about working with Tipple. She said there had to be confidentiality about the arrangements, and that confidentiality had been lacking. Nyman wrote back confirming he was on the team and had been retained by her and Tipple. Nyman said she had the choice of lawyers and none of the team would act unless they had the full confidence of Lindy. Nyman also wrote to Tipple telling him the work he had undertaken to do should be finished by December.

Tipple had given them a full briefing on scientific evidence. Lindy told Nyman he should leave the scientific material to Tipple and he should proceed with the affidavits on the primary evidence. He replied: "We are surprised that our visit has been misrepresented. We appreciate your sensitivity; no doubt you realise that we were unable to say where we stood as to status, when support groups enquired whether we had been retained or not, as Stuart Tipple was. We wish to re-emphasise that your choice of lawyers is entirely for yourself. Neither

Mr Lloyd-Jones nor Mr Steirn nor the writer wish to act unless we have your full and complete confidence; and that position will remain throughout." He said his team was not to do any work on the scientific evidence but that they proceed post-haste with affidavit preparation which he estimated should be completed within four to six weeks.

Betty Hocking said Lindy would be released by Christmas. She said independent experts in the United States were examining new evidence including scientific material that had been put together by Stuart Tipple. It would be presented to the NT Government in a few weeks. Tipple asked the NT Government to release Lindy on licence, in accordance with the normal treatment of a woman who had committed infanticide. On 31st October, the NT Attorney-General, Jim Robertson, replied: "As indicated in previous correspondence, I am not persuaded to consider your client's application for release upon the ground that she should be dealt with as if she had committed infanticide. As to psychiatric assessment, I had merely sought your client's approval in principle and have noted what you have had to say on her behalf in that regard. It is not intended to proceed with any such examination at this stage. You are no doubt aware of the efforts being made from many quarters to bring pressure of bear upon the Northern Territory Government in regard to some form of further inquiry. Noting that you and your client have previously disassociated yourself from the activities and efforts put forward by some others, I have let it be known that the government will only consider representations made by your clients authorised legal advisors. Recent press reports have indicated that other lawyers may now have received instructions from Mrs Chamberlain and I would be grateful to receive your comments." Robertson said the Northern Territory did not accept the proposition that the Territory was the only state or territory in Australia that made the offence of infanticide punishable by imprisonment.

Tipple noted Robertson's reference to pressure being brought onto the Northern Territory. The NT Government was adamant that it had followed the due processes of law and that it would not be dictated to by the mob, in whatever form that "mob" appeared. Tipple thought the tone of the letter did not indicate that the Territory was going to give favourable consideration to releasing Lindy Chamberlain. Michael Chamberlain said the tone of Jim Robertson's letter indicated that the Territory had rejected the application outright. He said his wife had been examined by a psychologist and a psychiatrist, and that the report of the psychiatrist, Dr Metcalf, had led to Lindy's release on bail to look after new-born Kahlia. The NT Government had indicated that Lindy might be subjected to a psychiatric assessment. Tipple said that if that were to happen, her lawyers should be present. "I would like to say that Lindy is now the longest-serving prisoner in modern Australian legal history for the alleged offence of infanticide," he said.

At Cooranbong, Michael Chamberlain was under continuing stress, working in college archives and looking after Aidan and Reagan. Both Aidan and Reagan were having trouble at school, enduring taunts of other pupils, and getting into a number of fights. Reagan was now adjusting to life with the full use of only one eye and ongoing medical procedures. Now there was another complication. Wayne and Jenny Miller, who had been foster parents to Kahlia, were to move to Brisbane. The question was whether Kahlia should stay with them or whether another set of foster parents should be found in Cooranbong. Either way, there were problems. Kahlia in Brisbane would be separated from Michael and her brothers. Staying at Cooranbong, she would suffer the dislocation of being swapped around between families. On 1st November 1984, Tipple and Michael Chamberlain flew to Darwin to meet with Lindy.

At least some of the details of the visit were leaked to the media, which infuriated Tipple, who made an official complaint. "Mr Chamberlain and the writer then met with the Acting Superintendent, Mr Dewsnip and he approved a further visit between Mr and Mrs Chamberlain in the afternoon between 1 pm and 1.30 pm," he said. "Mr Chamberlain was in the writer's company all the time except for the time he went to visit Mrs Chamberlain between 1.00 and 1.30 pm, met at the airport again at 1.45 pm, and departed Darwin at 2.00 pm. Prior to our departure we were accosted by a television news crew and received messages that Mr Brian Johnstone, a reporter, had been attempting to contact Pastor Donaldson and Mr Chamberlain. At arrival in Sydney, Mr Chamberlain and the writer were confronted by a large number of media and it was noted with interest that from their questions it was apparent that they had received the following information: That Mr and Mrs Chamberlain had discussed the welfare of their youngest child; They had become upset; The matter was not raised until the end of our conference; Mr Chamberlain was subsequently allowed a further visit; Mr Chamberlain signed some papers in gaol. We further understand that Mr Brian Johnstone had confirmed to another Darwin resident that he received a report of this matter from within the prison." Mr R.F. Donnelly, director of NT Correctional Services, replied that he did not believe there had been a leak from the gaol. "As I have notified you informally by telephone, I have myself investigated this matter and despite my earlier fears that the information was released by Correctional Services staff, I now believe this not to be the case," he said. "I propose to take no further action in the matter unless additional evidence is placed before me."

At the San Hospital in Wahroonga, a group of SDA medical professionals met on 4th November to discuss whether there was anything they could do to help the Chamberlain family. As outlined them in a letter by Dr Carolyn Butler to Pastor Walter Scragg, president of the Australasian Division of the SDA Church, they decided this was an Adventist family in desperate need and they recommended that professional assistance be engaged to assess them. They recommended that Dr T. Ludowici and/or Professor Beverly Raphael should be engaged to assess the social and emotional needs of the family. Pastor George Rollo, a wise and seasoned cleric who had been a friend of Lindy's parents and grandparents, and had written a booklet, *A Reason to Kill,* proclaiming Lindy's innocence, should provide pastoral counselling.

Tipple again tried to get Lindy released, this time on compassionate grounds. In a letter dated 7th November, he told Attorney-General Robertson that because of the difficulties presented by Kahlia and by Michael Chamberlain's difficulties as a single parent, Lindy should be released on compassionate grounds. Tipple acknowledged that he had failed to persuade the government in his submissions on infanticide, but there were other grounds for release, such as the dilemma of what to do with Kahlia as her foster parents were moving to Brisbane. In addition, there was the problem of who was to foster Kahlia. The best solution, he said, would be to release Lindy on compassionate grounds to look after her. Jim Robertson replied: "I refer to your letter of 7 November 1984. I have carefully considered your client's application but I am not satisfied that the matters advanced on her behalf warrant my recommending her release with or without conditions."

Lindy, in a letter to Tipple dated the same day, said: "I have to keep reminding myself that I promised Kahlia to God and he promised to look after her. Trouble is I keep trying to tell Him how. He hasn't gone wrong so I must trust him now. He won't let me down. I wonder sometimes at His plan." She said she had increasing communications difficulties with Michael. "I spent one hour on the phone yesterday and after going over everything three times, I am still not sure a word had been heard as he tried to repeat the main points to write down and was still mixed. I tried to dictate, but I'm not sure even then. I had to close the phone call as Michael was asking me a fourth time, so I've written it all down. He went home last Friday with the exact opposite of what I'd said firmly in his head, and (Monday phone call) I can't convince him otherwise."

Ultimately, Kahlia did not go with the Millers to Brisbane, but instead went to a new set of foster parents at Cooranbong, Dr Owen and Jan Hughes after a traumatic handover. But in other theatres of this war, elements within the SDA community wanted immediate action. There was now continuous pressure to remove Tipple from the case and have the Nyman team take over. In *Intrasyd*, the official news magazine of the Greater Sydney Conference of the SDA Church, conference president Robert Parr said on 10th November that he fully supported the team led by Jim Driscoll, his wife Cavell Driscoll and Mr Lyn Knight. That group, he said, were dedicated people, but it was costing "a mint of money". "Guess how much the support groups expects to pay out in the next few months," he asked. "No, you're not even close. $300,000!!! Where is the money coming from? Glad you asked that. It's going to come from people like you and me. Not only from the rolling-in-the-stuff people; it's going to come from the little people who sacrifice to send ten or twenty dollars. You can be assured that every tiny cent will be used directly to continue to fight to have a terrible wrong righted, and an innocent lady (as we believe Lindy to be) restored to her family again. And thanks 300,000 times for what you will do."

Tipple passed on the Ward/McNicol material to John Bagnall, an SDA lawyer with whom he had previously worked in the legal firm, Hickson Lakeman. Bagnall had been "one of the few people that supported me," Tipple said. Tipple asked him to assess the Ward/McNicol material. He knew Bagnall, who was later to go to the bench as an Arbitration Judge, would be "honest and forthright". In a letter dated 14th November, Bagnall said: "I spent a part of last evening reading through your summaries. At the end of the night I had the distinct feeling that there is very little substance in the so-called fresh evidence. I find it hard to believe that an appellate court would come to the view that any of the additional evidence is so material as to make the jury's finding unsafe and unsatisfactory. The jury after all had the benefit of the evidence of Lindy and Michael Chamberlain and of Mrs Lowe. They rejected the very best evidence that the defence had. The High Court has indicated that the jury was entitled to do that and to accept the scientific evidence and it was not unsafe and unsatisfactory for them to do so." He added: "There seems to me to be a deal of confusion and contradiction in some of the statements given by the lay witnesses. This may not be deliberate but in the hands of a competent cross-examiner, the witnesses can be made to look unsure of themselves. There is also the problem of 'recent invention'. It could certainly be suggested that some of the witnesses' versions of the events have been 'improved' following the conviction."

In Brisbane, Paul Gerber spoke to the Queensland Medico-Legal Society on the Chamberlain case. They then had a re-enactment of the trial in which Gerber played John Phillips. Dr Weston Allen, one of the participants, wrote to Tipple on 24th November describing how the audience had been invited to vote in a secret ballot what they thought the verdict should have been. One lawyer protested that this would be a great embarrassment if the result were leaked out. Allen said that some time before, he had appealed to Amnesty International on the grounds that Lindy had been persecuted because of her faith. "But they don't want to touch it," he said.

Lindy Chamberlain, aware the pressures on Tipple to have him step down from the case, stuck with him. In an open letter dated 22nd November, she said: "This is to confirm that Mr Stuart Tipple is my official solicitor, and that he holds my utmost confidence. His credibility and conduct are of the highest value and I have found him to be trustworthy and confidential in all dealing with him. He has taken the brunt and the blame of many accusations levelled at him for carrying out his duties at my behest. He has never neglected his duties or worked contrary to my benefit at any stage of his engagement in this case since he first became involved, and indeed his supportive attitude, straightforward truth even when difficult news, and straightforward results are much appreciated, and not often found amongst lawyers. A request for work never needs repeating and reactions and input prompt and correct."

Word got around among some Chamberlain supporters that Lindy was in love with Tipple. When Lindy heard that she laughed and ignored it. Tipple rejected it and said he was used to seeing things twisted. Anyone who was in the trouble that Lindy Chamberlain was in would feel very positive to the lawyer who, through thick and thin, year after year, was battling for her. That is perfectly natural. But Lindy was looking for positive vibes in different directions. She hoped that perhaps a changing of the guard at the top of Northern Territory politics might be to her advantage. Jim Robertson had maintained the government's hard line. He was stepping down and she thought that Marshall Perron would take a different attitude. She thought the new Chief Minister, Ian Tuxworth, who had taken office on 17th October, might be able to do "a good job". She felt it was now time to put more public pressure on the NT Government.

Tipple was now playing a game of perceptions. Long ago he had realised this battle was not going to be one on the strict letter of the law. On 30th November, he wrote to Lindy telling her he could arrange a psychiatric consultation if Lindy felt she needed it. He added: "We can see a danger however in you seeking the services of a psychiatrist, as this could be used against you in suggesting that you were suffering from some psychiatric illness which would help bolster the old theory that she was somewhat of a psychopath. Let's stress however, that if you require any assistance then that should become the primary consideration."

Tipple continued to grapple with the campaign by the support groups who retained Nyman's group of lawyers as their champions. Tipple told Lindy in his letter of 30th November that there had been a meeting with support group members Lyn Knight, Eddie Long, Jim Driscoll and SDAS pastors Walter Scragg, Wal Taylor and Andrews which had been most helpful. "The [SDA] Division made it clear that they would not be forcing you to have legal representation other than as chosen by you," he said. "The support groups led by Lyn Knight accept that you may want other legal counsel to argue other matters but insist that John Lloyd-Jones be retained to argue any materials that it prepares. They seem concerned that if any material is handed over to either you or us it will become secondary to any further forensic evidence we have obtained. We do not believe that their fears on this point can ever be pacified. We stress that we cannot and were not prepared to force you to have any legal representation other than you chose but could see a compromise being reached whereby Lloyd-Jones could argue any material he has prepared and the balance could be argued by other counsel. It was generally agreed that the Lloyd-Jones team would continue to prepare their material to Affidavit stage following which it would be submitted to the Northern Territory."

Lindy considered now that the only way to fight back was through the media. On 19th December, she wrote to Tipple: "I feel quite strongly that we should let the press have it [the new scientific material] when the Govt gets it so no more cover ups. I have a plan to discuss with you: Send info to Greg [Cavanagh]; Set time for press conference with TV doco at their station; Release some of the pre-advertising bits to whet appetite for program; Greg, or you preferably, to have appointment with [the NT Government]. To hand over the material and discuss etc at the same time as the press conference. This stops them plotting a veto on letting it out. They will twist it and leak it their way otherwise. I know you thought this may annoy them, but I don't think they can get any worse. It's time the truth was told clearly (I'm still open to a bit of negotiation on the subject)".

In Newcastle, Barry Boettcher received replies to letters he had sent to Senator Peter Baume and to Jim Robertson. Among other things, Boettcher claimed that two witnesses had knowingly provided incorrect information in the Chamberlains' trial. He told Tipple: "Peter Baume has sent copies of my correspondence to Paul Everingham saying, basically, that the NT needs to show an interest in material sent to them, and to be seen to be showing an interest. Would he, Everingham, please ensure that the situation was looked at and brought into good order?" Robertson replied that Boettcher would be assured his communication had been "understood and give full consideration".

On Christmas Day, 1984, Boettcher received an invitation to attend the following year's World Congress on Law and Medicine in India. A member of the congress's steering committee, Justice R.S. Pathak, told Boettcher he had received glowing reports of Boettcher's "crusading contribution to the forensic debate in the famous Chamberlain case". Professor Krishna Sharma of the Law School of the University of New South Wales had "spoken with admiration of your intellectual honesty and integrity", he said. "It is my proud privilege to extend to you an invitation to attend this conference." Boettcher asked Tipple whether he thought it would be in the Chamberlains' interests to attend. "I would be happy to go to India to speak about it, with the possibility of drawing further international attention to the case," he said. But, I wouldn't go to India unless I was given the opportunity of speaking to a major audience." Boettcher thought he would be given a position in the program for a major session and he had written to Mr Pathak to confirm that he would have a major audience."

So, 1984 came to an end – a gruelling, bitter, exhausting year in which the highest court in the land had seemingly slammed the Chamberlains' hopes. The Northern Territory Government could at any time have ordered a judicial inquiry. That had been done in other states in other cases and the inquiries had not brought down governments. That would have been a solution. But here, a government decided it should stand on principle. They were intent on bringing an end to this solution by telling everyone to shut up. Perhaps George Orwell's spectre of the all-encompassing "Big Brother" of 1984 had become, in a sense, a reality.

CHAPTER ELEVEN

CIVIL WAR

> "
>
> *We are only as strong as we are united, as weak as we are divided.*
> — J.K.Rowling
>
> *It isn't the mountains ahead that wear you down. It is the pebble in your shoe.*
> — Muhammad Ali

As 1985 began and controversy over the Chamberlain case continued, the Northern Territory Government was deeply entrenched in its position. Popular clamour was not going to shift it. If they succumbed and conceded that they might be wrong, what was the legal system, and the millions of dollars that had gone into it, for? And what of the thousands who had been convicted and punished, many of them nursing grievances about being unjustly treated, who never had popular support? Cases were to be decided by careful objective consideration of the evidence, not by popular clamour. That principle, of holding firm, had been upheld time and time again in any legal system which strove to work on objective principles, and that was the principle that the Northern Territory, quite properly, adhered to.

In more recent times, When Schapelle Corby was arrested at Bali's International airport in 2004 with 4.2 kilograms of cannabis in her boogie board bag, there was overwhelming support for her within the Australian populace as she confronted the Indonesian legal system. She was a pretty girl, and she cried, holding her head in despair. Many thought she was probably guilty and there was at best, a lukewarm response to the suggestion that corrupt customs officers had used her bag to transport drugs. She was a pretty girl who had made a mistake. Let her go! People walked around with "Free Schapelle" t-shirts and bumper stickers. White powder was sent to the Indonesian embassy in Canberra in 2005, sparking fears of an anthrax attack. By 2014, after the clamour had died down and Schapelle had served years in Kerobokan prison in Bali, a research poll found that only 19 percent of people thought she was innocent. So, justice, in accordance with Indonesia's legal code, had been done, not dictated by popular sentiment but by evidence.

It might be argued that the Northern Territory placed far more significance on the Chamberlain case than it should have. In other states, cases that had been through the legal system up to the appeals courts had been subjected to continuing campaigning. Governments had responded by appointing royal commissions or special inquiries. In New South Wales, the Ananda Marga three, Tim Anderson, Ross Dunn and Paul Alister, gaoled for attempted murder of an extreme right-winger, were exonerated by an inquiry in 1985 and they were each to receive $100,000 in compensation. That did not put the legal system into jeopardy, though there was criticism of police and prosecutors. It certainly did not reflect on the NSW Government. But the Northern Territory Government saw the continuing campaign for the Chamberlains as a challenge to itself.

In Darwin prison, Lindy herself dug in, protesting her innocence. But she was also fighting another battle. There were now concerted attempts by others to have her change legal teams. Some of her visitors, like Pastor Bob Donaldson, who had replaced Graham Olson as SDA pastor in Darwin, were very supportive of Stuart Tipple. But others said she could have been better represented. "About 12 months ago I was told I should accept Phil [Ward] and his team or there would be repercussions," Lindy said in a letter. "Later it was, 'Accept or we will pressure you until you have to'. There has been an insidious and subtle and quite far-reaching campaign to do just that. When I continued to ignore the pressure, I was told that people would be sent to 'straighten me out'."

Lindy said she had received several visits from people she knew very well telling her to dump Tipple. Her supporters in Darwin had been rung up and had had pressure put onto them. She said: "Some folk in Darwin were rung up and some (like Pr Donaldson) abused because they said they would not pressure me into accepting the team. As I understand it, Michael had several threats of revealing details of his resignation, when he told them he could not dismiss Stuart – he was my lawyer and only I could do that. 'They' then threatened me again, telling me if I didn't cooperate they would campaign the churches for money for their team, and apply pressure to the division to have their support of Stuart stopped, so minus personal support or division backing I would have to accept this team as 'they' had placed their teams and reputation on the line and a lot of their money and others had been invested in this team and I must accept it regardless – besides the team 'never loses cases'."

Lindy said: "Win or lose my case is going to be a clean fight with no payoffs or dirty methods and God controls the outcome – not them. The doubt campaign …. concerning Stuart's objectivity and usefulness and professional ethics being brought into question has also had far-reaching results and prepared the ground, along with the massive publicity campaign on the so-called 'new' evidence, while I have had to keep the real new evidence silent still. I had hoped my church brethren would have realised the falseness of this campaign, but so subtle has it been that leading people in our church have been misled. They don't realise the harm that they are supporting, nor the splits it is causing. The church wanted to pray for me, now it is beginning to fight over me. How sad am I at this? You cannot begin to imagine my distress and horror when I learned Pr Parr was now campaigning in his conference churches for funds. If the money was put to building the college church, I would sleep better at night! "

She continued: "Their campaign is working well – and they are getting the Division involved as threatened. The West Australian group mainly were Adventists, and a number of newly baptised and beginning to attend because of their support involvement are fund-raising for [scientific analyst] Julie Fry's lawyers and expenses, as are several other groups for their lawyers. What are these new lambs of the fold when they realise what is happening? I have seen the disillusionment of new members over far less. Can the Division condone helping these people? I feel very strongly the devil's hand in this. I cannot condone this. If the division gets itself involved, or any conference, officially, it will soon be referring far more than this group. I beg you not to. If only I could get out of here and tell those good people the truth – alas I cannot. I can only weep and pray that those in charge of God's church will not be blinded of the truth. The Devil uses every excuse to stop the truth. When the first inquest closed, I felt strongly the call of God to accept certain selected media invitations to explain my Christianity and faith. I reluctantly accepted Division counsel from Pr R. Taylor to let things lie while Adventists had a good name –'a good note to fade out on'. The conviction to go and speak has never left me, and when it was reopened, I promised God I would not do the Jonah act again, but would use every opportunity to speak for him, if not personally then by mail or whatever means I could. After much prayer, I wrote what was in my heart in my earlier letter this year, and it was censored by Michael as he felt it was too long. He cut out what I said about my love of the Lord – he is sensitive about raising extra opposition because of religious bias. I still felt God urging us to repeat this. People continue to ask. I want to share. In my letter this time, I determined that I would keep my promise to God. I got Pr Donaldson to contact Pr Gorrie at the *Signs* [an SDA church magazine] and see if we could cooperate in mailing the special issue to all non-Adventists on my list, along with my circular letter."

Lindy wrote to Pastor Scragg, the President of The South Pacific Division, explaining why she had made a public statement that she preferred Tipple to the Nyman team. That had caused furore within the supporting group. She told him: "I purposely included that paragraph, as mildly as I knew how, to try to let people know who to support and not to be misled, and hopefully to try to forestall the kind of collecting now taking place as Pr Parr is doing, and to let all legal teams realise there are more legal groups than theirs working," she said. "A separate letter to each group explaining this would cause more unrest and misquotes than an open paragraph. Those unaware of the conflicts would not realise the significance of the paragraph and so no harm would be done. Those involved would realise they are not the only ones involved. This paragraph is holding up the whole letter. It stays put. In hoping to keep my feelings quiet, these people are only misleading the people more. This is my statement of my faith and my court case. I must make it. Your sermons are not censored by the Division before you deliver them. My mind must not be either. That is the Devil's wish, not God's. I have appreciated the assistance of the Division, yet some of its members, and my fellow church members, have caused me more pain than any other single factor in the last five years. Never can you understand the pain and frustration I feel when I write this letter. My church is dear to me and that I should be the cause of any disruption causes me great pain. What can I do from here? I cannot even write an open letter without those who have no business in church business misconstruing it to newspapers, and I cannot even write direct without the censor knowing church business. How can I let them know? This is why I write via Stuart and ask you to do the same if further discussion is necessary. It is legal enough business doing this, even though I risk losing the privileges of private legal letters by so doing. Fortunately, the press hasn't latched onto the split as yet, although 'they' are threatening this (Non-church members are asking why, though.)"

Tipple said: "I think the biggest disappointment to me was that the attacks were coming from Adventists. I got more attacks from Adventists than from outside the church. That was a real disappointment." Tipple was under such pressure that he and Cherie often went to friend's home for refuge. The friends were Pastor Cecil Ogg and his wife Audrey, Cecil being the SDA pastor at Erina, on the Central Coast of New South Wales. "We had two other special friends, Rick and Rosalie Belford, in Gosford," he said. "Rosalie and Cherie had been friends in Western Australia and we renewed the friendship. We certainly needed that. Lindy liked the letters that helped her escape from reality. One letter she received from Rosalie described how our friends arranged a surprise party for Cherie and Cherie and Jaemes ended up dancing to the tune of the Mickey Mouse Club. Lindy enjoyed that."

Michael Chamberlain stuck with Tipple. He wrote later: "There was a time when people were saying, 'Why don't you get a hit-man? Why Tipple? The boy in short [pants]. Get someone in long trousers!' I stuck with him because it's better to have someone you can trust, even though he might still be learning the ropes, because God can add the difference."

Lindy said in a letter to Walter Scragg: "I know certain people have tried to influence them [her parents and brother] to influence me as they have mentioned it to me. Alex [Lindy's brother] was not impressed! (nor I gather were they). You know dad I think from long ago. I hope this is the last time I ever write on this matter. If the division decided there was too much strife to continue to support Stuart, I have decided to drop any further legal action unless I can raise the finance by interviews or some other way. I feel convinced I should not use that team under any circumstances. When God shuts one door, he opens another, and if I am prevented from using Stuart, then I know God has a better plan in mind, not a worse one. Hard though it will be I will wait. God help me." Referring to a resolution by a number of SDA medical professionals to offer their support, which Scragg had relayed to her, she said: "I don't need their counselling! I need their support! The only problems I have are ones caused by pressure groups, some supporters of which were signatories on that letter. My family needs their support also, not their censure ... Stuart and Cherie need our support also. Please give it to them. We are only human and we need the strengthening of our brethren. Please pray for us all. God help me keep my head high and courage up no matter what. I cannot live without this support. He daily keeps me sane and keeps me going. How I long for His return."

Tipple told Lindy his telephone had been "running hot" over the controversy. He said support group members had begun "dropping into the office complaining about the fact that Pastor Scragg did not want anything more to do with the Lloyd-Jones team". He said: "Our standard response to the query was that as far as we were concerned you had retained Trevor Nyman and Company to consider their investigation and prepare affidavits following which they would consult with you or ourselves to decide whether these affidavits should be made available to the Northern Territory Government seeking an inquiry or some alternative." Tipple was concerned that disinformation was being put out. He was particularly concerned about talk that there would be another appeal, and that the Nyman legal team had no doubt that a further appeal would succeed. He said: "From our discussions with the other legal team we do not believe that any of the above allegations can be supported as they do not now believe that another appeal should be attempted and rather representations should be made to the Northern Territory Government and secondly they have accepted that the task is a difficult one and is not guaranteed of success."

That was no reflection on the competence or integrity of Trevor Nyman and either of the counsel he had engaged. They had been entirely professional in their approach. They had unwittingly been drawn into battle of wills not of their making, and had taken the entirely professional approach that retaining them was a matter for Lindy. Tipple, sticking doggedly to his own agenda, essentially meeting the Crown scientific case point by point, kept plugging on, trying to ignore as best he could the torrent of scorn being directed at him. He was greatly encouraged by the result of the Shannon inquiry into the conviction of Edward Charles Splatt, which had seen the scientific evidence against Splatt taken apart piece by piece. He thought that if a similar inquiry could be established in the Chamberlain case, a similar result would be achieved.

In a letter to Lindy, Tipple said there should now be particular focus on: the clothing damage; the hairs; the blood analysis; the spray; and Keyth Lenehan's position in the car. He said: "We have spoken to Senator Mason a number of times recently and he is now adamant that the best course is to make these submissions as soon as we can to the Northern Territory and then give them a two to four-week period in which to announce further action. If the further action is not satisfactory then Senator Mason is more than happy to raise the matter again in Parliament. We know from your last instructions that you wanted us to make the material available to the Northern Territory and at the same time release it to the media. Senator Mason believes this would be counter-productive to our case as it will look as if you have not given the Northern Territory a fair go and may well be that you will lose some support from Federal Parliamentarians. Please think about that matter as we do agree with Senator Mason's view."

Tipple saw that one of the critical questions was the relatively large amount of blood, or what was identified as blood, around the hinge of the front seat in the car. The Chamberlains had said from the outset that any blood must have been Lenehan's. Two High Court judges had been confused about where Lenehan was in the car. Tipple told Lindy: "As far as Lenehan is concerned you will remember that two High Court Judges fell into error in deciding that Lenehan could not have caused the blood staining around the seat hinge. We therefore plan to arrange for Lenehan to be photographed in a similar Torana Hatchback and use these photographs to show the defects in the High Court Judgements in support of our submissions to the Inquiry."

On 1st February 1985, Lindy wrote to Nyman asking about progress by his team. In his reply, Nyman referred to the growing international concern about the case and suggested that might be used to her advantage. He said the main thrust of the submission to the Northern Territory should be along these lines: exculpatory evidence for the Chamberlains had not been presented at the trial; much of the Crown evidence at the trial was wrong or misleading; there was "widespread pubic disquiet throughout Australia and overseas" at these aspects of the case; and the disquiet was injurious to the reputation of the Territory as a just administration of the criminal law. Nyman said there was evidence that some of the material evidence had been suppressed and that some of the procedures adopted might have been unfair or misleading.

In a joint letter on 7th February, Tipple and Nyman said that material was virtually completed and could be sent to the NT Administration within a fortnight. There were to be two "books", one having primary witness evidence and scientific evidence produced since the trial, the second a refutation of the scientific evidence by the fresh scientific evidence. They presented Lindy with a number of options for senior and junior counsel, and instructing solicitors, who could represent her in presenting the submissions and at the later inquiry. Her choice of counsel, they said, might be John Lloyd-Jones QC, Andrew Kirkham and Kevin Murray QC. The first two had detailed knowledge of the case, Murray, a firebrand in the court room, would have to read it up.

In Glasgow, Barry Boettcher was hard at work garnering international support. In a letter to Tipple on 12th February 1985, he said he was about to attend a conference in India and that the former Governor-General of Australia, Sir Zelman Cowen was listed as a participant. "Since I am now one of the guest speakers, and since he and I will be Australians together in a foreign country, I think it is likely that I will have a good opportunity of getting his ear – and he certainly moves in influential circles in Australia," he said. Boettcher was confident that political pressure was being ramped up in other ways. "I trust that you have copies from Jim Robertson [the former NT Attorney-General] and [Federal politician] Peter Baume … I now have had the originals forwarded to me," he said. "I now hope that enough pressure can be exerted on politicians for an inquiry to be forced on either the Northern Territory or the Federal Government."

Boettcher was also homing in on the crux of the scientific attack. He could now demonstrate that a positive ortho-tolidine test result on the under-dash material was misleading. He thought Joy Kuhl's had been misled by getting blue specks (the usual positive indication that blood may be present) when she conducted her tests. of Boettcher wrote: "You can see from one of my letters to you that the Dulux product HN1081 (I think!) gave me some blue specks in the test. But the result was very slow. The actual batch on Chamberlains' car may have been an even greater tendency to give a positive O-tolidine test. All it needs is a bit of oxygen to be liberated from the hydrogen peroxide along with a bit of rust – and the product is not pure by any means! (It would be nice to get a bit of spray from under the dashboard of the Chamberlains' car)." Bryan Culliford, the British forensic scientist who had carried out tests on five samples sent to him, had obtained positive presumptive results in four of them.

While this grand strategy of political pressure and scientific exactitude was being implemented, the opposing factions within the Chamberlains support community kept ripping into and weakening each other. Michael Chamberlain thought the NT authorities, seeing this, might try to drive a wedge deep into the movement. He might have been exaggerating a little, attributing some degree of malice to such authorities, but the support groups were doing enough of it themselves. Despite the cooperation between Nyman and the Tipple team, the agitation against Tipple continued.

Greg and Sally Lowe joined Lindy in supporting Tipple. In a letter dated 14th February, they told him: "Just a short note of moral support. Understand that you continue to cop flak from less informed quarters. We would like to confirm our confidence and faith in your actions on behalf of Mike and Lindy. We know you have always performed in a manner to suit their best interests, and will continue to do so. Whatever we may have learned about the legal profession and its pitfalls, you stand out as a shining example of unceasing dedication and application (no bullshit). We respect your confidentiality in matters pertaining to the case and given a chance when it is all over, we will publicly (albeit suitably) commend your persistence. I doubt that any of us will be forever free of rumour and innuendo, but from us laypersons who are fortunate to have sort of total overview of the case, you are a bloody marvel and we salute you."

Representing the alternative point of view, Phil Ward wrote to Lindy two weeks later alleging that Tipple had brokered a secret agreement with the Northern Territory Government.

He told Lindy he believed God had a special purpose for her being in gaol because people would turn to God when they saw how she was able to cope with the tragedy.

Ward retracted what he alleged he had heard from Senator Mason's office about a secret deal between Tipple and the NT Government and admitted he was wrong.

Lindy was unimpressed. On 28th February, she wrote to two women who were taking a lead in the Ward campaign. They had told her they were disappointed that she was so unappreciative of their efforts. Lindy said: "Thank you for your letter. No, I don't hate you and your family and whatever expression it was you used. I do feel sorry that certain members of your family continue to release statements to the press and public about my supposed future intentions though. I will work out my own press release when ready and all these other statements just tend to give the public an, 'Oh, that again', attitude like the boy who cried wolf – when the truth comes out it isn't believed either as a consequence ... My lawyers have finished and I'm not going to hold them up any more. Giving people to understand I'm under stress and therefore cannot reason correctly may work in the short term but not in the long run – too many people know it to be false – and when I've got out, what then? I do not appreciate interference in my private life or misrepresentation of my public life. I may be here unjustly but it is my case and me doing the time. Your actions only compound this. Over 12 months ago, I asked you to stay clear of the legalities as all was not as you had heard and money was being wasted. Now it has snowballed out of control. This is the last non-public letter I will write to you asking for your support, not your hindrance."

In a letter to Tipple the same day, she said: "Now I've done it! I'm sick to death of what's going on down there. I don't suppose you'll be real pleased with me but you must admit you'd have to do the same. There comes a time when one must speak out. Reckon things will get worse before they get better, but things should start to improve after that (I hope!). The NT can have the minimum time you suggested only – they are sitting this week or next week too – they can do things in a day or two if they wish. You can go ahead without." She thought the new NT Attorney-General, Marshall Perron, would "give us a fair go". Then she turned to what the evidence would be in a new inquiry. She said his idea of getting photographs of Keith Lenehan was a good one. "Make sure you get the right positions for him and me and straight and cornering head positions," she said. She also looked at use of the media, and referred to an approach to her to do an interview with TV personality Mike Willesee. "Do you think it premature to do that Willesee thing?" she said. "I am beginning to think it may be the time to do an in-jail interview with someone before any worse legalities blow up to stop it. You can let me know what you think next visit."

At Nowra, on the NSW south coast, Pastor Cliff and Avis Murchison, Lindy's long-suffering parents, an "apple pie couple" as one journalist called them, fell back on their Christian faith and on a total reliance on Stuart Tipple. In a letter on 28th February 1985, they said: "Courage in the Lord! Just a little note to tell you we love you and pray for you constantly. The way has been pretty rough, hasn't it and so needlessly. But God is at the helm. If we accept our trials in the right way, they can bring the greatest blessings of our life. God understands each of us and knows it all ... So, take courage, victory is on the way we believe. The devil is angry, he will do all he can to discredit God, those who serve God, and His church. Keep bravely on. God has promised to see us through all our trials. We are so grateful that God has given you to us to care for Lynne's case. We know we can trust you and this means so much to us just now when there is so much dishonesty and corruption everywhere. We had a reply from Colin Mason. He said that Lynne has asked him to deal with you only when he talked to her on the phone and had done that all along ... We are praying for the Holy Spirit to go before you and give you wisdom and guidance. Chin up, we are in this together, let us stand shoulder to shoulder in God's promises – that is a secure place."

A few days later, on 6th March, Cliff Murchison said: "There are times when Avis and I feel almost overwhelmed with gratitude for what you and Cherie have done for our little daughter. Fighting corruption on such a scale is indeed a daunting task, but to have erstwhile friends malign and sabotage your work is beyond belief. To say you have gone the second mile is a gross understatement. There is no way we could express how deeply we appreciate you. We believe that you are a tool in the mighty hand God, and that victory of a nature that may surprise our highest expectations is before us. God bless you Stuart and keep at it. More than humans are fighting in the warfare and the Lord may take the battle far beyond anything we have dared hope for. We never cease to uphold your hands in prayer & earnestly look not only to see Lindy freed but to see God's name exalted marvellously before men. Thank you simply and sincerely from our hearts."

While all this was going on – academics arguing at overseas conferences and lawyers and government administrators poring over documents – Lindy continued to endure the hellish conditions of her incarceration. On 7th March 1985, she wrote to Tipple: "Just turned lights out and it's going to be a bad night – there is a certified off and running hot opposite me and keeping everyone awake – 3rd one in a row we've had. One now in Adelaide mental hosp. One sent back to Alice and they've just sent us their 3rd one! Aboriginal curses at the moment mixed with English, very lucid – with some curses! Wow! I'll be a zombie tomorrow and I have kitchen too – oh well ….! Such is life. What an education. Three men to hold her and a wrecked cell (broke 'unbreakable 'glass in the bargain). One was yelling at her and another yanking her hair while the 3rd tried to sit on her. They belted and cuffed her eventually but with some struggle. I thought they had her round the throat at some stage she sounded like she was choking. All she wanted to do was watch TV and be happy. They goaded her into going off because one officer is scared of her and didn't want her out … Five minutes of tact and she would have stayed like a lamb. It totally disgusts me. She is only begging to be treated like a human being. Surely a right of all?"

Prison, from the perception of the normal, law-abiding citizen, is hell. People who end up there have done something really bad. They are demoralised and often vicious. Their attitude tends to brutalise their guards. For the normal, law-abiding citizen, to be incarcerated in that company is unthinkable. A woman like Lindy, with all her education, refinement and Christian conviction, should never, ever have gone there. But she was stuck there and had to do something about it. Though there was cooperation between the Nyman team and Stuart Tipple, ultimately Lindy had to make a choice. On 18th March, she wrote to Nyman terminating his services. She could no longer use the two teams. When Jim Driscoll heard about her decision, he was bitterly disappointed. "Tens of thousands of people have contributed money to get to the bottom of this case," he said. "We sent this team all over Australia to see witnesses and more witnesses. Everyone we spoke to said Mrs Chamberlain would never be vindicated on forensic [scientific] evidence alone." Nyman replied to Lindy, acknowledging her decision, and said he would "make allowance for your rude and peremptory communications". He said she for her part had made demands which were "physically impossible" to fulfil, namely getting a 1,500-page opinion photocopied and sent to her at very short notice. Nyman told Jim Driscoll that he and his team had compiled a "good deal" of the information that had been collected but had never been presented to the courts. The team Driscoll led had raised more than $117,000 to retain the services of the Nyman team, which had compiled a mass of affidavits, which they said was circumstantial evidence that a dingo had taken the baby. But Lindy stood by her decision. She felt Tipple was "well worth the wait" and she hoped the material compiled by the Nyman team would be passed on to Tipple. Jim Driscoll said he thought Lindy was being "unreasonable" and he was not sure whether the Nyman material should be passed on to Tipple.

At Newcastle, Boettcher continued the attack on the Crown scientific evidence. If deemed not to have been successful in the witness box, he was certainly showing his colours now. On 26th March, he wrote to Bryan Culliford, of the London Metropolitan Forensic Science Laboratory, who had supported the Crown case on identification of blood, and put to him that he had been wrong in one of his test results. "From the information you gave at the trial, you were sent five samples relevant to the case and responded by identifying blood on four of the samples, but not on two metal clips from the front passenger's seat," he said. "The material which we now know was not blood was on one of the five samples tested by you and this was not the two metal clips. Consequently, you indicated that you had detected blood on an item whereas we now know that the substance being tested was not blood. Because of my interest in the case and, quite honestly, my belief that there was a serious miscarriage of justice in this case, I would like to resolve the position." Culliford did not reply.

On 7th April, Lindy wrote an open letter to supporters: "False reports of incompetence by Mr Tipple have been circulated to cover the real facts. As stated in my letter, I am still hoping someone will send the evidence in. It can only be sent to Mr Tipple now in order to be confidential, as direct access to me passes through normal prison channels. If any of the witnesses have anything to add I hope they will contact Mr Tipple immediately. The forensic material has gone to the senior counsel for the preparation of the books, and if additional eyewitness material is not sent in, we will proceed without it – and it will not be omitted because Mr Tipple didn't want it – but because it has been withheld by those who have it. My apologies to those who are unaware of the legal hassles behind the scenes but this is the only way I can inform the support groups the truth of the matter without being as public as my letters become – I hope. It is nearly 18 months since I warned about the wasting of hard-earned money, I was promptly 'gagged', informed I didn't know what was really happening, and was under stress and a long list of more uncomplimentary explanations. I've also been told in rejecting the theories in the book, *Azaria! What The Jury Were Not Told* that I'm saying I'm guilty. NO WAY! But I do not want to see anyone else railroaded like I have been. The interviews are fact – the conclusions merely a scenario, most of which can be proved untrue by hard fact (not yet released to the Northern Territory and the public) except for a small portion which is not quite as it appears on the surface, I believe – I won't be more specific at this stage – I know there is legal action pending (have known for two months incidentally) which can only further cloud things at this stage, and not as straight forward as it would appear later. "

Lindy said: "It would be much easier if all this was quiet for a while so we can work faster without hindrance. I will say though that when the new evidence is released you will be amazed, shocked and thrilled. It's worth the wait, believe me. I've no intention of giving up or making 'sweetheart deals' (that was fabrication). I want total exoneration. Rumours that I would have been out if others had handled the case are false. Absence of intervention by a well-known gentleman may have got me a licence, that's all. Absence of impending appeals to the press would also help. Rumours like that need checking first, I'm afraid. The law turns slowly but it does turn, and we must wait for it, I'm afraid." She said that the wheels of justice turned slowly but they did turn. "I'm no exception to the rule, and what is Time on the clock of the universe?" she said. "God has eternity to set the record straight and He can see very anguished tear and pain. He will not ask what we cannot give. Let God have a fair Go instead of trying to dictate to Him. I've found it pays."

Lindy wrote to Sir Reginald Sholl thanking him for speaking out in her favour and for his involvement with the Chamberlain Innocence Committee (CIC). "I have intended for the past year or more to write and thank you for speaking in my favour in a most positive manner, and recently your involvement with the new forensic material and the Innocence Committee," she said. "Now I must speak and delay no longer. Thank you very much for caring and interesting yourself with myself and my family. If there were more men of integrity around like you this country would have a justice system to be proud of instead of the mess we now have. Once again thank you. Would you please be so kind as to convey to the other members of the Innocence Committee working with you my heartfelt thanks for their support also. Incidentally I had a lovely meeting with Pro and Raylene Hart and Elizabeth Rae recently. It was great to meet someone you only know on paper through mail. I was able to explain to Pro a little of the local scene re my case and the involvement of Phil Ward and the Driscolls. As good as their [the SDA laymen's campaigners] may be, their efforts have been disastrous on the Government attitude here. I have given instructions to Mr Tipple that none of these people or any of their hard-core supporters are to have any place on the Innocence Committee. Much as I hate to do this, I realise all the hard work recently coming to fruition will be 'down the drain' if they are in any way connected. I realise you have been under quite a deal of pressure to amalgamate some of their [material] into the C.I.C. but I would like you to know I am totally opposed to this. I have recently corresponded with Mr Jim Driscoll asking him again to cooperate with me, and once more he has refused to do anything except on his own terms … I have told him he is welcome to work for the C.I.C. under his area controller, Dr Weston Allen, as long as he gives no press interviews but he did not refer to that in his reply. He did assure me however that we 'had all the bones' of the material they had, it just differed in the inferences drawn from it and the way it was presented. I do not agree with these 'inferences' in any way."

Barry Boettcher who had taken 1985 as sabbatical leave and was working at the Beatson Institute for Cancer Research in Glasgow, was himself moving onto another plane. He was inspired by research into, of all things, Egyptian mummies, which had apparently turned up DNA. It had applications for the Chamberlain investigation, he thought.

While Boettcher was pursuing these ideas – which might have appeared a little eccentric, the mainstream media were working on a much more practical level – the news value of the personal stories of the Chamberlains, in particular Lindy. On 30th May, Henry Plociennik, editor of the *Woman's Day*, wrote to Lindy asking for her story when she was released from gaol. He said there would be "considerable pressure" from sections of the media for her story when she was released, but *Woman's Day*, which had already published interviews with Michael, would be able to do a responsible job, and it had association with the Fairfax media organisation, including the *Sydney Morning Herald*, the *Age*, the *Sun-Herald* and the *Sun*, and Channel Seven. "As you are aware, Michael has been most impressed with *Woman's Day's* response to his interviews and this would be maintained in your story," he said. "In addition, the newspapers I have mentioned have an enviable reputation for responsible and accurate journalism." Lindy replied through Tipple that she would keep it in mind. The media, when seeking a vital interview, will always present themselves in the best light, and a lot of that is true, but not entirely true. Lindy had many balls to juggle – from the confines of her Darwin cell – and she had to make sure she got things right.

Tipple understood that when people heard the primary and circumstantial evidence that a dingo had taken the baby they properly wondered how was

Lindy convicted?

They thought who could possibly argue against tracks of a dingo going into the tent and coming out dragging something? It was certainly enough to have left Denis Barritt in no doubt as to what had happened. But Barrit never heard the Crown case, that the car was awash with blood ,including an arterial blood spray from a baby under three months of age, that the clothes had been cut most likely by scissors found in the Chamberlains car. The cuts had produced cotton tufts like those found in the car and the Chamberlain's camera bag. The scientific evidence had overwhelmed the primary and circumstantial evidence of a dingo attack and allowed the jury to even reject the evidence of Sally Lowe who was emphatic that she had heard the baby cry out when en the Crown Case was that the baby was already dead and stuffed in the camera bag.

Tipple said long afterwards, "The defence never regarded the primary evidence as a sideshow, it had been put firmly and emphatically at the trial and had clearly persuaded the judge."

After the trial Tipple reviewed all the evidence and had a private investigator take fresh statements from the important witnesses just to make sure nothing had been missed. At the same time he realized it was no longer good enough to raise a reasonable doubt about the scientific evidence, it had to be destroyed. Tipple said, "When the Ward-McNicol material was presented to the NT Government and Crown, it was an easy matter for the Government to say that the primary evidence had all been 'done before'." But Tipple endured the scorn and vibes of those convinced he was on the wrong path. None of the criticism was lightly passed over by Tipple. But Lindy, forced to make a choice, decided to stay with him.

CHAPTER TWELVE

HEAD BUTTING A GOUVERNMENT

"

I think Jesus was pretty radical. I don't think he was a Conservative. I didn't really understand that until after my experience at Uluru in 1980. When I realised that being a status quo person was going to get me nowhere. Trusting the Government sure wouldn't help! So, I began to change my attitudes. I became more attuned to social issues, like the plight of the Aborigines. I started to pray what I never thought I'd say, 'God help me, because the Government won't – they're too bound up in conservatism.' That's precisely what I was thinking when we lost the High Court Appeal when there was nowhere for me, or the Chamberlain Support Groups, to go."

— Michael Chamberlain, Beyond Azaria, Black Light/White Light

In mid-1985, Tipple, working with the Chamberlain Innocence Committee, a group of eminent people led by Sir Reginald Sholl, was ready to make a move. On 4th June, Tipple delivered a package containing new material to the NT Government and applied for an inquiry into the case. He said it was his opinion that the new material, which dealt with such things as the under-dash spray and the cuts in the baby's jumpsuit, was cogent and raised grave doubts on the Chamberlain convictions. The under-dash spray was not blood, the damage to the jumpsuit had been done by canine teeth, the hair removed from Azaria's jumpsuit was canine, not cat, and the anti-serum used by Joy Kuhl was not suitable on its own for the identification of foetal haemoglobin.

That same morning, Tipple, appearing on TV's *Good Morning Australia*, confirmed that the submissions had been handed over. He gave some brief new details of evidence. The Chamberlains Innocence Committee held a national media conference at Australia Square in Sydney. A media kit was distributed detailing all the new evidence, and a small booklet summarising the scientific evidence. Phil Ward turned up. Tipple refused to let him inside. Ward, true to form, set himself up at a desk outside the entrance, beamed at those entering, shook hands vigorously with those who stopped to ask what he was doing, and proceeded to take notes. Nothing was going to stop Phil. He believed he was right, and he was going to pursue it. But in naming people adversely without cogent evidence to back himself up, he had put himself in an untenable position. Inside the meeting room, Sir Reginald focussed on what always had had to be addressed first, which was the scientific evidence upon which the Chamberlains had been convicted. He said the Crown scientific evidence was "so unreliable as to make the convictions unsustainable". The other material was from eye witnesses which were "all tending to establish that a dingo had taken the baby".

The media conference was followed by a panel discussion which was aired on Channel 10. Tipple was happy enough with most media coverage, though an article in the *Weekend Australian* on 8th June 1985 disappointed him because in Tipple's view it was dismissive of the new evidence. Les Smith had a meeting with Malcolm Brown. A leading article in the *Sydney Morning Herald* on 11th June said: "A formal application for a further judicial inquiry has now been lodged by the Chamberlain Innocence Committee. The inquiry should be granted. None of the doubts concerning the verdict against Mrs Chamberlain have been answered in the past three years. The new evidence that has been gathered is significant and should be tested. The case, in other words, still cries out for review."

The next News Ltd article, in the *Weekend Australian* on 15th June, was positive. That day, Michael Chamberlain had a letter published in that paper saying: "Almost one thousand days have passed since the conviction of my wife and I. This event, her subsequent incarceration in Her Majesty's Darwin Prison and the adverse publicity on a macro scale have made life virtually intolerable for my family. While we remain indebted to those objectively-minded persons who seek our exoneration it gives us little comfort to read of people who want now to free Lindy because 'she has been punished enough'. Although such people are possibly well intentioned, the fact remains, we are innocent. Our consciences are free and clear. Our convictions were wrongful. Lindy's continuing incarceration is vindictive. In this matter, we do not seek mercy. We await natural justice and total exoneration."

The NT Solicitor-General, Brian Martin, requested a Chamberlain Innocence Committee's media kit. On 25th June 1985, Tipple wrote to the NT Attorney-General, Marshall Perron, asking for the submissions that had been made on the

Chamberlain case to be considered as a matter of urgency. "As you are aware our submissions included submissions that had already been prepared and forwarded to you by Professor Barry Boettcher in March 1984," he said. "Mr Robertson, the then Attorney-General, replied to Professor Boettcher in a letter dated 6th April 1984 acknowledging receipt of the submission and went on to advise that he would arrange for the 'submission and accompanying material to be examined from a scientific point of view.' We understand that Professor Boettcher's submissions have been evaluated and we would ask that you please confirm that this is so and provide us with a copy of this evaluation."

Tipple received further information on dingo attacks at Ayers Rock. On 6th August 1985, he wrote to Lindy acknowledging the material and saying: "Although as you know we do not support the 'Ding' theory we would be disappointed if the terms of reference of any inquiry were not wide enough for this story to be fully investigated and finally determined. We agree with you that the trackers should be available to give evidence." He did not think people in the media should attack the Northern Territory, 'particularly whilst it appears they are seriously investigating the submissions [presented by the Chamberlain Innocence Committee]'." He said a recent editorial in the *NT News* was "the first positive article that they have written for some time and is a very important about-face change". He said that on 22nd August, it was intended an outline of submissions of the Chamberlain Innocence Committee be presented to Federal Parliament. It was also intended to have Ita Buttrose interview Lindy Chamberlain in prison and have an article published in the *Woman's Weekly*.

On 13th August 1985, Tipple told Martin that there were many new aspects that needed to be considered, preferably by a new inquiry. He said among other things that there was now "substantial evidence of dingo attacks which were not able to be given at the Chamberlain Trial or Appeals including the incident involving the Cranwell child". He said the eye-witness evidence "was either neutral or very favourable to the Chamberlains, such as the evidence of Mr & Mrs Lowe". To convict, he said, the jury had to accept the evidence of the Crown forensic experts. "We believe that further investigation and identification of this matter will have to be carried out by overseas experts," he said. "We submit that this further work should be carried out under the control of an Inquiry as it will involve the removal of samples and therefore damage of relevant exhibits. Professor Boettcher is presently in Glasgow and has advised that he will be prepared to return and provide that further information. We consider that this further information be provided under the direction and control of an inquiry and should not delay you in setting up such an inquiry."

On 20th August, the *Bulletin* published an article by leading journalist Bruce

Stannard discussing all the fresh evidence. Stannard had interviewed Sir Reginald Sholl, who said he believed there had been a serious miscarriage of justice. Sir Reginald was critical of trial judge Muirhead who he said had left the jury with the "almost impossible task of resolving conflicting scientific evidence". Stannard quoted Sir Reginald saying: "In cases involving such a conflict of scientific evidence, there ought to be not a jury but a panel of scientific advisers which the court can call upon. How is a jury of laymen able to make up its mind on conflicting scientific arguments? That bothered me so much I climbed onto my hobby horse and rode into the controversy." The Northern Territory's response to this relentless pressure was to dispatch Martin, along with Dr Simon Baxter, to Germany to visit Behringwerke, to investigate the specificity of the haemoglobin. Sir Reginald thought that was a very poor response. He told the Federal Attorney-General, Lionel Bowen, that it was "like appointing an accountant to audit his own accounts," and "meanwhile, Mrs Chamberlain has remained in gaol".

At Cooranbong, Dr Norman Young, a one-time fitter-and-turned turned theologian, then on the staff of Avondale College, was following Smith and Ken Chapman in their scientific inquiries on the jumpsuit and the under-dash spray. They concluded that canine dentition was quite capable of causing the damage seen in Azaria's jumpsuit, and that the spray under the Chamberlains' dashboard was not blood. Deciding that a media strategy was the way forward, Young presented the findings to Malcolm Brown. Dr. Young told Tipple in in a letter of 24th September: "I have a very fine preliminary report from Dr Andrew Scott supporting the Dufix data and criticising Mrs Kuhl's work." He said Professor Chaikin was "cagey and will be well armed to defend himself if he ever comes before an inquiry ... he is now Pro-Vice-Chancellor of the University of NSW ... prestige is a difficult thing to handle".

There were informal reports, based on apparent leaks, that Brian Martin was going to recommend against a review of the case. But the pressure on the Northern Territory increased when on 2nd October, John Bryson's *Evil Angels* was published by Penguin Books. Bryson, a lawyer by training, had attended the trial and believed that the evidence did not support the convictions. The book was well reviewed and went onto the best-seller list. One reviewer dared anyone to read it and not have doubts about the convictions. The NT Government was unimpressed. So were some individuals mentioned in the book, including Frank Morris who had been first on the scene when the baby's clothes were found. Unhappy with what was said about him in the book, he sued for defamation. The case would eventually be settled.

On 10th October 1985, Justice Michael Kirby, as he then was, was reported in the *Sydney Morning Herald* saying that contempt laws needed to be reformed to ensure fairer trials, especially for celebrities such as Lindy Chamberlain and the mafia figure, Robert Trimbole. Speaking to an International Criminal Law Congress in Adelaide, he said that pre-trial publicity made it difficult to find juries ignorant of allegations and uncontaminated by the widespread coverage given them. The injunction by judges to jurors to put everything they had heard outside the court out of their minds was probably ineffective. He referred to an article in an issue of the *Journal of the Law Institute of Victoria* which said the combination of leaks from police and public prosecutor's office and sensational media reporting on charges brought or considered against celebrities represented a threat to civil liberties.

This of course could work both ways. Would O.J. Simpson and Michael Jackson have been acquitted in their sensational cases – Simpson charged with murder and Jackson with child molestation – had they not been celebrities with legions of fans and the proceedings reported across the world? Simpson did not survive the civil litigation process, but how many less renowned individuals would have survived the prosecution itself?

On the same day that Kirby was reported in the *Herald*, Sir Reginald Sholl wrote directly to Lionel Bowen calling for an inquiry into the case. He said: "Our latest belief is that the Northern Territory legal advisers have advised that a judicial inquiry should be ordered, but we fear that the politicians in Government may decide against one or order an inquiry so limited in its terms as to inhibit a full re-examination of the whole case. This would surely be a narrow or parochial approach, and it might lead many people to wonder whether the Northern Territory Government was afraid of the effect of such an inquiry on the reputation, or even the integrity of some of its own employees or other inhabitants of the Territory – especially if it is established that a dingo took the baby and third-party intervention may have occurred before the child's clothes were found.

"Furthermore, the alleged actions of the prosecution in limiting the evidence of the Crown witnesses may be called into question. This is such a case where, on the scales of justice the possibility of an innocent young woman spending the rest of her life in gaol must far outweigh any considerations of possible criticism of political disadvantage which the Administrator or any individuals might suffer from such an inquiry." Sholl's concluding remarks were: "There must be some way in which the Group in control of what is still a Territory of the Commonwealth can be prevented from perpetrating without a full and thorough and comprehensive inquiry, what appears to many thousands of

Australians to be one of the worst miscarriages of justice in the history of Australia."

On 16th October, the NSW Ombudsman, George Masterman QC, made his final report on his inquiry into Tipple's complaint about practices in the NSW Division of Forensic Medicine. He concluded that: it was unreasonable for the laboratory not to have retained test plates or slides; the practice of destroying test slides immediately after conducting the tests was unreasonable; photographs of tests should have been taken both for recording and court purposes; the failure to retain or photograph test slides prejudiced the defence and made it difficult for the court to determine facts. The testing of anti-serum had not been wrong, but some formal review of it should have taken place.

Tipple now continued to work on the media front. In a letter to Lindy on 22nd October 1985, he said: "We will now proceed to contact the *Bulletin* to determine whether they are still interested in interviewing you. We should also add that Michael is apparently not happy with you giving interviews and would rather that you reserve your availability for future interviews until after the Northern Territory have as he suspects refused to grant an inquiry. We are very pleased at the way the *NT News* has become more favourably disposed towards you and we are doing whatever we can to foster this new attitude. To prod the Northern Territory into some reaction we recently forwarded a letter to the Attorney-General dated 15th October 1985, and owing to the mail dispute, forwarded it by telegram on 16th October 1985. Further, we enclose a copy of a letter that we have received from the Australian Associated Press Pty Limited and Channel 10 both seeking interviews. Please let us have your instructions on these matters but our advice in respect of both of them is that there is little point in granting interviews at this stage to any media groups which will not be reported in the Northern Territory. Pressures outside the Northern Territory would be focused once the Northern Territory have made their decision to grant an Inquiry. Up until that time then the media pressure should be focused on the Northern Territory."

People supporting the Chamberlains, if unable to participate in the ground strategy, found different, even odd, ways of offering their support. One Fred Roy, then living in England, wrote to Tipple saying he wished to leave his estate to the Chamberlains to help them in their fight for justice. Roy had said he had 10,000 pounds which he wanted to leave the Chamberlains, and a pushbike he thought the Chamberlain children might be able to ride. Tipple sought Lindy's instructions on that. On 1st November 1985, Norman Young took out a paid ad in the *NT News*. It said: "Lindy: Oct 29 – Year Three. No motive. No weapon.

No witnesses. No opportunity. No confession. No arterial spray. No scissor cuts. No foetal blood in the car. No crime and no case. Yet STILL no inquiry ... WHY NOT"

Michael Chamberlain had taken his campaign to Canberra. Tipple told Lindy in a letter written on 4th November that Michael was seeking as much support as possible from Federal politicians who might move in and initiate Federal action if the NT Government refused an inquiry. Tipple said that Michael was "getting a brief together with which we are assisting him combining articles that are supportive and obtaining statements from eminent and interested persons showing that the Northern Territory Government is not unbiased in this matter and that the best forum for a review would be in the Federal sphere ... this brief will only be used with its full weight in the event that the Northern Territory Government refuses to order an inquiry. The latest rumour has it and no doubt you have already heard it that Brian Martin's almost completed report re the Inquiry has been made available to the acting Attorney-General Jim Robertson".

In the same letter, Tipple said he had discussed Mr Roy's kind offer. Michael had said that half the money should be paid into the Aid the Chamberlain Fund, which would be used mainly for personal projects and the *Azaria Newsletter*. "Michael says that at the present time he is having to finance himself to go down to Federal Parliament and lobby other members of the Federal Parliament that are interested in coming to your assistance in the event that the Northern Territory refuses an Inquiry," Tipple said. "The balance of the money would be paid into the Church Fund earmarked for Chamberlain Innocence Committee projects." Tipple had discussed with Michael the use of money that had come from the interview with Ita Buttrose. Lindy instructed Tipple to pay most of the money to the church fighting fund but to also pay her tithe and retain enough to let Michael buy the video camera he wanted to record the children's growing years that Lindy was missing out on.

On 11th November 1985, six of the primary witnesses at Ayers Rock took out a paid ad in the *NT News*. Signing themselves Greg and Sally Lowe, Bill and Judith West and Max and Amy Whittaker, they said: "We, the undersigned, who were present at Ayers Rock camping ground, the night Azaria disappeared, know that Mrs Chamberlain had no opportunity to commit the alleged homicide for which she is now serving a life sentence in Berrimah Jail, Darwin. Though we were all Crown witnesses at the trial, we feel that insufficient weight was given to our evidence and all of our evidence was not elicited. We demand, therefore, that there be an unfettered Judicial Review of this terrible miscarriage of justice."

Marshall Perron decided that that demand would not be met. In a letter to Tipple on 12th November, he said: "I refer to your submission and material in support of it seeking a judicial inquiry concerning the verdict and subsequent conviction of your clients Mr and Mrs Chamberlain. I enclose a copy of a report prepared by the Solicitor-General. After careful and detailed consideration of the submission, the material in support and the report, I have concluded there is nothing raised by you which is cogent, or of such substance, whether new or otherwise, as to warrant the holding of the inquiry sought. Given media speculation, it is proposed that a copy of the submission and the material in support and the Solicitor-General's report will be tabled in and authorities to be printed in the Legislative Assembly today."

Martin's report, *Chamberlain – Request for a Judicial Inquiry,* otherwise known as "The Martin Report", effectively closed the door on an inquiry, at least from an official point of view. Martin said the claim that infant blood had been found in the Chamberlains' vehicle had been "enhanced by everything learnt since the trial emanating from the manufacturers of the serum". The report went before the NT Legislative Assembly. Perron told the Assembly that he was rejecting the Chamberlain' application for a judicial review. He said: "The submission sought to identify cogent new evidence to support the case for a judicial review, as all avenues under the Northern Territory system of justice have been exhausted, including appeals to the Federal and High Courts of Australia. I find none of the nine matters in the case for a judicial review ... convincing. Most of the material presented was dealt with extensively during the trial and reviewed by two courts of appeal. Some of the claims were untrue, others irrelevant. I have concluded that there is nothing raised which is cogent or of such substance as to warrant the holding of a judicial inquiry."

The statement did not satisfy the Commonwealth Attorney-General, Senator Gareth Evans, or the Shadow Attorney-General, Senator Peter Durack, both of whom said Lindy should be released immediately on licence. On 13th November, Michael Chamberlain released a media statement from Parliament House. He said: "I am obviously greatly heartened by the comments of Senator Gareth Evans and Senator Peter Durack recommending my wife's immediate release on licence. Whether or not my wife is released on licence from the Darwin Jail, we will continue to fight for a just conclusion and for our names to be cleared. We have always ultimately sought an open Commonwealth judicial inquiry and this remains of supreme importance to me and my family."

Senator Mason still had his private member's bill to put before Federal Parliament, but that faced formidable obstacles. The matter was at least debated in the Senate. On 16th November 1985, Tipple sent a telegram to Perron: "We request on the grounds contained in our earlier applications and in accordance with views expressed today in the Federal Senate, Mrs Chamberlain be released on licence immediately." The Northern Territory refused to budge. It insisted it had control of the case, and their conclusion now was that Lindy should serve her sentence. Malcolm Brown spoke to the Chief Minister, Ian Tuxworth, and his media adviser. The media adviser said that for every bit of stirring "down south", for Lindy it was, "in for another six months". Tuxworth concurred, repeating the dictum of the Northern Territory that it was not going to bow to the pressure of the mob. What he did not go on to say, but could have, was that the government was prepared to release Lindy, but only when everyone shut up. Brown said later: "I was absolutely flattened by what Tuxworth and his adviser said. There seemed something terribly wrong with this. Lindy was being kept in gaol not to punish her but because the Northern Territory wanted to save face, or so it seemed to me. I formed a view for the first time that all the media stirring I was doing was just keeping Lindy in gaol."

Lindy Chamberlain for her part decided on a frontal attack. She decided she would release a "Letter to All Australians and My Friends" and she thought she might go on strike and not perform her duties as a prisoner, and she wanted everyone to know she was doing it. She carefully composed a statement over several days for public distribution and sent a draft to Tipple. It said in part: "For over 5 years now I have lived with rumour, innuendo and accusation over the death of my baby daughter Azaria. I have tried to cooperate in all ways possible, but still this farce continues. For nearly three years, I have worked as an inmate of this prison for the NT Government for 30 cents per day, trying to do whatever I was asked pleasantly and politely, whether I liked it or not, without causing trouble. I have used available legal means and sought an inquiry whereby the NT Govt had a chance to redeem their own name. In return, they have ignored decency and justice and still scoff at it. Tues 12 Nov 85 they have refused an inquiry without even asking to see the evidence or offer a reason for part of that inquiry. As an innocent person who has gone the second mile and turned the other cheek I will no longer stand quietly by and serve a corrupt system. As from 1.00 pm Darwin time today (Friday 15th) I am refusing to work in any way whatsoever for this Prison and the Court it represents. I did not kill my beloved daughter and refuse to be treated as a criminal any longer."

Sending the statement to Tipple, she said in a covering letter: "I know it's long and you and Al [Alex Murchison, her brother] can change the spelling where necessary. It's nearly 3 o'clock am and I want to make sure these [statements] are both well and truly out of the prison before Friday and hopefully you can get a copy of the press release to Bob Collins Friday also ... I am prepared for all mail to be stopped, all visits cut and to be put in solitary. Anything less will be great of course. I have an information service set up where possible that should work well. Tell Michael at the last minute but keep him from coming up. It is possible that they could use Michael as a lever on me. A frustrated husband up at the gate might be the last straw. I need to ride this one out for a while. Tell him and mum and dad and his parents that I'm mentally prepared and I'll be OK. Jesus and I will handle it together. All this precious No has done is make me fighting mad. Censor my letter as little as possible so I can't get sued for libel and let it go. It's time for the knuckle dusters. Teeth and nails, if necessary, too! Don't let Michael reduce it – it needs to go – it's time."

Lindy expected an intense media response. She asked Tipple to stop Michael coming to visit her on 16th November. "I hear the international media will be here in force, and that makes for tense visits (parliament is tabling the gear, or debating it)," she said. "High chance he wouldn't be able to see me due to recent plan discussed with you which would start that weekend probably – negotiations are under way now to get your letter and parcel out, Collins and [a Corrections officer] Barrier in on Friday. I want that done on my terms if done, without pressure of visits denied, or look as if it's Michael's idea after a visit. If there is as much internal fuss and pressure as I think there will be, I want it to settle before it's time for the kids' next visit. My plans must remain secret at the moment. I hope Michael understands. He must work in the way he thinks best, and I in my way. If this plan does not need to be carried out, he could come about a fortnight later with no worries. Give him my love."

The problem for Lindy was that the NT Corrections Department was well geared towards handling difficult and uncooperative prisoners, and the pressure Lindy sought to exert was not likely to shift officialdom. Tipple saw that. When Lindy's statement was released on 21st November, the part that she was going on strike was excluded. However, there was plenty else Lindy had to say. Five years before, she had been an "average citizen, with the idea that, in court, the facts could be presented so that an intelligent assessment could be made by the jury as an independent 'referee' of the truth". She continued: "The law, of course, favoured those who told 'the truth, the whole truth and nothing but the truth' and the police (although they are known to have set some people up at times, only did it to those known to be guilty but were too smart or too corrupt to catch, because they 'eliminated witnesses or something!'), well the police were there to see that right and justice were followed. Oh, how wrong I was!

Do you know I still clung vainly to the idea – despite evidence to the contrary – until the trial. Now I no longer believe a bar of it. 'Sadder but wiser now'... yes, indeed....

"No longer, in Australia, are you innocent till proved guilty – that is a mere myth perpetrated in the hope of keeping 'Mr Average Man' as gullible and trusting as he is now. Now in Australia, one is guilty until one can prove one's innocence – but one is given little chance to do that. In Australia, a person may have a number of court appearances before they are committed on a charge. And of course, they are instructed by counsel to present a neutral face in the court, since any other is open to misinterpretation. Now when a plea of innocence is entered, and they go before a jury, the jury wonders why they do not look shocked, or penitent, or whatever emotion the jury themselves feel appropriate on being presented with the facts for the first time. The frustration of sitting listening to this without being able to answer back, added to the anger pent up over months of the same treatment, leads to an impression the jury may interpret badly, thinking it is the 'don't care' attitude of a hardened person all too often (I have seen a number of times where a trip to court is like a picnic in a dull life, lending excitement and change. Think of this next time you do jury duty or see someone on television going in or out of court. The hassle of the press can also cause tremendous strain. It takes something getting used to having cameras in your face every move – and to look natural – well I think the only way to do that is to ignore their presence altogether. Very difficult at times when they have lenses in front of your nose and then obligingly hit you on the head (hard) as they swing away in the melee.)"

Lindy spoke about all manner of petty events in court that disadvantages the accused, including statements made by counsel to which the other side "objects", but not in time for the original statement, though withdrawn, not to have reached the ears of the jury. She spoke about the unfairness of the Crown, with huge resources compiling their case, compared with the accused with far fewer resources. She said: "This is your Australia – now it's me inside – next time, it maybe you, and if your case doesn't catch the national imagination, you won't have any chance of doing a thing. No-one will want to know, and only a few close friends will care. You'll rot in obscurity like others I could name. It's time the legal system treated everybody the same and was allowed to determine truth and justice, and not depend on political intervention when the appeal process is exhausted. Something needs to be done to tighten up methods and practices used in our courts today before it is too late for your sakes.

"My own conviction is totally against the evidence of eyewitnesses and –

now – the available scientific evidence as well. The set-ups and cover-ups and concoctions used are obvious. The millions – yes, I mean millions – spent by the Territory to put me here, and keep me here would have a gone a long way towards that railway and airport they keep on mentioning up here. No wonder they don't want their finances checked out, or an inquiry into my case. Either would reveal far too much. Whoever dreamt up the atrocious story or what I was supposed to have done to my darling daughter must be sick and in need of psychiatric care. It is totally untrue and abhorrent. And local leaks which claim if I would admit it, and blame post-natal depression, I could be out and go home are equally sick. If I lied, I could go home, but to tell the truth, I must be punished and stay. What are they hiding? Even if someone thinks I'm guilty an inquiry would only serve to reveal the truth, so there is nothing to lose is there! I have nothing to hide. I'm totally innocent of their accusations. I want truth, justice and the clearing of my name and that of my family, with a public apology, and nothing less will do."

In a message to Avondale College graduates, Lindy pitched her appeal in theological terms: "Man's extremity is God's opportunity. Always remember this when you are feeling as if things are getting tough and you don't know where to turn or what to do in your new life work ahead. Step out with faith and courage, and keep your hand in God's hand. He will never send you where He does not lead. God be with you as you live for Him and serve Him. Congratulations and love, your friend, Lindy."

Lindy's heartfelt appeals struck home with the supporters. But the effect on some was to turn with renewed fury onto Tipple. Dr Caroline Butler, a doctor at the San Hospital, was very critical of his approach and accused him of ignoring the work done by the Nyman team and Lloyd-Jones. In a letter of 3rd December 1985, Tipple told Butler that Nyman and Lloyd-Jones had since agreed that pursuing a judicial inquiry would be a better course of action. "I was most surprised when you advised me on Saturday the 1st December that you had concluded that I was unethical, unprofessional, incompetent and a liar," he said. "I thought you would have raised these matters with me previously rather than waiting until I had contacted you ... I also noted that you had understood that inquiries had been made about my previous work experience in the Public Prosecutions Office. As I have advised you, I have never worked for the Public Prosecutions Office but I have worked for the Public Solicitors' Office. I would certainly welcome inquiries being made there as to my experience and expertise."

The political pressures on the NT Government continued, principally the

Private Member's Bill of Democrats leader Colin Mason was to put before Federal Parliament to have an inquiry into the case initiated at Federal level, but it faced huge obstacles. It all depended on whether the ruling ALP Government decided to back the bill, and there were strong signs that members were unwilling. On 25th November 1985, the NT Government rejected another application by Lindy Chamberlain for release on licence.

Tipple continued to negotiate the forensic obstacle. What now attracted his attention was DNA technology, a branch of science which was destined to bring about profound changes to forensic work, to the extent that prisoners in the United States would be released from death row and the law of double jeopardy would be reviewed because of the capacity of DNA identification to produce irrefutable proof. A medical scientist, Dr Malcolm Simons, gave Tipple information on its potential and Tipple saw the immediate application in the Azaria case. If only DNA technology had been available in 1981 when the blood, or supposed blood, had been found in the Chamberlains' car! On 6th December 1985, Tipple had a conference with Marshall Perron and Brian Martin in which he referred to research on DNA testing and work that had been done by Dr Simons. He said that the new technology could be applied to the remaining staining in the Chamberlains' car and possible traces of dingo saliva in the baby's nappy, as well as what appeared to be fragments of flesh found in the baby's jumpsuit. In a letter some days later, he asked for cooperation in obtaining "further samples for testing" and "advice on your further requirements and suggested procedures".

Perron replied that the matters Tipple raised were "important and complex" and he would have to receive proper advice. "Your proposals are already being examined and I do not believe that you can expect me to respond in a responsible way to such matters without adequate investigation which, of course, takes time," he said. "I can assure you that as soon as I have sufficient information before me you will be advised of my decisions. I wish to add, however, that I support your view that should any further analysis be agreed to, it should be carried out jointly under agreed processes and experts."

Reagan Chamberlain, then aged nine, wrote a letter pleading for his mother's release. Addressed to "Mister Tuxworth, Mr Hawke, Prince Charles and Princess Diana", it said: "I can still remember the dingo walked on my chest. I loved my bubby Azaria so did mummy. We want mummy at home because Kahlia needs a mummy. Can you let my mummy come home to me?" The letter was published in a newspaper, and a reader wrote in a malicious tone to Reagan: "Dear Reagan, re your letter which was printed in our daily newspaper.

It is very easy for your mother to get out of jail. All she has to do is tell the truth. To the very experienced police officers that questioned her it was most obvious that she was lying (Even a novice could tell). So just tell her to tell the truth."

In the background, the national media was stirring. On 18th December, Hector Crawford, chairman of Crawford Productions Pty Ltd, wrote to Tipple: "Brian Wright [working for Crawford Productions] tells me it may be mid-January before it will be possible to arrange a meeting with you and Michael Chamberlain. While I am eager to start work on a programme which will properly inform the public about Mrs Chamberlain's situation, naturally I look forward to meeting you both at your convenience. May I take the opportunity to express my pleasure at having the chance to give a true and effective presentation of the case through our powerful medium of television. I believe it to be in the public interest for my Company to use its skills and facilities to make such a statement."

Avis Murchison wrote to Tipple saying she had had a flying visit from Malcolm Brown. "He is quite disturbed as he feels Mason's bill is going to fail," she said. "He thinks the best way is for Lynne to accept her conviction, get out and make the best life she can for the family – before she is irreparably damaged herself. He seems quite despondent about it. I will write to him and see if I can lift his spirits a little."

At some point at about this time, in a moment of depression, Malcolm Brown wrote to Michael suggesting his first priority would be to get Lindy out and back with the family, not to give up his campaign for innocence but to stop the dreadful suffering. It was not a wise thing to do. A journalist, despite the abuse he or she might get in going about a job, has an accepted status as a non-participant. To write to a party proffering advice is to step over the line and become part of the action, and once a reporter does that, he is subject to the same retaliation as any other participant. I said: "Carefully consider beating a strategic retreat, as any good soldier does who wants to win a war... It is time to get out of this purgatory, Michael, give ground, get Lindy back into the fold and put this whole tragic ghastly business behind you.... I know that your whole instinct is to keep fighting harder than ever (as you have said) but is it the best response?"Michael received the letter and responded aggressively, saying the letter would be published, suggesting that someone might have put Brown up to doing this, and telling him to get out of his hair, which under the circumstances was probably a reasonable response.

The Martin Report, which might have settled the matter for an inquiry for all time, went nowhere. It drew plenty of criticism. Boettcher said the Report had not represented the Behringwerke evidence correctly. Behringwerke had agreed with Boettcher that the anti-serum Joy Kuhl had used was not suitable to test for foetal haemoglobin in the denatured samples. Boettcher wrote to Tipple: "On January 14, I telephoned Baudner [of Behringwerke]. Baudner advised me that he was writing a letter to Martin "at this moment". He hoped to have the letter sent by the end of the week, and he would forward a copy to me. Baudner would repeat the points that he considered important and hoped his letter would make a difference." Boettcher said he had pointed out to Behringwerke that what Martin had said in his report contradicted what Baudner had told him. Baudner had not given that advice to Martin and Baxter that Martin said he had. According to Boettcher, Baudner agreed to write once again to Martin, pointing out that he apparently had not understood the information he had given him. Kuhl had used the anti-serum in test procedures for which it was not designed and that some of the results in her work notes appeared to be nonsense at least uninterpretable. "Consequently, she had come to conclusions that could not be supported," Boettcher said.

On 20th January 1986, Baudner and his colleague at Behringwerke, Dr Storiko, sent a letter to Martin saying the tests Joy Kuhl had used should not have been "crucial to a criminal procedure" and it appeared Martin had misunderstood what they had said. Further potential ammunition was provided for Tipple when he received a letter from the inventor of a test Joy Kuhl had used, Professor Orjan Ouchterlony, a Swedish bacteriologist and immunologist. He told Tipple that after reading the transcripts of the case he had concluded that Joy Kuhl "did not have a sound understanding" of the principles of some of her tests. He said she had made an error which could have led to "an erroneous interpretation of the tests".

On 21st January, Andrew Scott, who had been retained by the NT Opposition leader, Bob Collins, to review the Martin Report, said the Martin Report was an inadequate assessment of the new evidence and summarized his major concern. "It appears to have been written from a prosecution perspective in that it is sometimes selective and biased in its treatment of the evidence," he said. Collins went to see Boettcher at Newcastle University to discuss the matter further.

On 24th January, Michael Chamberlain said in a letter to his family and supporters: "I've just completed my thirty-fifth 'tour' to the NT. A futile, useless exercise except for an attractive, intelligent and innocent, loved mother and wife, who remains a hostage at the NT Government's whim. This vindictive show of strength suggests that the Territory has little but the harshest and most archaic method of dealing with people from the South." He then referred to Malcolm Brown's letter, saying that a "respected senior Australian journalist" had written "a lengthy letter labouring with me to give away my 'fruitless' struggle for freedom for Lindy". He said: "Well, you know what my reaction will be to this, but what is yours now that our backs are really against the wall?" He ended with a quote from an author, Lowell Tarling: "The forensic scientists made their memorable comeback proving beyond doubt that the Australian Public has faith in the unseen if it is packaged as science rather than religion." Upset by Michael's response, Malcolm Brown contacted Stuart Tipple, who had seen the letter. "I was never telling him to give up," he said. "I was presenting an alternative to Michael. You don't have to endure extreme torture to make a point in arguing a case." Tipple took a conciliatory approach. "Don't worry, we've all felt like that!" he said. He was not going to take it any further.

At Ayers Rock people still climbed to the top. It was a practice the Aborigines did not condone. It was a dangerous place. A number of people exerting themselves to get up in previous years had suffered heart attacks or slipped trying to retrieve hats that had blown off. A hump on a lower part of the rock, at the beginning of what was then the normal tourist climbing route, was known as "Chicken Rock", when people having exerted themselves enough and seeing what was ahead of them turned back. There were areas where the curve of the rock increased, a little deceptively. Brown thought later there might have been a mystical element. "Ayers Rock might well be referred to as Hanging Rock," he said later. "It is a place where dreams occur and where strange l things happen, a place where events perhaps drift into the realms of Aboriginal mythology, and nobody can really tell what has happened."

At about 8 pm on Sunday, 26th January 1986, an Aboriginal couple saw a man, later identified as David Brett, a 31-year-originally from Kent in England, climbing in an area of the rock off the beaten track. It was Australia Day, referred to in some quarters of the indigenous community as "Invasion Day", when European man strode uninvited and in numbers into the Aboriginal domain. Here was an Englishman striding uninvited in the same way. Nobody can ever be sure what happened next. On one view, he got too far away from the safe incline, lost his footing and plunged to his death. Malcolm Brown in his later reflections thought that perhaps "a spirit" had pushed him, "a spirit of vengeance perhaps, outraged that the outsiders have dared set foot in a sacred domain, the same spirit perhaps that induced a dingo to sneak into a tent put up by other invaders and snatch their baby".

Brett's body lay at the foot of Ayers Rock for a week. Then he was discovered. A terrible event, but a misadventure that was going to open a whole new chapter in the Chamberlain saga.

CHAPTER THIRTEEN

LINDY OUT

"

Whoa, tie a yellow ribbon 'round the ole oak tree
It's been three long years
Do ya still want me (still want me)

— Irwin Levine and Russell Brown

Some prisons don't require bars to keep people locked inside.
All it takes is their perception that they belong there.

— Lysa TerKeurst

The yellow ribbons were always going to come out when Lindy was released. Her son Reagan had them already prepared. There had to be some abrupt, enlightening event – the discovery of a baby's skeleton in a dingo lair, for example – that would allow authorities to get past the impasse and for the reality to emerge. Lightness would penetrate the darkness and the yellow ribbons could be brought out. In the event, it was going to involve someone's death. Lindy would be out, and her well-wishers would flock to her. But what of the mindset of millions of others? As long as that mindset was there, the yellow ribbons would only be for those who fervently believed in her. In the broader context, Lindy was never going to be truly free.

There was an element of mystery about David Brett, the man who fell off Ayers Rock on Australia Day, 1986. It could hardly have been part of the Chamberlain case if not mysterious. Brett's family was to say that when he bid farewell the previous year, he appeared tormented. He had told his mother: "If anything happens to me, I have been made a sacrifice." He had moved out of his Sydney flat but left behind newspaper cuttings about Azaria's disappearance.

When his body was discovered by a tourist on 2nd February, it was badly decomposed and limbs were missing. Police were alerted and this time there was not going to be any of the casual procedure suggested of police in the aftermath of Azaria's disappearance in 1980. This time the area was sealed off, photos were taken and a line search was organised.

John Beasy, a motor mechanic at Ayers Rock, who had helped search for Azaria in 1980, joined the search, walking between two policemen. After searching 300 metres to the east of where the body had been found, he turned and began walking back in a westerly direction. Moving into a small bushy area between two trees, he noticed some material and picked it up. As he did, he felt the ground breaking from around it. He recognized this was a small sized baby jacket – a matinee jacket. It was in all probability the matinee jacket Lindy had insisted Azaria was wearing the night she disappeared. If Lindy in gaol had prayed that God would intervene for her, this might have been the moment, because of all the searchers, Beasy was the one who recognised the significance of the find. There were other odd bits of clothing found at the base of the rock, including a pair of women's panties, probably blown from the top when someone decided to bare, and they were properly dismissed as irrelevant. How easy it might have been for Beasy to have discarded the matinee jacket as well. But no, Beasy was on the ball.

It did not take long for news to get out. The discovery of the matinee jacket – even though it had not then been positively identified – was like the pin that ruptured the balloon. Or, expressed differently, Brett's tumble, tragic as it was, started a landslide. Michael Chamberlain was alerted the following day and told Tipple. Lindy had been telling the truth about that all along! Why hadn't she been telling the truth about everything else? The Northern Territory Government saw this as a genuinely new development. Prior to this, it had locked itself into a position. The Martin Report had said the supposedly new evidence presented by Tipple was not considered sufficiently cogent to justify an inquiry. Now, there was something irrefutably new. Like the jumpsuit, it was a grubby piece of material that might have been discarded by a less discerning searcher. But what a difference it made!

The NT Police treated the investigation stemming from the discovery of the matinee jacket at top level. This time there was to be extreme caution about the testing. Neither the police nor the Chamberlains wanted any of the problems that had developed over the jumpsuit. The Melbourne *Sun-Pictorial* ran a cartoon depicting a hydraulic jack lifting Ayers Rock from its foundations and one police officer saying to another: "We're leaving no stone unturned this time!" But despite the far greater caution now being observed, Tipple rang Martin and asked for immediate access to identify the jacket before it was subjected to any testing. He sent a telegram to Martin: "Request immediate access for identification to jacket found at Ayers Rock and your undertaking that it will not be subjected to any testing or further examinations until then." On 4th February, Martin replied by telegram to Tipple: "Suggest you advise me forthwith of your proposals concerning examination of the garment recently found near Ayers Rock Stop It is anticipated that it will arrive in Darwin later today and will be in the custody of police."

Police soil sampling at the site of the discovery of the matinee jacket on 4th February revealed a button, a label and "organic material" below the surface. The *NT News* speculated that this might have been Azaria's "burial site", but nothing more was to come of this. Tipple said that while Brett's death had nothing to do with his case, the fact that his body was partially eaten was significant. "We have always known that dingoes will eat human flesh," he said. "It makes it all the more possible [that Azaria was taken by a predatory dingo]." The same day, Perron wrote to Tipple saying he would accept further testing of blood samples taken from the Chamberlains car and on bloodstained exhibits held at the High Court. "If the procedures are agreed to I propose that, depending upon the quality of material available, part of it be tested for HbF [foetal haemoglobin] by a suitable qualified person who has had no previous connection with the case and using accepted immunological methods," he said: "I understand that after five years the denatured blood may not be suitable for testing by immunological means and the results may be inconclusive. However, in the event of a positive identification of the HbF is made, do you agree that would be the end of the matter?"

On 4th February 1986, Perron replied to Tipple's letter the previous December regarding DNA testing. "The techniques referred-to by Dr Simons require further consideration," he said. "I note that in your letter you refer to 'recently developed techniques'. Dr Simons speaks of 'recent advances in DNA genetics' which 'may be applicable for forensic aspects' concerning the matter. Dr Simons' work so far has been related to paternity testing which involves fresh whole blood as opposed to aged blood stains. He refers to the 'RFLP' technique as the 'next development in genetic resolution of Disputed Paternity'. The point is that the technique proposed appears to be one of recent origin. It may be that in some respects the scientific knowledge put forward has arisen since the trial but I wonder if it is accepted by the scientific community generally and in particular by those engaged in forensic science as opposed to being postulated advances."

Perron said that for him to take Simons' proposals on DNA testing further, he would need: "The names, addresses and qualifications of, say, five other suitably qualified scientists who support Dr Simons' proposals, identifying which of them are practising forensic scientists. In particular, I seek support for the proposition that the techniques suggested by Dr Simons will, as you put it, determine whether, what appears to be tissue in the baby's jumpsuit is the body tissue of Azaria Chamberlain; copies of, or references to, reprints in accepted scientific journals dealing with the subject; the views of Dr Simons and others (including reprints from the journals) on the application of the techniques to: (a) aged blood stains as opposed to fresh whole blood (the subject of paternity cases) and; (b) comparisons between results derived from fresh whole blood and aged blood stains."

Perron was very reserved about Tipple's request for ultraviolet fluorescence examination of blood samples from the car and associated items, together with control samples of Dufix from the Chamberlain car and blood samples from the baby's jumpsuit. He said: "Please advise the purpose of such an examination. As I understand the position, analyses of substances such as Dufix and aged blood will simply say that the two things are different and perhaps identify the nature of each. I would also invite your comments as to who should bear the cost of the engagement of experts and other expenses in relation to the proposed new sampling and testing."

Perron then made direct reference to pressure that had been put onto the Northern Territory Government. He said: "I take the opportunity to express my concern that the clear understanding reached at the meeting between, yourself, the Solicitor-General and I, that the current submission and any discussion thereon be kept confidential, has been breached by your client, Mr Chamberlain. Recent media reports demonstrate that he has been publicly talking about the 'new procedures' and the anticipated results. I can only assume he did so with a view to trying to embarrass me by exerting media and other public pressures. Please inform Mr Chamberlain that I will not be swayed by such reports and perceived pressures. I would have thought that by now you and your clients would understand that I will not be persuaded or bullied by media attention and subsequent public responses. My willingness to give careful and detailed consideration to representatives authorised by your clients has been demonstrated even though my decisions may not have been acceptable. The time taken to respond to media inquiries and representations from the public as a result necessarily detracts from the attention which my officers and I are able to give to the substantive issues which are raised."

On 5th February 1986, Tipple flew to Darwin. On the plane he met TV reporter Mike Lester who introduced him to Senior Sergeant Henry Huggins, Victorian Police Crime Scene Squad. Lester was very supportive of the Chamberlains but was to admit that he had lost his objectivity and Channel Nine replaced him as the reporter. To Lester, however, the developments were a vindication of the line he had taken, that the Chamberlains were innocent. Tipple said: "Mr. Huggins confirmed he was on his way to take over the investigation of the site where the jacket had been found. He told me he had been a crime scene investigator for over twenty years." A soil specialist from Huggins' squad and two arid zone botanists not associated with any police force were recruited in Alice Springs.

Tipple said: "On my arrival at Darwin I was met by a lady police officer. She told me she had been instructed to immediately drive me to meet with the Police Commissioner at the Police Headquarters at Berrimah. I arrived at about 1 pm and met with Commissioner McAulay and Superintendent Plumb. After some discussion, it was agreed that Lindy would be brought from Berrimah Gaol to inspect the jacket. The inspection would be recorded on video and by still photography. Solicitor-General Brian Martin arrived shortly afterwards. He confirmed John Beasy had found the jacket but no photographs had been taken. We went downstairs to an examination room where Lindy was already waiting with two prison officers. I was shown a sealed package and the seals were broken in our presence and the jacket was removed. I was surprised at how well preserved the jacket was. I could see it matched the detailed description given by Mrs. Chamberlain when Azaria disappeared. The top button had become detached but it was stuck in the top buttonhole. The lower button was missing. The jacket was inside out and whilst being photographed it was turned to the right way."

According to Tipple, Plumb became agitated while Lindy was examining the matinee jacket and had said: "Well is it the jacket?" Tipple could see Lindy was red-eyed and trying to control her emotions. Plumb said: "Well it's not ripped to pieces as you'd expect if a dingo had been involved ... Now what would you like to say about that?" On Tipple's account, Lindy asked whether she could speak to Tipple alone. "When we were alone, she told me, 'I've got no doubt it is the jacket but it is quite weathered'," Tipple said. "We returned to the examination room and after she identified the jacket, she was taken back to Berrimah Gaol. I met with Commissioner McAulay and agreed on a press release."

Police Commissioner McAulay said that Victorian experts would be involved in the examination of material reportedly found 10 cms under Azaria's matinee jacket, to avoid any perceived conflict should that material have anything to do with Azaria Chamberlain. Tipple said he accepted the Commissioner's offer to fly him in his plane to Ayers Rock that evening and on his arrival at the Rock at 10:30 pm he was met by the NT lawyer, Michael O'Loughlin, who had been part of the prosecution team. They agreed to meet at 7.30 am the following day to agree on further investigation protocols.

In Canberra on the same day, Betty Hocking told the ACT House of Assembly that the Martin Report was "a whitewash". In Darwin, journalist Brian Johnstone, who was then media adviser to Bob Collins, announced that Collins had retained Andrew Scott to review the report. At Ayers Rock on 6th February 1986, Tipple reunited with Vern Pleuckhahn, whom he had asked to come from Adelaide. "After a briefing from Sergeant Huggins, we went out to the Rock to inspect the site," Tipple said. "The site where the matinee jacket was covered with a tarpaulin. As Huggins pulled the tarpaulin back, he joked, 'I'm wondering whether we might find a dingo mother and a litter of pups under here!'" Huggins walked around the site taking soil temperature readings with a thermometer. It was February and the heat was oppressive. "As he walked towards me, I heard a flip-flop and saw the soles on his track shoes had delaminated in the heat," Tipple said. "Sergeant Huggins impressed me as being an experienced and capable investigator and there was no need for me to stay in a supervisory role. I made plans to fly out."

Collins had provided copies of Scott's review to the *NT News* and the Adelaide *Advertiser* on the condition that its details remain confidential until they attended a press conference he had scheduled for 2 pm that day. After receiving that material, an *NT News* reporter, Frank Alcorta, rang Behringwerke in Germany, and was told it had written to the NT Law Department expressing concern that its position had been misrepresented in the Martin Report. Commissioner McAulay ordered that a letter be couriered to Tuxworth's office, calling for a judicial review of the Chamberlain case. It arrived there at 9.30 am and staff had it sent directly to Tuxworth who was at a local school function. Tuxworth wrote immediately to Perron, saying: "It also seems to me that you, as Attorney-General, will need to consider whether the Northern Territory Government should take action in respect of Mrs Chamberlains' detention." Alcorta, utterly frustrated by the government delay, drafted an article and showed it to the NT Government. He said that unless Lindy was released from gaol by midday, the *News* would publish it. Two reporters sought comment on their proposed story from within the Government. Fifteen minutes before the paper's publishing deadline, Tuxworth contacted the *News* and proposed that it delay publishing the story pending a significant announcement in connection with the case. Following that, Perron announced that Lindy would be freed and a judicial inquiry into the case would be held. Further, Lindy would not return to prison, irrespective of the outcome of the inquiry. The media had often been condemned for its treatment of the Chamberlains. On this occasion, it might be said to have done them some good. Alcorta, who in the past had been so bullishly defensive of the reputation of Territorians and scornful of the southern media, showed his worth as a journalist.

Tipple flew from Uluru [Ayers Rock] and was waiting at Alice Springs airport for the connecting flight to Sydney. At 2 pm, he heard his name paged requesting that he come to the office. On arriving at the office, he was handed a telephone and heard: "Mr. Tipple, it's Marshall Perron here. I would like to formally advise you that Mrs. Chamberlain will be released on licence. I have ordered an inquiry into her conviction. Whatever the result, Mrs. Chamberlain will not be required to return to jail." Tuxworth wrote a letter to Bob Collins: "Dear Mr Collins, you have for some time taken a strong interest in the Azaria Chamberlain case and have expressed your view as to the course of action which the Northern Territory Government should adopt in respect of Mrs Chamberlain. The Government has consistently indicated that the integrity of the judicial process must be maintained and that only in the event of significant new evidence becoming available would a judicial inquiry be initiated. I have to advise that the Attorney-General, acting on the advice of the Commissioner of Police and the Solicitor-General to the effect that there may be significant new evidence, has decided that a judicial inquiry should be undertaken. Subsequent to advice, the Attorney-General will be introducing suitable legislation, including terms of reference together with details of membership of the inquiry in the next Sittings of the Legislative Assembly. I also advise that His Honour the Administrator, acting on the advice of the Executive Council has now signed the necessary papers to effect the release from prison of Mrs Chamberlain. I attach for your information a copy of a statement by the Attorney-General on this matter. I would draw your attention, in particular, to the indication by the Attorney-General that Mrs Chamberlain's release from detention may be considered permanent, regardless of the outcome of the judicial inquiry. When the garment was found in the area where the English tourist fell to his death, we considered this to be new evidence. It was obvious that an inquiry must be held and it would be proper to release Mrs. Chamberlain on bail or parole or whatever until the outcome of the inquiry was known." Boettcher's comment was: "It seemed that, at last, this was the beginning of the end. A feeling of relief!"

Some were prepared to say the discovery of the matinee jacket was virtually the sole reason for Lindy's release. Sydney lawyer and newspaper columnist Charles Waterstreet said that but for that she would have, at the time of writing, still be rotting in gaol. Boettcher had doubts whether the discovery of the matinee jacket had been as important in the NT Government's thinking. He said the letter from Baudner and Storiko of Behringwerke on 20th January saying the anti-serum should not have been used as it had, had broken the deadlock. Although the media reported that the matinee jacket had broken the deadlock, he thought the real reason was the totality of pressures that had then been placed on the government. "The matinee jacket had been found more than a week earlier and Lindy had not been released when the jacket was found; the Northern Territory Government had already stated that the finding of the jacket did not have any bearing on the case; and there was a party still working in the area where the jacket had been found, looking for any other items of possible interest, without success," he said.

Whatever the ifs and whys of the decision process, the decision to release Lindy was nevertheless made. Tipple was, in his words, "stunned" by the news, but decided to continue his trip to Sydney. He was exhausted. He'd won the battle but there was still a war to be fought. In the early afternoon, prison superintendent Fred Mercer told Lindy she was to be released. She left Berrimah Gaol at 3.45 pm local time by car. Supporters took her to a safe house in Darwin. The incarceration had lasted for three years and four months. Tipple arrived in Sydney at 6 pm. "I was exhausted but rang Lindy hoping she would not hold me to an earlier promise I had made to go to Darwin and bring her home," he said. Lindy was unmoved, "A promise is a promise" she said.

On 8th February, reports on the Behringwerke letter appeared in the *NT News* and the Adelaide *Advertiser* and events surrounding it, though with some detail omitted. That day, Tipple returned to Darwin. In Epping, in Sydney's north-west, John Bagnall speaking at an SDA church said hearts rejoiced at the news. "We do not always understand the ways of the Lord," he said. "But we must always trust Him. We cannot fully understand why John the Baptist died in prison or why Peter was released from prison by an angel only later to meet a martyr's death, or why Lindy should lose her baby and then lose her freedom. She was convicted of the cold-blooded murder of her child – a conviction obtained without body, weapon or motive. Lindy has displayed great strength of character in the most appalling circumstances. She is a Christian much to be admired. Lindy has been misunderstood as she has witnessed her faith. She has been persecuted and reviled to an extent that has bewildered us. The events surrounding Azaria's disappearance must have touched some deep and hidden qualities in the Australian psyche we do not understand or admire. Michael Chamberlain has been in a prison of his own, bound by events beyond his understanding and the responsibilities of parenting alone his sons and new daughter. He too deserves our admiration. We are grateful to the Church Organisation. The Church has had to be seen to uphold the law and at the same time to uphold the Chamberlains in the profession of innocence. The Church has employed and housed and protected Michael and the family and has ensured that they have funds to exhaust the legal processes and then continue to fight. We are grateful to the various support groups and individuals who have worked for Lindy's release, especially Guy Boyd, Pastor George Rollo, Greg and Sally Lowe, Malcolm Brown of the *Sydney Morning Herald* and recently the members of the Chamberlain Innocence Committee. We are grateful to the scientists in Australia and overseas who have continued to question the scientific conclusions upon which the conviction was obtained."

Bagnall expressed appreciation of the efforts of politicians and lawyers. Of Stuart Tipple, he said he was "a man of two worlds – the world of his church and his God and the world of law and politics ... He is, to many of us, a modern-day Daniel or Moses or Joseph. Stuart Tipple has worked relentlessly, intelligently and thoroughly in the interest of his clients under great provocation from those who misunderstood his role and questioned his dedication and his competence". Bagnall said the Chamberlain supporters looked forward the new inquiry, and hoped that it would lead to improvements in the justice system and that "as a society, Australians will learn more tolerance and understanding of minorities in our midst."

In the early hours of 9th February 1996, Tipple accompanied Lindy from Darwin. Prior to the flight leaving, Lindy hid in the cargo shed till 1 am till loading began at 2.15 am. She and Tipple arrived at Sydney at 9 am. Tipple was to publicly thank the Australian Federal Police and Ansett for their help to the Chamberlains in avoiding the media. But they were recognised by the general public and a yahoo at Sydney Airport gave them a dingo howl. When Lindy was driven into the main entrance to Avondale College, she was greeted with an array of yellow ribbons, just as the released prisoner in the song, found the old oak tree festooned with ribbons.

Lindy was being welcomed back by her own people with all their hearts. But in the eyes of others, and on the official records, she was still a convicted baby-killer. "We believe we have won a decisive battle," Tipple said. "We've got a mopping-up exercise to carry out to win the war." But winning the war would be no mean feat." On 10th February, John Bagnall, following Lindy's release said in a letter to Tipple: "It would be helpful if the support groups ceased at once talking about compensation for Lindy and Michael. Public goodwill is very fragile and could well be destroyed if there are strident demands for compensation even before the inquiry, let alone before an exoneration of Lindy and Michael." There would forever afterwards be people who would ask Malcolm Brown: "What really did happen? Did she do it?" And as he discovered, the further north he went in Australia, particularly in the Northern Territory, that scepticism became more apparent. Tipple knew that all he had done so far was facilitate Lindy's release. He had been charged with the responsibility of getting them exonerated and there was still much to do.

CHAPTER FOURTEEN

REPERCUSSIONS

"

I feel I have seen the jaws of hell and survived. I've thought there was no point in life, and then suddenly out of the storm came a touch of blue. And then the thought came, 'Hang on a minute, there is life after a character assassination, there is life after a reputation annihilation. I'd better stick around.'

— Michael Chamberlain, Beyond Azaria,
Black Light White Light

The repercussions of Lindy's release in February 1986 were perplexing. There were serious questions to be answered. Was she being released because she had been punished enough? Was it because there was too much doubt about her guilt? Should she have been convicted at all? Did the Chamberlains, caught up in the hothouse of hysteria and bigotry that surrounded them from the outset, ever have any chance of a fair trial? Could their defence have been handled better?

Stuart Tipple, after having endured such intense and harrowing criticism for his handling of the case, was at least entitled to feel vindicated. Richard Nairn wrote to Tipple: "You are deserving of the highest praise for your tenacity in the cause of justice for Lindy Chamberlain. I have never ceased to hope that you might achieve the seemingly impossible and have lost no opportunity to publicise your cause in the special avenues open to me in Australia and overseas. However, the miracle has happened, it is a splendid tribute to you all. If there remains anything I can do to contribute you your fight to clear the

Chamberlains' name, you have only to ask."

In a media conference at Avondale College on 10th February, Tipple said Lindy Chamberlain was deeply distressed by her portrayal in the media, and blamed the media in part for what had happened to her. He said a lot of new evidence had been presented to the Northern Territory and that the discovery of the matinee jacket was "just the catalyst". In Darwin, Marshall Perron, when questioned about the Martin Report, said that Martin had sought advice from one of the Crown prosecutors in preparing his report on the new evidence. Tipple wrote to Perron that day, asking whether the NT Government would support the application by the Chamberlains to have their convictions struck from the record and whether the NT Government would support the Chamberlains' application to be legally represented. The new NT Attorney-General, Daryl Manzie, replied that he did not intend to enter into such discussions at that stage.

In the meantime, Bob Collins called for the resignation of Brian Martin because of criticisms of his report. In Canberra, Bob Brown, Member for Carlton, announced a Notice of Motion put to the Federal Labor Caucus, proposing: "Caucus notes with satisfaction the decision of the Northern Territory Government to release Mrs Chamberlain and establish a judicial inquiry. Caucus notes with concern that in its panic to respond to recent developments in the case, the Northern Territory Government has been unable to indicate what the composition of the proposed enquiry will be and who will head it and what its terms of reference will be. These recent developments include the letter of 20th January 1986 to Solicitor-General Martin of the Northern Territory from Drs Storiko and Baudner of Behringwerke and the commentary on the Martin Report dated 21 January 1986 by Dr Andrew Scott, Forensic Scientist of South Australia, which was commissioned by Bob Collins, Leader of the Opposition in the Northern Territory. Caucus notes the call made by Mr Bob Collins for Solicitor-General Martin to stand aside and the compelling reasons for that call. Caucus notes the clear expression of concern about these developments by the Hon N.K.Wran, Premier of NSW and National President of the Australian Labor Party. Caucus requests its Legal and Administrative Committee to examine the composition and the terms of reference of the judicial inquiry of the Northern Territory as soon as they are announced and, as a matter of urgency, to report to Caucus on the suitability of the composition of the inquiry and its chairmanship, and the adequacy of the terms of reference to allow the enquiry the widest possible areas of investigation including a comprehensive examination of the prosecutions side of the case." Brown urged caucus to inquire into developments leading to the release of Lindy Chamberlain.

The same day, Alan Morison, editor of *Saturday Extra* for *The Age* in Melbourne, wrote to John Bryson, author of *Evil Angels*, which had just been released in Britain. "On the evidence as it now stands, Mrs Chamberlain should be freed pending a full inquiry. Yet her chances of going free and eventually winning a pardon now seem to depend almost solely on the Federal Caucus and Federal Parliament next month. I can only suggest that Mrs Chamberlain has nothing to lose and everything to gain from speaking out now, before Caucus meets. If Mrs Chamberlain cared to write an open letter, we would certainly be prepared to publish, in an unsensational way, her thoughts on the latest twists in the case. Could you please convey this to her?"

Lindy was the subject of attention from many different angles. She even got a proposal of marriage. A letter written at Finley in the Riverina in New South Wales, dated 29th January, said: "Dear Mrs Chambers (sic), When you come out of prison if you want to get married, I will marry you ... I'll look after you Mrs Chambers. There's plenty of food in the refrigerator. We will have plenty of sleep, rest and quiet."

Not everyone was prepared to join the victory parade for the Chamberlains. Many considered Lindy guilty. One letter addressed to Lindy said: "You Lying Bastard. You Murdered That Baby and Planted the Jacket at the Rock. I Know God Will Judge You. You Have Got Away With It on Earth. But God Will Judge You." A letter dated 4th February 1986 said: "Congratulations on Your release. But we know you did it." One said: "Murderess – Murderer. You will have your freedom but you will never go free." Another said: "We hear you are all going to New Zealand. Please, please, please, go quickly and stay there. A kiwi bit a three-year-old girl on 27 September. Gives you any ideas?" Yet another, dated 10th February 1986, from Moruya on the NSW south coast, said: "Dear Sir and Madam, as you consider that you are beyond reproach in the eyes of God you face a higher judgement ... I hope your conscience never lets you get a moment's peace. You must think everyone is as stupid as yourselves if you think anybody could believe that impossible story about Azaria's death. For many loose ends, it was a very tidy dingo must have cleaned the tent up before he folded the clothes up. Of course, the tracks could not be followed, none to follow were there? I feel sorry for you and your crazy religion..."

One letter said: "I have watched your interview on TV with Ray Martin, listened to your address to the church congregation and read many articles in the newspapers about you and your crime. I was particularly interested in your statement to the congregation in which you said, 'It's not just for our freedom and our name to be cleared, it's for every Australian'. Now, I would like to remind you that in no way are you supposedly speaking for or representing me in your quest to clear your name." An anonymous Victorian, signing himself/herself "Disgusted", wrote to Tipple saying: "I'm just one of many people who found the jury in Lindy Chamberlain's case was right, even Justice Muirhead nearly pleaded with the jury to let her off, but God has seen the jury to be fit and tell the truth, have you ever felt sorry for little Azaria who was murdered by her Mother, some women go off for a while in a state of depression after having a baby and that's what has happened, she soon got her track suit pants dry cleaned and what about the blood under the dash in the car and the police found a small knife at the Chamberlains' car bloodstained. What do you want? Do you feel a big shot or are you short of a few customers what if she was black or ugly woman you wouldn't be interested, she only got pregnant so she would get off on pity? I bet the jury will all be Seven-day Adventist well she going free so they may as well let all the Melbourne Pentridge prisoners out."

From someone at The Entrance on the NSW Central Coast came this contribution: "You people must hang your heads in shame. How many people go short because of the many millions the government has spent on you? How much do you pay people to lie for you? You have even tutored your son to lie. It does not matter what is decided, that heathen bitch called Lindy will always be known as a convicted criminal. How she glories in all the media attention. She should be shot the way she flaunts herself dressing up like a little child. May God forgive you both for your cruelty and your money grabbing. This is your money. Hanging would be too good for you pair." Another wrote: "Dear Mrs Chamberlain, I was amazed when I learned of your release from prison, for the crime you committed you should be locked up for life and your husband with you. The only people to think you are innocent are from the church you belong to. The rest of Australia are sure of your guilt."

Money was certainly a very important consideration to the Chamberlains, but at this stage the question was how much was owing to others. On 11th February 1996, it was reported that the SDA Church had lent about $200,000 to the Chamberlains to cover their expenses once legal aid had stopped. That had happened when the Federal Court appeal was dismissed in 1983. Pastor Ray Coombe, public relations officer for the church's Australasian Division, said there would be discussions shortly between Tipple and officers of the Church. One way of making money was through media interviews. *New Idea* magazine wanted an interview with Lindy's mother, Avis Murchison, who was keen to do the interview but required a fee, which would go towards defraying costs. On 11th February, *New Idea* sent a telegram to Tipple about a suitable arrangement.

On 18th February, the Melbourne Age reported: "Professor James Cameron, who gave evidence for the prosecution that bloodstains on a jumpsuit worn by nine-week-old Azaria Chamberlain indicated her throat was cut, has defended his testimony and insisted that the child was killed by a human, according to a London newspaper report." The report concluded: "These remarks partly bear out the fears of senior Victorian policemen that it is forensic science which will be on trial during the renewed inquiry". Kenneth Brown, meeting Malcolm Brown in Adelaide, was initially put off by because he had identified Malcolm with the innocence campaign. Then he said of the developments in the case: "It was politics, politics. Bring politics into it and people will believe anything!"

Forensic science, of course, was never on trial. The capability and fallibility of forensic scientists was. And, sadly, the closing of the ranks continued. In a letter to Daryl Manzie, on 21st February, Tipple complained that the Victorian police had been denied access to trial transcript before they carried out an examination of the matinee jacket, button, tag and organic material which were then held in the Victorian Police Forensic Laboratory. "We are concerned that following a briefing session from NT Police officers, the Victorian Police requested access to the trial transcript in order that they could properly assess what testing should be carried out," he said. "For reasons unknown to us, the NT Police have refused such access. Will you please advise us of their reasons for doing so as it appears to us this would be the proper course. Will you please confirm that you will be consulting us on appropriate terms of reference and the Commissioner for the forthcoming Inquiry prior to any legislation being introduced? We look forward to hearing from you."

Tipple was also returning to intense examination of the one item that had triggered off the entire ghastly process: the baby's jumpsuit. He corresponded with Michael McHugh QC, who had represented the Chamberlains in both appeals and was now a High Court judge. In a letter on 26th February, Tipple discussed a photo of the damage to the baby's clothing which contained in the middle of the damaged section a single unbroken thread. "I do not believe the unbroken nylon thread and the similarity of damage in the samples of Azaria's jumpsuit ... could ever be duplicated by scissors," he said. When an experimental carcass dressed in a jumpsuit had been mauled by dingoes, it was seen that small portions of flesh were found embedded in the damaged areas. "Upon further examination of the Chamberlain jumpsuit similar 'flesh' samples were observed in [one of the photographs]," Tipple said. "There are several such samples and they are distributed in a similar manner to those observed in the experimental samples."

Then Tipple, referring to the newly-evolving DNA science, said: "A new process developed over the last few months would allow this material [remnants of flesh in the baby's jumpsuit] to be identified as being the flesh of Azaria Chamberlain or otherwise as it is able to detect and identify small amounts of DNA. DNA like fingerprints are unique to the individual and so this technique could also be used to demonstrate that the material still on the under-dash bracket is not Azaria Chamberlain's blood. We also intend to carry out a very thorough examination because if we are able to find any further blood at all from around the hinge areas this technique could similarly be employed. The real advantage of this new technique is that it only needs minute samples and DNA is not affected by denaturation."

On 1st April, the NT Legislative Assembly passed the Commission of Inquiry (Chamberlain Convictions) Act. The next day, Letters Patent were issued appointing a Federal Court judge, Trevor Morling, as Royal Commissioner. The NT Government offered to pay part of the legal bill the Chamberlains faced to be represented at the inquiry. The media tide was then well and truly in favour of the Chamberlains. A Christchurch radio stationed telegrammed Tipple that day asking for a telephone interview with Lindy Chamberlain. It said: "Interview would be sympathetic and could be pre-recorded rather than live." Nine days later, as though Nature were chiming in to underline the pathos of the entire situation, a pack of wild dogs, apparently led by a German Shepherd-dingo cross, attacked a five-year-old girl in the Cooloola National Park, north of Brisbane. The girl was badly mauled. Police later shot the crossbred and set out to trap the other dogs.

In an attempt to improve the system, Tipple had submitted an entry for the NSW Law Society young solicitors' essay competition. In his essay Forensic Science – *The New Trial by Ordeal*, he referred to the Chamberlain case. Tipple said some of the NSW Health Department Laboratory practices were flawed and wondered why the failings had not been exposed before. He said the laboratory had been very busy dealing with 600 crimes a year and doing some 50,000 tests. But the control systems for these tests, and not keeping the slides or photographs, was lamentable. A better system of documenting case notes and independent checking of all major observations needed to become part of the NSW system. Furthermore, important test specimens should be kept so that they could be retested or subjected to any new test that was developed. The system of not keeping the slides or photographs had been going on in the laboratory since 1974, but the legal profession had failed to uncover or challenge it.

The resources and practices of the laboratory were pro-Crown and prejudiced the defence which did not have the resources of the Crown. Tipple's essay won the award.

On 21st April 1986, Tipple said the Chamberlains did not have the funds for legal representation at the royal commission. The Chamberlains, who had built up heavy debts to the SDA Church, did "not have any resources to draw on". "We are finding it impossible to properly retain anyone until we know we are going to have any funds," he said. Then he said the NT Government should pay the Chamberlains' full bill, not just part of it. On 3rd May, the NT Government refused an application for an unconditional grant to Lindy Chamberlain but said it would consider a loan. Tipple said that would prevent the Chamberlains from having proper legal representation and asked it to reconsider. He told Brian Martin he felt full funding would be appropriate. The government then offered to pay for a legal team for the Chamberlains.

The Royal Commission into the Chamberlain Convictions began in Darwin on 8th May. Counsel assisting the royal commission was Chester Porter QC, a Sydney silk known for his razor-sharp cross-examination. A good-natured, ebullient man with a ready sense of humour, he had been dubbed by Sydney journalist John Slee as "The Smiling Funnelweb". His junior was a Sydney barrister, Bill Caldwell. Representing the Chamberlains was a Victorian silk, John Winneke QC, more aggressive in his style but an equally sharp intellect. With him were Brind Woinarski (now QC), and a Canberra counsel, Ken Crispin (later an ACT judge). Tipple, as always, sat at the back, taking in everything. He was accompanied by two solicitors he had employed. The NT Government retained Ian Barker, QC, who was now supported by Michael Adams, (later a QC and NSW judge), and Elizabeth Fullerton (later a SC and a NSW judge), with Michael O'Laughlin instructing.

On the first day, Morling agreed with a submission by Porter, supported by Winneke, that the matinee jacket should first be tested in the Victorian Forensic Science Laboratory. As before, the centrepiece in this massive saga was a tiny, pathetic little baby's garment, whose role had simply been to fit snugly around a tiny body.

Soon afterwards, Phil Ward put in an appearance. He wanted to be represented at the royal commission as well, and had briefed counsel, Audley

Gillespie-Jones. Porter told Ward his views were without foundation. Ward disagreed. He thought Porter did not have a good grasp of the Aboriginal evidence and said: "I cannot imagine the Crown would want to ask Aborigines the questions I would want to put…" Morling, referring to ongoing defamation action against Ward, said he would not be making an adverse finding against him. People suing Ward would be giving evidence at the inquiry, but it would not be relevant to Ward's case. The seven plaintiffs against Ward were represented by Marcus Einfeld QC, who told Morling on 6th June: "Part of Your Honour's inquiry is the public disquiet that has surrounded this case almost from the disappearance of the baby. Part of this public disquiet has been fed by a bundle of scurrilously irresponsible allegations that have been made against my clients, apparently without the slightest regard for the truth or the evidence that supports them."

Arthur Hawken, who had experience with the Aboriginals of the Centre, and had obtained statements from Nipper Winmatti, appeared in the witness box. He said Winmatti's statements supported the dingo attack scenario and he had the tape-recording of what Winmatti said in a bank vault. A good bushman though he was, he was unprepared for the mauling he received from counsel at the inquiry, in particular Michael Adams QC. Hawken had translated Winmatti's statement, mainly spoken in Pitjantjatjara, into proper English and said those were the "exact" words Winmatti had said. They were not the "exact" words, rather they were Hawken's translation of them into proper English, and Adams put to him that he was lying. Hawken could not recover his ground after that. He left the witness box and never returned to the hearing, though his wife did put in appearance next day. Tipple was at pains to comfort her. The Aboriginal trackers were called to give evidence. But Tipple noted that they did so reluctantly. "They always knew from their own skills what had happened," he said. "We had the contrast of what we regarded as a primitive race having all the answers and our sophisticated system, 'the best in the world', getting it so wrong. It's little wonder they did not want to give evidence because they had seen what had happened to Lindy Chamberlain. They knew a terrible injustice had been done to someone who was innocent and probably wondered what could happen to them."

The Aboriginal trackers were always underrated, but there were some very funny moments. When Barbara Winmatti gave evidence of seeing dingo tracks outside the tent, the Crown counsel put to her that the tracks might have been made by a dingo carrying a kangaroo, the question was put to Barbara through the interpreter. After some interchange in the Pitjantjatjara language, the interpreter translated Barbara's response: "Was there a kangaroo in the tent?" That produced mirth in the hearing. "She's priceless!" one observer said. On another occasion, tracker Nui Minyintiri was answering Michael Adams line of questioning in the negative. When Adams continued the same line of questioning, Minyintiri started getting agitated. The interpreter told Adams it was insulting to Aboriginal people to keep asking them the same question. When Adams put much the same question again, Minyintiri reacted with an extraordinary display of exasperation. He stood up and began gesticulating and at the same time crying out in Pitjantjatjara for what seemed several minutes. Everyone in the court was in total wonderment and craned forward to hear the interpreter's translation of all that had been said and done. The answer was just "One word "No"."

Of course, there was always a premium on what Michael and Lindy had to say. On 7th June 1986, as Tipple sat next to Malcolm Brown at an SDA church service in Darwin. Brown jokingly pulled out a cheque book saying: "I thought I'd bring it just in case I had to speak to the Chamberlains ... I saw Michael yesterday and nearly said a penny for your thoughts ... but of course I should be saying $250,000 for them".

The evidence that had gone before five previous tribunals was trotted out again before the royal commission. But now those standing up for what had been the Crown case were on the back foot and Tipple knew that. Tipple took a trip around the world to get expert statements. On 31st July, flying back to Sydney with Barry Boettcher beside him, he sat back, closed his eyes and thought of the helter-skelter of the previous fortnight: Hong Kong, London, Frankfurt, Marberg, Kiel, Falconberg, Gotronberg, Lund, Kiel, Frankfurt, London, Cambridge, San Francisco, Sydney. He had a lot on his mind. His wife, Cherie, was heavily pregnant. "I smiled to myself thinking it sounded like a great holiday but at least the statements were dictated," Tipple said. "I needed to make up for all the lost sleep. I had to get those statements typed up, couriered back around the world, signed and filed with the Commission by the end of the month. It didn't sound like a lot of work when I thought about it quickly."

Tipple's wife Cherie was at the airport with their son Jaemes to drive him back to Gosford. For Tipple, the drive to Gosford seemed to take an age. "All the way home my mind kept racing back to the big task ahead," he said. "I wondered whether the Northern Territory legal team had found any experts to bolster their flagging fortunes. No, surely not, I kept telling myself, 'No way!' The statements I had now meant there is no way we could fail this time.

Tipple went to his office the next day. "The work desk was hardly visible covered in mountainous piles of files and mail," he said. "I slumped into my seat and started to attack the mail pile. Suddenly my whole body began to shake. Slowly at first but then increasing intensity and frequency. The last two weeks had finally caught up with me. I needed to sleep."

The sleep did not last all that long. At 5 am the next day, his wife woke him to tell him the baby was coming. "I was incredulous," Tipple said later. "I said it couldn't be, the baby was not due for another month ... I was leaving for Darwin the next day and wouldn't be back for a month!" The baby came quickly, and then there was concern. The baby, a boy, had a cleft lip. The doctor thrust his finger up into the baby's mouth and said, 'He's got a palate ... Don't worry. I can fix that lip, no one will ever know except for the smallest of scars'". Tipple's mind was in rather a whirl. How could he leave his wife and baby in these circumstances to go to the other end of the country, where all the fuss and bother was over another baby? Then he looked down at the newborn. "I began looking down at his little face. I saw the most indescribable magical moment," Tipple said. "I saw the way Cherie was looking at him, I saw the love and immediate bonding. I knew then that I didn't have to worry about anything. Tears welled up in my eyes and as I turned away to look out the window, I felt the peace of knowing everything was going to be okay."

Then, from that spiritual moment, when Tipple experienced harmony, it was back into hell. As the evidence before Morling continued, and again went into the intricacies of blood testing and fabric damage. With that segment of the hearing over, Tipple returned to New South Wales to take his wife and the baby, Anthony, home. With the baby and Cherie, he visited Cherie's cousin, Marrilyn, who was in hospital waiting for a lung transplant. She had kept herself alive determined to see the baby and died two days later. Tipple knew he had important family matters to attend to, principally to get a medical history for his new-born son. He needed to find the biological parents of Cherie, who had been adopted as a baby in Tasmania. But like everything else that had to wait. The Chamberlain case continued to come first and demand priority treatment.

Lindy Chamberlain was being continually tortured. She received, by airmail from Melbourne, a Christmas card for a six-year-old, with a picture of six candles, and the words: "I never lit a candle. I never made a birthday wish. Why didn't you come and look for me? I was so cold and so frightened." How cruel, how horribly, horribly cruel, people can be. It is said of the Chamberlain case that it was like a war, it brought out the best and the very worst in people. It displayed the ugly side of the Australian psyche, the yahoo element that had bedevilled the case from the start. On 15th August, Tipple, in Darwin, confided in his diary that he was feeling lonely and depressed, missing his family and feeling depressed about the outcome of the royal commission. "I wondered whether we could win against such odds," he said.

But things were looking up. The Crown flew Peter Martin, a forensic expert based at Scotland Yard, to Australia. "His initial statement indicated that he was going to support the Crown but as it turned out he did not," Tipple said. "He actually completely discounted a number of her [Mrs Kuhl's] tests including the scissors test. Forensic scientists were now delivering the death blows to the Crown scientific case it had presented at the trial. Tony Raymond, head of the Victorian State Forensic Laboratory, said on 3rd October 1986 he applied an ortho-tolidine test and the Kastel-Mayer test to Azaria's matinee jacket and obtained positive presumptive reactions for the presence of blood even though it had been out in the open for six years. When he had carried out tests on the Chamberlain car, he did not get any significant indication of blood. He had not been able to obtain a positive reaction for blood anywhere in the car except in the remains of a nasal secretion between the two back seats. What in the trial had been identified as blood, in Raymond's view, turned out to be things like spilt grape juice and "caramelised milk".

No blood in the car? Did that mean that all that vast amount of inquiry, testing, reports, expert testimony and cross-examination had been about something that was not even blood? Surely not! No forensic biologist could have been so incompetent to have identified that not only as blood but as baby's blood! But one explanation went as far as indicating that. The fruit juice and the caramel milkshake, along with the Dufix sound-deadener, had been sticky. The trapped copper oxide dust in Mt Isa had produced the positive reactions for the presumptive presence of blood. Joy Kuhl had concluded it was blood and had proceeded to analyse it. Not even the Chamberlains' lawyers could accept that there was no blood. Surely, they thought, some of it must have been blood, but the source had most likely been Keyth Lenehan. Tipple formed the view that at least some of the samples, in particular those taken from the side of the front seat and the floor, were blood, but the source was Lenehan. Other samples were not blood at all. "Kuhl", Tipple said, "claimed to have found blood everywhere!"

The Crown case kept collapsing. On the day Kuhl started her evidence she was wearing blue, which might have signified depression. Boettcher was sitting next to Tipple and revealed his matching cufflinks with Japanese inscriptions proclaiming happiness. On 20th October, Joy Kuhl finally admitted that in the tests she conducted before the trial she had got reactions against adult blood with the anti-serum she claimed was specific to foetal haemoglobin. She had not recognised the significance of those results at the time, having regarded the bands as mere "artefacts". She had not got those bands when she re-tested. But her admission was enough. Boettcher was vindicated at last. On 4th December Joy Kuhl stepped down from the witness box, Tipple heard Elizabeth Fullerton ask her how she was. Kuhl replied: "Furious!" On 10th December 1986, after Dr Lincoln gave his evidence that he had been unable to detect any foetal blood on the items, Tipple took to him for testing in London before the trial. *The Sydney Morning Herald* carried a headline: "Chamberlain Blood Tests Questioned by Biologist". The same day, the *Australian*, carrying a report on the same evidence, had as its headline: "UK Expert Backs Blood Tests Used by Locals". Tipple commented: "A good argument for Mr Murdoch not owning every newspaper in the country!"

The evidence that surprised Tipple the most came from Constable Barry Graham. He confirmed that acting on instructions from Charlwood he had carried out a search of the Chamberlains' car in Mt Isa in October 1980 when Aidan was giving his statement to the police. His search, using a Big Jim torch, had not turned up any evidence of blood or the scissors let alone any murder weapon in the car the Crown claimed was awash with blood and contained the scissors 13 months later. Graham indicated in his evidence before the commission that his search had not been very thorough. From Tipple's point of view, it was an attempt to explain why blood might have been present despite his search. Chester Porter took him to task about this apparent change in his evidence to the statement he had given the Royal Commission.

In the midst of what now seemed to be demolition of the Crown case, Barker tried a little humour. He composed a letter, dated 6th November 1986, addressed to Chester Porter. Giving a return address as "Blowfly Downs via Birdsville", he said: "Dear Mr Porter, in response to your public appeal, it may help you to know that in 1943 my late father, Mortimer Hangdog, who was known throughout the district as 'Mort' Hangdog, told me that in about 1932 he was what may well have been a dingo looked menacing at my father's Blue Heeler dog, called Harold. The menacing look caused Harold to become extremely excited, and he leaped from the back of my father's model 'A' utility. Regrettably, he was then run over. Harold's death was a great blow to my father, who thereafter regarded all dingoes with considerable reserve. The sad circumstances of Harold's passing certainly suggest that a dingo is not to be trusted. I hope the above is of some help to you. Naturally, I would be prepared to give evidence before the Inquiry, subject to reaching some agreement with you about return, airfares, accommodation, appointment of a manager etc."

The letter was signed "Frampton J. Hangdog (JP)". On 26th November, the *Sydney Morning Herald* noted in its Column 8 that Suzie, the three-legged Kelpie / Border Collie cross that had done so much service to the Chamberlain case by biting jumpsuit material in experimental conditions and produced scissor-like cuts and tufts, had died at the age of 17.

On 18th December, Barker finished his cross examination of Barry Boettcher. Barker was tired, Tipple said. At one point where Barker was questioning and harping endlessly on just one aspect of the evidence, Brind Woinarski, counsel assisting the Chamberlain team, sighed. Barker thought it was Ken Crispin and spinning round snarled: "There is no need for you to sigh. I have endured you for four days!" Quick as a flash Crispin shot back: "Yes, but not on the same point!" As tired as he was, Barker never lost his sense of humour. As Boettcher walked out of the witness box, Barker leant over to Tipple and said: "I wouldn't know an immunological reaction from a coffee stain!". Tipple walked back to their chambers with a very happy and relieved Boettcher. "It wasn't as bad as the trial," Boettcher said. "At the trial, I sweated so much it formed crystals in my shoes." Tipple remembered how Boettcher's shirt was saturated and how his hands perspired so badly he had to keep wiping them with a handkerchief. "Boettcher kept saying how good it was to be all over and then suddenly he grabbed me and gave me two big bear hugs and through his tears," Tipple said. "He said, 'Thank you, thank you.' Here he was thanking me when he more than any one had given so much to achieve the victory we would finally savour."

At Christmas, Tipple received a letter from Greg and Sally Lowe: "Those of us who have been swept through the stream of life via floods, dams, droughts, underground cave-ins, super-tides, anything else you like to name – pay homage. Sincere thanks for your perseverance, prolonged insight, thorough research and identification of barriers. May never see you again but nothing comes your way from us but admiration. If justice prevails above the law, shall raise a toast of orange juice to you."

The year came to a quiet close but it was a far more joyful occasion than the 12 months that had preceded it. When 1987 arrived, the Chamberlains had their tails up. This was an inquiry not bound by formal rules of evidence and procedure. Now there was an experienced jurist with access to all the facts. But Barker and his team had their brief to execute, and did so diligently. They got wind that Michael Chamberlain had a private diary and subpoenaed it. Tipple made an entry in his diary for 23rd January that he had to drive to Cooranbong and go through Michael Chamberlain's private papers, with two royal commission officers in attendance. Michael, he noted, was very upset about this extraordinary intrusion into his private life. "I talked to him as being a hell of an experience and found it difficult to stop tears filling my eyes as I thought of the tremendous effort, loss of enjoyment of life and physical damage to all of us," Tipple wrote. "Lindy was talking throughout the search. She kept sharing everything and a lot of it was totally unnecessarily. It took twice as long as it should have. By the end we were all fed up with the Crown wanting this stuff and the fact we had wasted time getting it."

On 28th January 1987, James Cameron, travelling from England to give evidence at the royal commission, was subdued but obstinate. He said he had been wrong in saying there was a bloodied handprint on the baby's jumpsuit. He agreed that the handprints comprised red dust. He had assumed the staining was blood because Scott, had tested the jumpsuit and found it had blood staining. He had not known that Scott had found bloodstaining around the neck and sleeve areas but not on the torso. Cameron said he had relied on what Kenneth Brown had told him. His fluorescent photography had indicated to him that there had been a full handprint on the left shoulder and a partial handprint on the right shoulder. He had not checked with Dr Scott because of distance problems. Cameron agreed that even if he had tested the stained area it could not be relied on because of the age of the staining. But he had gone on to talk about bloodied handprints. How scientific was that? When Winneke's examination had finished, Barker asked Cameron: "Now is there anything that you have heard ...". He was in the process of asking the the same question that he had asked at the trial, when Cameron had said nothing he had heard in the trial had changed his view. Cameron's answer at the trial seemed to have a decisive effect, but Winneke was not going to let this happen again. Cameron did answer in the negative but his answer was overshadowed by Winneke's strong objection. And now, the negative answer carried no weight.

There was now too much doubt about Cameron's evidence, and that really removed the last plank from the Crown case. The multi-stranded rope that had made up the Crown case, was no more. If the handprints on the jumpsuit were in fact handprints – and that was increasingly unlikely – then it meant absolutely nothing because it was not blood. The jumpsuit could have been picked up by someone with dusty hands at any time. A suggestion by the Crown lawyers that the baby had been killed somewhere other than in the car got short shrift. Morling said the entire crown case had been centred on the car and that was where it would have to remain.

With the tide flowing well towards the Chamberlains, the media was climbing on board to get more interviews. On 11th February 1986 Bob Cameron, who was bureau chief of *New Idea*, telegrammed Tipple asking him to consider an appropriate fee for an interview with Lindy Chamberlain, following a letter from the chairperson and chief executive, Dulcie Boling, proposing the interview.

Ken Crispin, who was of a literary bent, and was writing a book, Crown versus Chamberlain, became amused by the lawyers representing the Crown, who were apparently under instructions to defend the Crown's position. He took note of the efforts of Michael Adams QC, who had focused on the blood evidence, and wrote a ditty, *Ode to Adams*:

> *The expositor of blood flew into the fray, made himself ready to be carried away / Swept into court to answer the call and exhume the Crown case Joy Kuhl and all.*
>
> "It's outrageous to say that her test was a dud/ for no better reason than it showed paint was blood
>
> If they murdered the kid to cause us confusion, they probably gave it a paint transfusion.
>
> "The serum's no good we're obliged to confess/ and the records are in one hell of a mess.
>
> The samples are dubious the tests make you puke but how do you know they weren't right by a fluke?
>
> True the bloodstain that came from her hand now turns out to be eighty per cent sand / But it isn't fair of these quibbles to linger a fifth of a handprint still leaves one finger!
>
> The dingo is innocent! That's what they say! And damned if we'll let facts get in the way!
>
> The accuracy of our experts is anyone's guess But if she weren't guilty the dingo would confess!"

It is, of course, easy to mock the opposition when it is at a disadvantage. Adams, who would go on to become a NSW Supreme Court judge, was only executing a brief and within the limitations of his instructions was his normal proficient self. Crispin, who was later to go onto the bench himself, knew that no counsel should ever be personally identified with his brief, or with his client, and Crispin's *Ode to Adams* amounted to just a dig. The real problem lay with those giving the instructions. The Chamberlains, so long on the receiving end, were happy enough to see the discomfort of others. Tipple noted in his diary that on 5th February 1987, Morling wanted to know whether Lindy Chamberlain would be giving evidence, but in error asked John Winneke: "Will Mrs Winneke be giving evidence?" Winneke replied: "My wife is more guilty than Mrs Chamberlain." Then, referring to Errol Simper, covering the case for *The Australian,* whose coverage of the case had not endeared him to the Chamberlain team, he said "I make an immediate application that my remarks not be reported by Mr Simper". Tipple recorded: "Malcolm Brown on his way out rubbed his hands together and with a glint in his eye said to me, 'That application does not include me!'"

On 12th February, Tipple noted in his diary that as he arrived at the court, he heard the raucous laughter of John Winneke coming down the corridor. "When I went in there, I saw he was reading Michael's diary that had been produced under the Crown's subpoena. Winneke had said: "It is nice to see yourself as others see you." Winneke then read Tipple the diary entry Michael Chamberlain had made after their first meeting: "Winneke on first impressions was a friendly, mild-mannered man. He reminded me a little of a benevolent ferret." Winneke laughed again before observing: "And Michael wonders why people don't think he's the full quid."

On 3rd March, Tipple recorded how Malcolm Brown turned up in an ill-fitting safari suit with rolled-up shirt sleeves protruding. When Tipple asked him: "Where did you get that suit, Malcolm?" Brown replied: "My father-in-law just died and I'm wearing his clothes." Tipple recorded: "He told me that the night before he was woken by a young man knocking at his door at 2 am. The man introduced himself as the night manager and wanted the TV for a family that had just booked in. Malcolm had said, 'Take it and get out'. Next morning inquiries revealed that there was no night manager. The real night manager had left at 10 pm. Neither the person claiming to be the night manager nor the TV were ever seen again." Brown reported the theft to the police, who were delighted that he had been shown up as such a chump. News of it went around Darwin and some NT Police even rang interstate newspapers to ensure it was reported. Brown was taunted mercilessly, and when one lawyer came to him and made an order for a television set, Brown snapped, at least verbally. When Lindy heard about it, she gave Brown heaps too. Of course, having been incarcerated with toughened convicted criminals, she had developed her own street cunning. Brown was going to say: "Well, I don't have the benefit of your extensive criminal experience!" But he held his tongue. She was no criminal, but Lindy was most happy to celebrate's Brown's misfortune. In her book, saying that from one perspective he was the seasoned reporter –"been there, done that"– but from another just a naïve little boy from the backblocks. And that is fair enough. Any reporter, sitting in judgement on others, recording meticulously all their travails, must be prepared to cop it sweet when his own turn comes.

On 7th March, Tipple, disengaging himself from such an amusing diversion, noted in his diary that he had discussed final submissions with John Winneke. Chester Porter was not critical of the police and had pointed out that the police had not tried to "verbal" the Chamberlains, Tipple had observed: "They could hardly verbal them. To come up with a verbal, they would have to say how they did it, which was impossible.

Tipple and Winneke surmised that Morling was not going to criticise the police and it would be a mistake to begin their submissions seeking that finding and was better left for the end.

Ken Crispin pointed out the Crown would now have to say: "We have not got a cause of death, we have not got a place of death, and all they could put to Lindy Chamberlain was that 'somehow, somewhere in the world you killed your daughter'." The Chamberlains told the royal commission that with them at Ayers Rock had been a water bottle, an esky and they and a serrated vegetable knife. They also had with them a small spade. This was not known to the police at the time of the search. Had they become aware, each item would have been forensically examined and, who knows, Joy Kuhl might have found foetal haemoglobin on them. When the Sydney *Sun-Herald* reported this on 15th March, some radio shock jocks in Sydney said words to the effect: "Ah ha! The esky! That's how they did it! That is where they put the body!" But such bigoted attitudes could now, at least in this case, be consigned to history.

The Crown made final submissions but Barker, utterly dismayed by the collapse of the forensic evidence upon which he had built the Crown case, was resigned to the inevitable. When Adams finished his own submissions, Barker said to him: "Michael, you are putting in more passion than conviction." Tipple recorded later events in his diary. Winneke finished his submissions at 12.30 pm on 19th March 1987, the occasion of his 49th birthday. After the submissions, Cliff and Avis Murchison came and warmly thanked the team. "By chance or design, I was the last to be thanked," Tipple said. "Avis extended her hand and I brushed it aside and embraced her. Her voice broke as she said, 'Thank you... thank you'. Cliff came up and we embraced and his voice broke as he said, 'You were the kingpin'. Nice words but this was never a one-man band. My mind raced back to the beginning of the fight back, to Patricia Fleming's tuition, the crafting of the Kuhl cross examination with Andrew Kirkham, and then the herculean efforts of Boettcher, Smith and Chapman." The note concluded: "It's been a wonderful effort but, will it be good enough to stop a tragedy like this happening again?"

Morling had no choice but to exonerate the Chamberlains. On 22nd May 1987, he presented his 390-page report to the Governor-General before flying to Darwin where he presented his report to the Administrator on 25th May. Attorney-General Daryl Manzie said the report would be released on 2nd June. Tipple asked for an advance copy. The request was denied. "I was advised that I would have to go to Sydney to attend the office of the Commission's solicitors and be locked up with the report two hours before it was tabled in the Northern Territory Legislative Assembly," he said. Morling found that the presence of baby's blood in the car and on the Chamberlains' possessions found in the car had not been demonstrated. "Taken in its entirety, the evidence falls far short of proving that there was any blood in the car for which there was not an innocent explanation," he said. "The evidence at the trial was that there was baby's blood on a towel, a chamois and its container found in the car and the camera bag which had been in the car. I am satisfied that the presence of baby's blood or any blood on these articles has not been established."

Of the under-dash spray, Morling said: "There is compelling evidence that the spray was made up of a sound-deadening compound and there was no blood at all. The new evidence casts similar doubt on the reliability of other evidence that there was baby's blood on some of the contents of the car. With the benefit of hindsight, it is unfortunate that the defence did not become aware of the chemical composition of the spray on the metal plate removed from under the dash of a Torana car similar to the one owned by the Chamberlains. If this had been ascertained, it seems likely that the defence would have been alerted to the possibility that all findings of blood relied upon by the Crown would have been suspect ... The evidence leads me to conclude that if there was any blood in the car, it was present only in small quantities in the area of the hinge of the passenger's seat and beneath. It has not been established that any such blood was Azaria's. The blood shed by Mr Lenehan could well have been the source of blood in that area."

Morling dealt with the cut-throat theory advanced by Cameron. "In the light of new evidence, the opinion expressed by Professor Cameron at the trial that the pattern of blood staining on the jumpsuit was consistent only with a cut throat cannot be safely adopted, nor can it be concluded from the pattern of blood staining on the clothing that that the baby's throat was cut by a blade," he said. "Professor Cameron's evidence that there was a handprint in blood on the back of the jumpsuit has been weakened, if not totally destroyed, by new evidence that what was thought to be was blood on the back of the jumpsuit was, in fact, red sand."

Of Cameron's judgement that a dingo was not involved in the attack, Morling said Cameron had strayed beyond his field of expertise. "With the benefit of hindsight, it can be seen that some of the experts who gave evidence were over-confident of their ability to form reliable opinions on matters that lay on the outer margins of their fields of experience," he said. He put the onus of responsibility for what amounted to a disaster in the legal system squarely on the shoulders of the Crown forensic experts. He disagreed with the contention by the Chamberlains' lawyers that the way the NT police had conducted the investigation had prejudiced the trial. "I am not persuaded they did," he said. "The great difficulties for the defence arose out of the scientific evidence and the police cannot be held responsible for that."

Morling then addressed evidence of the dingo attack, on the night Azaria disappeared. "Although Azaria's clothing might have been buried, the quantity and distribution of sand on it may well have been a result of it having been dragged through sand," he said. "The type and variety of vegetation on the jumpsuit was more consistent with it having been dragged through vegetation, rather than buried, dug up and placed at the base of Ayers Rock. Head ranger Derek Roff's evidence was that he had tracked a dingo carrying a load and that had been corroborated by an Aboriginal blacktracker, Mr Minyintiri. The Crown's expert has conceded that hairs found in the tent and on the jumpsuit which were said at the trial to be probably cat hairs and canine hairs. Dog hairs are indistinguishable from dingo hairs. The Chamberlains had not owned a dog for some time prior to August 1980."

Morling had requested Ward and McNicol to provide all the evidence they had to support the "Ding Conspiracy Theory". After reviewing it, Morling described it as "extremely tenuous", and determined that it did not make even the semblance of a case and did not support the allegations. But Tipple was surprised that Morling did not give more weight to the Aboriginal trackers' evidence. "Morling really dismissed their evidence," Tipple said. "That really reinforced the judgement that Phillips and Kirkham made in the first place not to call them for the trial." Of the damage to the jumpsuit, Morling said: "It cannot be concluded beyond reasonable doubt that the damage to it was caused by scissors or a knife, or that it was not caused by the teeth of a canid." He said there was no reason to believe that Azaria was not wearing the matinee jacket on the night she disappeared. The fact that she was in the matinee jacket made more explicable the lack of dingo saliva on the jumpsuit. Of the state of the clothing when found, Morling said: "While Mr Roff did not consider the state of the clothing was inconsistent with dingo activity, Dr Corbett and Dr Newsome were of the view that it would have been scattered had a dingo removed Azaria from it. The evidence affords considerable support for the view that a dingo may have taken her. To examine the evidence to see whether it is provided that a dingo took Azaria would make the fundamental error of reversing the onus of proof and requiring the Chamberlains to prove their innocence."

Morling reverted to pure common sense. He observed if Lindy had done all those dreadful things attributed to her in that supposed 11-minute window of opportunity, what about Aidan? He said that if Lindy had taken the baby to the car with the intention of murdering her, she would not have been likely to have taken Aidan with her. All the things she would have been required to do to carry out the murder were inconsistent with her having returned to the campsite in a calm demeanour with Aidan. One question Morling did ask from the bench was whether any of the children were afraid of their mother. There was no evidence that they were. Morling said: "I am far from persuaded that Mrs Chamberlain's account of having seen a dingo near the tent was false or that Michael Chamberlain falsely denied that he knew his wife had murdered his daughter. I do not think any jury could properly convict them on the evidence as it now appears." He concluded: "It follows from what I have written that there are serious doubts and questions as to the Chamberlains' guilt and as to the evidence in the trial leading to their conviction. In my opinion, if the evidence before the commission had been given at the trial, the trial judge would have been obliged to direct the jury to acquit the Chamberlains on the grounds that the evidence could not justify their conviction."

On the day of the report's release on 2nd June 1987, it was confirmed the Administrator of the Northern Territory had exercised the prerogative of the Crown and granted pardons to Michael and Lindy Chamberlain. But Tipple was not prepared to accept that, because a pardon amounted to forgiveness for what someone was supposed to have done. Tipple said: "I advised the Chamberlains not to accept these pardons because they were entitled to an acquittal to wipe away their convictions and restore their presumption of innocence."

Manzie circulated a 32-page speech to journalists before he tabled the Morling Report in the Northern Territory Legislative Assembly. The circulated speech said: "The Commissioner does not exonerate the Chamberlains ... his report is not a proclamation of their innocence". But Manzie realised, or had it pointed out to him, that that was wrong. He took that sentence out when he addressed the Assembly. He later explained he had omitted that sentence because, "you have to accept the fact that there is a presumption of innocence". But it had been too late to delete the sentence from the circulated speech or inform the officials conducting the lock-up. Tipple complained about the way Manzie handled the release. "In keeping with the established tradition of informing the media before the Chamberlains, the media was given access to the report one hour before it was available to me," he said. "My protest about that was ignored."

Tipple had won, if not the entire war, then so much of it that the rest really did now amount to mopping-up. On 10th June, the *Sydney Morning Herald* published a letter from W.J.Walsh, law lecturer at the Mitchell College of Advanced Education, as it then was, in Bathurst. Walsh said: "Congratulations are in order for a relatively small country practice of solicitors, Brennan, Blair and Tipple, of Gosford – the Chamberlains' solicitors. In particular, Stuart Tipple deserves the highest commendation for professional competence, tenacity and commitment over a long period and, at times, seemingly impossible odds."

Joy Kuhl, James Cameron, Malcolm Chaikin, Simon Baxter, Kenneth Brown and others whose evidence was important to the prosecution were able to walk away. It was a case they could have done without.

The NT Police and Government had their noses properly out of joint. What had the police done wrong? Morling said they hadn't. What had the lawyers done wrong? Nothing. They had vigorously pursued their briefs. Their reliance on the seemingly top-notch forensic science experts had been their undoing. Part of Ian Barker's brief had been the competence and credibility of Joy Kuhl, which he had been obliged to uphold. Now, that credibility was in tatters. In an informal discussion, someone suggested that it would have all been simpler if the Chamberlains had been out in the Timor Sea in a boat and it was alleged a shark had taken the baby. "Oh, don't worry about that!" Barker retorted. "We could rely on Joy Kuhl to find foetal haemoglobin in the seawater."

CHAPTER FIFTEEN

A TORTURED CONCLUSION

"

[There was] no suggestion that $25 million of public money would be wasted to ultimately conclude what Aboriginal trackers, Nipper Winmatti and Nui Mintinyiri, had told police within hours of the tragedy.
– Lowell Tarling

We spent a total of 360 days in court. There were 18,500 pages of transcript. To put Lindy in jail cost $25 million of taxpayers' money. And the Azaria Chamberlain case dominated my life for at least a decade.
– Michael Chamberlain

The demolition of the Chamberlains' convictions, which had been upheld by both appeal courts – and in doing so exposed some dreadful flaws in the justice system – had major implications. Not only had the Chamberlains lost their beloved baby in these horrifying circumstances, but the entire system had combined to tear them apart, to overlook the evidence of people who had been there on the night and to fall back on what emerged almost as black magic. The principal forensic scientists called on by the Crown, Cameron, Kuhl, Chaikin and others, had failed. They had gone beyond their expertise, arrogantly insisting that it was within their expertise. The justice system had bowed before them, brushing aside the primary evidence, and relied on their judgements. Given the advantage enjoyed by prosecuting authorities from dealing with government-run forensic laboratories, there was now intense scrutiny of forensic laboratories throughout the nation. What about giving defence lawyers equal access to the same laboratories? And what about the quality of the science itself?

Dr Malcolm Simons, a medical scientist, told Tipple: "It is pleasing that the role of Forensic Scientists is coming under scrutiny in the aftermath of the case. Hopefully, this will result in new standards of performance. The advent of DNA technologies is likely to be introduced earlier, and have a greater role in future forensic investigations. The absence of any DNA in the putative blood stains might have changed the course of the Prosecution's argument."

Royal Commissioner Trevor Morling's finding in June 1987 was a great burden lifted from the shoulders of Michael and Lindy Chamberlain. It should have followed, given the strength of Morling's finding, that the convictions would be quashed and verdicts of acquittal entered. After sustained pressure from Tipple on the 24th September 1987, the NT House of Assembly voted unanimously to allow the Chamberlains to appeal to the NT Appeals Court to have their convictions struck from the records. On 21st October, the Northern Territory Government amended its Criminal Code by adding section 433A, which then allowed the Attorney-General to refer the matter to the NT Court of Criminal Appeal, with the power to strike out the convictions. The amendment gave the Court very wide powers and allowed it to accept the findings of a commission of inquiry such as the Morling Royal Commission or to make its own inquiries as an investigative tribunal.

It seemed likely that the Chamberlains would succeed in such an appeal. How could the convictions be allowed to stand after a finding like Morling's? But even if this came about, there were other, more intangible effects of the dreadful ordeal, which would not be dealt with in any easy manner. In a letter to Tipple on 15th December 1987, Pastor George Rollo, who with the consent of the church had conducted a number of interviews with Michael and Lindy Chamberlain, expressed pessimism. The whole experience, the journey from naivety to worldly wisdom had been thrust upon them by "a tragic mishandling of the law", he said. The outside turmoil had been reflected in the inner workings of the Chamberlain family. The conflicts and problems in the lives of the children had serious implications for their future development. Rollo urged the Northern Territory Government to admit its error, pay compensation and let the Chamberlain family try to make a future for themselves. "They will never ever be the family they might have been had this tragic event with its legal bungling not occurred," he said. "The mishandling of the law is to blame. The system should pay."

In 1988, Michael and Lindy Chamberlain applied to the NT Supreme Court to have their convictions quashed. The Northern Territory Government, in a decision regarded by many as churlish, opted to oppose the application. It retained the services of Michael Adams QC, who was to represent the NT Attorney General. In the hearing, Adams submitted that the court should not accept the royal commissioner's conclusions. One of Adams' instructing solicitors told Malcolm Brown that Morling's finding was "only the finding of one tribunal", implying that another tribunal would not have made a decision favourable to the Chamberlains. Brown found it an odd statement. "How many tribunals do you need?" he asked. "Can a judgement of the High Court of Australia be dismissed because it is only one tribunal?" After Adams completed his submissions, Winneke tendered a copy of the official pardons granted to the Chamberlains. Given that these pardons had been issued on the advice of the Government, he said, there was little else that needed to be said.

In late August, while this latest hassle was being sorted out, the Ward saga was coming to an end. Griffin Press, which had published Ward's book, *Azaria ! What the Jury Were NOT Told*, and a number of newspapers that had repeated some of the book's contents, made an out-of-court settlement with the seven litigants. The settlement was said to have totalled $500,000. Terry Mahoney, general manager of Griffin Press, said $500,000 was not the correct amount, but that Griffin Press had lost "a significant amount", and the press had learned a harsh lesson about responsibility for a defamation.

Michael Chamberlain, in his book, *Beyond Azaria, Black Light/White Light* paid tribute to Ward. He said: "Not everybody got it 100 percent right – but there's a passage in the Bible that says, 'Love covers a multitude of sins', and I'd like to reinterpret it and say, 'enthusiasm' or 'passion' to cover a multitude of errors. And this is where Phil Ward comes in because, even if he didn't always get it quite right, there's no one who could have had a bigger heart during this case than Phil Ward. He would have thrown everything at this case to win for us. I'm sorry about his personal life where certain stresses about this time caused him and his family to suffer a bit."

On 15 September, the NT Court of Criminal Appeal upheld the Chamberlains' appeal and quashed their convictions. Chief Justice Austin Asche said: "I would not therefore agree with the submissions on behalf of the Attorney-General that we should so substantially differ from the findings of the Commissioner [Justice Morling] as to conclude that the material he relies on is not sufficient to support the conclusion ... that 'there are serious doubts and questions as to the Chamberlains' guilt'. That conclusion is clearly open to the Commissioner and, in my view, follows from the material he has assessed. In those circumstances, the only way in which this court could challenge that conclusion would be to examine anew the whole of the material before the Commissioner including in that exercise the calling of witnesses. Having regard to the view I have just expressed that the conclusion expressed by the Commissioner is appropriate on the material before him, that would be a fruitless and unjustified exercise".

Justice John Nader said: "In my opinion, upon consideration of the adopted findings, there is a real possibility Mrs Chamberlain did not murder Azaria and therefore the convictions of the Chamberlains ought to be quashed and verdicts and judgments of acquittal entered. Not to do so would be unsafe and would allow an unacceptable risk of perpetrating a miscarriage of justice ... I have expressed the opinion that doubt exists as to the guilt of Mrs Chamberlain. I would categorize that doubt as a grave doubt. The doubt has arisen as a result of considering fresh evidence, in particular, the findings of the Commission. It is the existence of that doubt that demands the quashing of the convictions and the verdicts and judgments I propose. The convictions having been wiped away, the law of the land holds the Chamberlains to be innocent. Accordingly, I would quash the convictions of Alice Lynne Chamberlain and Michael Leigh Chamberlain and enter verdicts and judgments of acquittal."

It was seemingly the end of the line. There was again well-deserved kudos for Tipple. John Bryson, the author of *Evil Angels*, said in a telegram to Tipple: "A long race but you lasted the distance and won. Personally and professionally I salute you."

There were some not insignificant ends to be tied up, principally what everything had cost and what was still to be paid. The case had cost the NT Government an estimated $20 million, meeting its own bills and portion of the Chamberlains' costs. Added to that was the potential payout to the Chamberlains as compensation. The Chamberlains had been carried by a long-term loan from the SDA church, supplemented by contributions from the SDA laity. The church was requested to calculate what it was owed and did so. The expenses were reimbursed by the NT Government.

On 16th September 1988, the *NT News*, whose views in the past had stridently reflected the NT Government's view that the integrity of the legal system was being attacked, said in an editorial that there had been little option but to quash the Chamberlains' convictions, because of "fundamental doubts" about the convictions, amply proved in the Morling Report. "And this simply means that Mrs Chamberlain should not have been sent to jail and the family should not have had to endure the agony of separation as well as the eight years of tragic publicity," the paper said. The *NT News* said the legal expenses had to be paid, and then the more difficult question of compensation for pain and suffering. "No doubt it will be expensive, but this is the price we pay for a system of justice on which our freedoms depend." The paper said that "hopefully this unhappy episode can then be put to rest."

Three days later, the *Sydney Morning Herald* said: "The quashing of the convictions against Lindy and Michael Chamberlain by the Northern Territory Court of Criminal Appeal has been described as proof that our legal system works. The opposite is true. The Chamberlains finally received justice despite the system. The saga of the Chamberlains' quest for justice showed that once the system gets something wrong, it can be incredibly difficult to turn things around. The people in control of the legal system begin to believe the system has to be defended rather than the rights of the individual it is intended to serve."

Michael and Lindy busied themselves with the production of *Evil Angels*, the film being produced about the case. They both spoke with Meryl Streep, who was to play Lindy. The session prompted Meryl to change her style completely, from being the innocent, bewildered young woman caught up in something beyond her comprehension, to a far more robust, tough woman that Lindy had become. Streep noted that when she walked along a Melbourne street with Lindy, everyone noticed Lindy but did not recognize her.

But someone did see the link between the two. When the rumours started Lindy had received a card with a black bootie in it. When Meryl arrived for rehearsal in Australia, she received a card and bootie identical to those sent to Lindy. The card said: "With love on My Birthday. Dear Mummy, from Me. I hope you will be as happy as happy can be."

Evil Angels, directed by Fred Schepisi and starring Sam Neill as Michael Chamberlain, premiered in Sydney and later opened in Darwin on 3rd November 1990 to a packed house. It was screened throughout Australia and would open in the United States with a different name, *A Cry In the Dark*, instead of *Evil Angels* which would have suggested to Americans it was a film about bikies.

Michael McHugh QC, then a High Court judge, wrote to Tipple after seeing the movie. Thanking him for his card congratulating him on his appointment, he said: "As I am sure I have told you before, I regard you as one of the two or three best solicitors I have seen in practice". He said he and his wife had seen *Evil Angels* but he felt it lacked "a real sense of drama". "Perhaps my reaction was knowing in advance every word which would be uttered and every scene which was about to happen," he said. "However, one thing that did come across very strongly was the darkness of the camping area on the fatal night. It showed how difficult it would be for Mrs Chamberlain to have killed and buried Azaria and later recovered the body as the Crown contends."

But there was still work for Tipple to do. The principal question was the right the Chamberlains had to compensation. One point of view was that the Chamberlains were not entitled to anything. The legal system had to operate and it would be a poor situation if the community faced the prospect of paying out massive damages every time the justice system got it wrong. But there were extraordinary features of this case. On 24th November 1990, Tipple wrote to Daryl Manzie: "No amount of money can compensate the Chamberlains for what they have suffered. The Chamberlains are not greedy or grasping people and have naturally relied on their legal advisers to properly assess what is a reasonable compensation claim not only taking into account what they have suffered but to also ensure they can establish their independence and rehabilitation.

Tipple said: "Although no counterpart legislation has been enacted in the Northern Territory or indeed within Australia all Governments should adhere to the principle enounced. We are not aware of a single instance where any person having received a pardon has not received an *ex-gratia* compensation payment. Following becoming bound by this covenant the United Kingdom carried out a review of compensation procedures. In 1985 the United Kingdom Home Secretary appointed an independent Queen's Counsel to assess proper compensation in such cases and for such assessment to be binding on the Government. There will no doubt be an irresponsible element in our community which will argue that the Chamberlains should not receive any compensation. However, the proper view, that is, that the Chamberlains should receive compensation, has been expressed in editorials in all of Australia's leading newspapers and was no more elegantly put than in an editorial which appeared on 16th September 1988 in the *NT News*."

More books came out, including Dr Norman Young's account of the fight for justice, *Innocence Regained*. Then in 1990 came Lindy's book was published by Penguin Books, *Through My Eyes,* a graphic and spirited account of her experience.

The shockwaves of the Chamberlain case continued through the legal system. Developed in Britain over centuries and implanted in Australia, taking up the careers of some of the finest minds, it had been intensively studied and refined and set with safeguards. There was an inbuilt uncertainty. If one person says one thing and the other the opposite, there must be some way of deciding which is right. The great control was that there had to be a verdict "beyond reasonable doubt". The traditional catchcry was: "It is better that 10 guilty men go free than an innocent man be convicted." But the innocents were convicted, in the face of what, even at the time of conviction, was reasonable doubt. The judge saw the doubt, the jury did not. Chester Porter, commenting on the Chamberlain case, was quoted in July 1990 saying that the prospect of an innocent person being convicted "could easily happen again". He said nothing had changed since the case. He was critical of the judicial system and the gathering of forensic evidence in Australia. Morling's call for a National Institute of Forensic Science had been ignored. "The main reason the Chamberlains were convicted was because of bungled forensic evidence," he said. And the evidence needed for a court of criminal appeal to reach an acquittal was too stringent.

The Chamberlian case was to go down in history. The National Library of Austraia began collecting all documents and everything else connected with the case, including the car that had taken the Chamberlain family to Ayers Rock. The case was to become instructive, no doubt for future generations, including law students, as an object lesson on how badly a legal system can malfunction.

In the meantime, in the aftermath of the Chamberlans' exoneration, others claiming to have been wrongly convicted spoke up and two of them contacted Stuart Tipple. One was Douglas Harry Rendell. In 1979, Rendell had had a row with his de facto wife in Broken Hill. She had produced a rifle and the rifle had discharged, killing her. Rendell was convicted of manslaughter and spent more than eight years in gaol before being released on parole. He sought and obtained a judicial inquiry into his conviction. It emerged in the inquiry that police had suppressed vital evidence: the tendency of the rifle to discharge accidentally. Rendell was exonerated and wanted compensation. His case was taken up personally by Barry Boettcher, who for a period had Rendell living at his home. Tipple handled Rendell's case and was successful. The NSW Attorney-General, Jack Hannaford, sent Tipple a letter telling him the NSW Government would make a $100,000 ex-gratia payment. Rendell would carry on, living in the bush, with a girlfriend beside him, riding horses, till one day he was kicked savagely by a horse, which injured him so badly that he died. Barry Boettcher and Malcolm Brown attended his funeral.

The other lost soul who turned to Tipple was Alexander Lindsay, formerly Alexander McLeod-Lindsay, who had been convicted for the attempted murder of his wife in 1964. The critical evidence, about blood spatter on the wall matching blood spatter on his jacket, the subject of expert opinion, was critical in his conviction. McLeod-Lindsay served nine years in prison. By the time he was released, the science of blood spatter analysis had moved on and it was now possible to cast extreme doubt on the previous expert evidence. Lindsay, who with his new wife, Valda, turned up at hearings of the Morling Royal Commission. They asked Malcolm Brown to take up his case editorially, which he did. McLeod-Lindsay did get a judicial inquiry and in the light of new evidence about blood spatter, it was concluded there was too much doubt about his guilt. He was acquitted. But getting compensation was a drawn-out process. When they got it, Lindsay and his wife drifted off into their own private lives. But the pall of conviction and imprisonment never went away. Brown went to interview him, and even the blue trousers of the *Herald* driver were enough to agitate him because they were the same colour worn by the prison officers over those purgatorial years. McLeod-Lindsay and his wife died in obscurity, within a short time of each other.

The personal lives of Michael and Lindy had continued to disintegrate. Michael lost his ministerial credentials while Lindy was still in prison. Lindy hoped things had improved but sadly shortly after her release she discovered they had not. Divorce was inevitable. When Malcolm Brown heard of the divorce proceedings, he broke the story. Michael said: "You'll pay for this! You think you're God, don't you, crashing into people's lives like this!" When the *Herald* hit the streets, News Ltd formed a task force in the early hours of the morning to carry the story, and rang Michael Chamberlain's father in New Zealand, who protested he had not been informed, and cried out: "Just give me a chance to talk to my son!" On 27th June 1991, the divorce between Michael and Lindy Chamberlain became final. Kahlia chose to live with Michael and visit Lindy. Reagan stayed with Lindy and Aidan opted to split his time between the two houses. Lindy Chamberlain strongly objected to what she saw as a suggestion that she was responsible for the break-up of the marriage. That was not so, she said. Years later Stuart Tipple, though mindful of the need not to denigrate a former client, who was now not in a position to stand up for himself, said that Lindy Chamberlain had "perfectly valid reasons" for wanting to divorce Michael. Lindy said she would not mind all the facts coming out, if the rest of the family agreed to that. But the family did not.

On 16th July 1991, the government announced that it had paid the SDA Church $395,500 to compensate for legal expenses paid out on behalf of the Chamberlains. In calculating the amount, the NT Government had deducted what it had calculated was the money received from donations and media and refused to pay any accrued interest. That was still not compensation for pain and suffering. Tipple had called for an independent arbitrator to assess the

Chamberlains' claim. The delay continued, to Tipple's increased annoyance. Tipple had a letter published in the *Sydney Morning Herald* on 26th September saying there was something wrong with the legal system that failed to provide a right to compensation for someone who had been wrongfully convicted and gaoled. It was reported on 6th November 1991 that the Chamberlains might complain directly to the United Nations about pain they had suffered in delays in compensation since 1987, when they were exonerated. It was possible because of the First Optional Protocol to the First International Covenant on Civil and Political Rights. The Chamberlains could have complained directly to the United Nations Human Rights Committee. Tipple studied that option. The UN Human Rights Committee had no power to compel a government to pay money. But Australia was bound by Article 14 (6) of the UN Covenant on Civil and Political Rights, which stated that if a miscarriage of justice had occurred, then subject to certain conditions, the individual "shall be compensated according to law". The NT Government finally acted, and appointed Justice Morling, who had conducted the royal commission, to assess compensation for Michael and Lindy Chamberlain.

Coincidentally, another controversial case was being wrapped up in New South Wales with a grant of compensation. On 16th November 1991, the NSW Government announced it had compensated former police superintendent Harry Blackburn for wrongful arrest, malicious prosecution and defamation, following his arrest in 1989 for a series of offences including assault and rape. The Royal Commission that followed, under Justice Jack Lee, had revealed an appalling performance by some of the investigating police, who made no proper identification of Blackburn as the perpetrator. Blackburn, it turned out, had had nothing to do with any of it. But after his arrest he was charged and publicly paraded for the media. Fortunately, a competent police inspector, Clive Small, reviewed the evidence, stopped the process in its tracks and the charges were withdrawn. After the royal commission, Tony Lauer, who was NSW Police Commissioner at the time of Blackburn's arrest, told Malcolm Brown that the credentials of the investigating police "looked good on paper". So had the credentials of Professor Cameron and Joy Kuhl when the Northern Territory Police, dissatisfied with the findings of the first coroner's inquest, had turned to them. The Blackburn family suffered dreadfully from a hopelessly unprofessional performance. In all probability, it was the cause of both Blackburn's wife and his daughter-in-law miscarrying. At least the prosecution process in Blackburn's case had been nipped in the bud. If only there had been a Clive Small in the Chamberlain case who would have intervened when the

Cameron Report landed on the NT Government's desk, and asked searching questions.

With their convictions quashed and their marriage over, Michael and Lindy Chamberlain set out to make new lives for themselves. Lindy, keen to make ends meet and support her family accepted speaking tours in the United States where, in February 1992, she met a business manager, Rick Creighton. On 19th May that year, they became engaged. Six days later, the NT Government announced it was to compensate the Chamberlains for pain and suffering, the amount to be kept confidential. The response to the report of compensation was generally positive but not universal. The reports on the royal commission had inevitably swayed the bulk of the public. But one group, describing itself as "10 Seventh-day Adventists", was to send a postcard saying: "The money you are receiving is blood money! Both of you are guilty, as God is your judge will eventually be found so". The other side of the card showed a dingo with a dictionary definition, finishing with the word: "They feed on kangaroos, wallabies and rabbits", to which the correspondent added: "NOT BABIES". Another letter said: "Mummy this is Azaria talking to you while you are telling all those lies. You know you killed me. I am going to haunt you for the rest of your life. You are a greedy person you didn't want me but to blame a dingo you undressed me remember if I was you I'd leave the country or are you going to lend a hand to all the starving in the world? No, you are too selfish. It's not being in jail that made you skinny and ugly. It's what you did to me. Love, Azaria."

On 20th December, Rick Creighton and Lindy were married and chose to live in Washington State, USA. On 10th March 1993, Michael announced his engagement to Ingrid Bergner, a divorced mother-of-three, a beautiful blond-haired German-born girl, had migrated to Australia when she was a little girl. She had been divorced in 1989 and studied Education at Avondale College. In April 1993, Lindy was awarded custody of both Kahlia and Reagan, at the request of both children, and they went to live with her and Rick in the United States. A year later, in April 1994, Michael married Ingrid at St John's Uniting Church, Wahroonga. In the process, Michael acquired two grown-up stepsons and a grown-up stepdaughter. Stuart Tipple officiated at the reception in Cessnock.

Lindy's brother, Alex Murchison, said: "I was the only one in the Murchison family who remained friends with Michael. Avis and Cliff would have liked to but they were too close to Lindy for Michael's liking."

Tipple was approached again to act for a man whose life had taken a desperate turn. Graham Gene Potter as it turned out was on much shakier ground than others whose cause Tipple had taken up. Potter had been convicted of the murder of Kim Narelle Barry on the NSW south coast in February 1981. Barry's dismembered remains had been discovered and Potter, after disappearing for a period, reappeared and was promptly arrested. He was convicted in April 1982 and sentenced to life imprisonment. Betty Hocking, the justice activist who had been so active in the Chamberlain case, took up Potter's case in the belief there had also been a serious miscarriage of justice. The Potter family asked Malcolm Brown for help and he obliged by interviewing Potter and writing an article in which Potter stated his case that he was innocent. But the evidence against Potter was too strong and the conviction stood. Potter was later released on parole, allegedly got mixed up in drugs, became a police informant and at the time of writing was at large, afraid of what might happen to him at the hands of other criminals if he were ever again incarcerated.

Meanwhile, Michael Chamberlain who had acquired a rural property in the Cooranbong area with a dream that he would build a retreat there and safely spend what was left of his life. Not content with working as an archivist at Avondale College, he decided to write a history of Cooranbong and neighbouring Martinsville and he undertook PhD studies at Newcastle University. He had the book published and Malcolm Brown publicised it. It just happened that the launch was on a Sunday, August 17, coinciding with the day of week and date of year that Azaria disappeared. Malcolm mentioned that in the article, to the utter annoyance of Michael. One of Michael's strong supporters at the university, Professor Ray Waterson, encouraged Michael in his academic endeavours. Chamberlain's thesis, "The Changing role of Ellen White in Seventh-day Adventism with reference to sociological standards at Avondale College", was accepted and in 1992 he was awarded his PhD in Education. He joined the NSW Department of Education and was assigned to a teaching position in Brewarrina, in far western New South Wales.

But there was another loose end that troubled Michael and Lindy. They wanted the finding by coroner Gerry Galvin that Azaria had been murdered struck from the record. They wanted the original coroner's finding, by Denis Barritt, that a dingo had taken the baby, reinstated. They got a new inquest. On 13th December 1995, NT coroner John Lowndes found that neither Michael nor Lindy Chamberlain was responsible for the death of Azaria Chamberlain. However, he did not make a finding that a dingo had taken the baby. His finding was open. It appeared to be an exceedingly cautious finding, and it did not satisfy Michael and Lindy. Some of their friends told them it was not worth worrying about. But to the Chamberlains, whose lives had been blown apart from this case, near enough was not going to be good enough.

In 1996, now a father again – Ingrid having given birth to a daughter, Zahra – Michael took up a teaching position at Gosford High School. In August 1998, Rick and Lindy, now Lindy Chamberlain-Creighton, returned with Kahlia to live in Australia to be closer to Lindy's aging parents, Cliff and Avis Murchison, and to Aidan. For a time, they lived at Cooranbong and then relocated to Mt Vincent, near Cessnock where they lived for a number of years.

On 3rd March 2002, Tipple was invited to be the keynote speaker at "A Celebration of Life", which was a function at Lindy's home to commemorate Azaria's life and to thank the many people who had helped redress the serious injustice that had followed. Most of the primary witnesses and significant supporters were there. It was "an emotional and cathartic day", Tipple said. His speech followed: "As fellow Mariners our journeys connected with Azaria. Her journey was short but significant. We would learn things about ourselves, about others and about our world. Humans are obsessed with memorials. From personalised number plates to pyramids to epitaphs we strive to be recognised, remembered, to stand out from the crowd. Of all of the great things we can do, the achievements, the qualifications, the high office, there is no greater honour, no greater challenge, no better way to be remembered than as a good parent. To lose a child is a terrible loss but to be wrongly accused of killing that child is beyond compare.

"In the extraordinary circumstances surrounding the loss of Azaria, it would be understandable if today was a memorial of recriminations, bitterness and garnished with revenge. I am glad it is not; I wouldn't want to be part of a day like that. You can't take that kind of baggage on a successful life journey, if you have any baggage like that, today is the day to discard it. Our journeys and our time are dominated with the insignificant and the unimportant. Today, we recognize this as being important and have left those everyday things behind. The windows I cleaned this morning will be dirty by the time I get home. The game of golf I could have played is probably a game I would want to forget anyway. Today is important because it is a celebration, a happy day. It is the celebration of Azaria's journey, and our individual journeys. A celebration of how we stood for what we knew to be true, a triumph of right over wrong.

"Now, twenty-one years later, I can finally and truthfully say it was an honour to be part of it. It has been an honour to connect with your journeys. Many words have been spoken and recorded in transcripts, books, and media. All of these words can be summed up in three lines, 'This is the story of a little girl who lived and breathed and loved and was loved, she was part of me, she grew within my body and when she died part of me died and nothing will ever alter that fact'. Now that's a great Epitaph! It is great because the lady who experienced and suffered and wrote those words is able to call us together today to celebrate. It is great because it doesn't end there or even here. Today we can celebrate life and re-focus on that question, 'What is the most important, your journey or your destination?' Let me be bold enough to suggest it's the destination, and the ultimate destination is finding 'the truth'. For without 'the truth', today could never be a celebration."

In October 2002, Sydney saw the extraordinary spectacle of an opera on the case, *Lindy*, performed by Opera Australia, in the Opera House.

If not enough had been learned from the Chamberlain case about the frailties of forensic science, another scandal emerged in Britain which again showed how wrong a forensic expert could be. One Sally Clark claimed two of her babies had died from cot death. That was not accepted and she was charged with their murders following advice from a pathologist, Roy Meadows, on the statistical improbability of the same thing happened twice. Meadows gave his evidence in her trial and she was convicted. Sally was gaoled for life and, like Lindy, was unable to keep her new baby while in custody. After the dismissal of one appeal it emerged that one of the babies had not died from cot death at all but from a bacterial infection. Meadows' statistics were also heavily criticised. The appeal judges said that if the flaws in Meadows' statistic evidence had been "fully argued" at the first appeal, in all probability the appeal would have been allowed. Sally Clark's conviction was overturned in January 2003, and she never recovered from the trauma of losing a baby – in this case two of them – and being convicted, imprisoned and separated from her new baby. She was to die some years later of acute intoxication.

Michael stood as a Liberal candidate for the seat of Macquarie in 2003, and achieved a 5.2 percent swing against the sitting candidate, a good result but not enough to win the seat. Marshall Perron, interviewed by an ABC reporter in November 2004, said it was only alleged that a dingo was involved. Newspapers carrying reports of the interview carried articles headed: "Perron says Lindy Guilty". He did not say that, and the state of the coroner's findings did have a dingo attack only as a possibility. But the world was moving on. In November 2007, Kahlia married. Aidan married in February 2008. In 2010, the eyewitnesses who had all supported the Chamberlains' story gathered together for a reunion in Melbourne.

On 17th August 2010, the NT Attorney-General wrote to Lindy

Chamberlain-Creighton saying she was going to have the registrar look into the "open" finding on Azaria's death certificate. There was some more terrible misfortune to befall Michael Chamberlain. In 2011, Ingrid suffered a devastating stroke which left her bedridden. Michael responded by becoming her full-time carer. It was such appalling setback, but Michael responded stoically and made the plight of full-time carers the subject of academic study. In early 2012, Michael had his own book on the case, *Heart of Stone*, published by New Holland.

Though the wheels of justice moved slowly, there was at least some light at the end of the tunnel when NT Coroner's Elizabeth Morris took submissions in February 2012 in a fourth inquest into the disappearance of Azaria. It was not surprising that Tipple was the last man standing and again representing Michael and Lindy in what he hoped would be the final legal chapter.

On 12th June, Morris handed down her finding that "the cause of her death was as a result of being attacked and taken by a dingo." She sympathized with the Chamberlains for the ordeal they had suffered. The death certificate issued that day stated: "The cause of her death as the result of being attacked and taken by a dingo. Body not recovered."

There was some room for frivolity. Just before midnight on 12th June, newspaper columnist Peter FitzSimons sent an email to Tipple asking about a tie Tipple was wearing that featured a dingo. He said: "Congrats on your win. Where did you get the dingo tie? And why did you wear it? And here is a Miranda Declaration – everything you say can, and will, be used in my column!" Just before 6am the next morning, Tipple replied: "Somehow, I knew you were going to ask me ... and yes there is a good story waiting to be told before I tell you just between us, without prejudice, do you think the tie was tacky or terrific?" Half an hour later, FitzSimons replied: "I think it was Oscar Wildean – right on the edge! Whatever else, it was an interesting choice. But I certainly would not present it as tacky. Just interested in your perspective. Lindy Chamberlain very classy, I thought, in not pursuing damages. And I was fascinated by her awkward hug between her and her former husband." Tipple wrote back at 8.25 am: "Deferring to my wife's sartorial sense of style, I asked her to find a suitable tie. Cherie produced the tie and asked what I thought I recognised at once it was perfect for the occasion. It has proved to be a wonderful litmus test. Those that support Lindy without hesitation love it and those that have reservations are somewhere between your answer and claiming it to be downright tacky. Why is that? It's not because of the colour or style, it's because it features a DINGO. They know that because they have been told, or read about it in the paper perhaps had the energy to google it for themselves. Right? Well NO, actually, now look at the tie again. Do you still see a dingo or do you see what is really there? Of course a country boy like you would never mistake a fox for a dingo, would you? Well not for long anyway.

"I hope the lesson we all learn from this tragic case is don't always believe what you are told or read in the newspapers. We can all make the mistake of seeing what we want to. Sadly, I fear we haven't learned too much in the last 32 years."

Tipple then related two other stories. "After running the press through at the Darwin Airport which threatened life and limb, Lindy and I were scrambling into the refuge of our car. I observed a gnarled old Territorian pushing his way towards us as he drew near, he shook his head and exclaimed, 'Ya can still pull a crowd. [But] just as you think everybody knows you and what you are about you learn otherwise. Although we were within spitting distance of the court, I decided to order a cab as a safety measure. I made the order at the hotel reception. The young receptionist asked where we were going and the name. I said, 'To the court and my name is Tipple'. 'Oh,' she said. 'I hope you are not in trouble.'"

So, there it was, much the same as the death certificate issued more than 30 years before – and all that trouble, tears, sweat and money has passed between those two certificates. Aidan, now an impressive young man, married with children, embraced his mother. Malcolm Brown, who had turned 65 and was being politely told to leave his employment at Fairfax during the great contraction of the embattled company, covered the story, satisfied that he had seen it through. Firebrand Sydney defence counsel Winston Terracini QC, who like so many in Australia's legal fraternity had followed the Chamberlain case with interest, said in a letter to Tipple on 25th June 2012: "Your dedication and steadfast commitments to your clients despite all the criticism, mockery and stressors is a profound example of a solicitor at his best. I think I can speak with some insight into cases of this type, but I do not claim to understand the depth of commitment that you must have held quite rightly to your clients and this case. Sometimes as we both know, the justice system fails to provide simply that – justice. However, it is at least some small comfort that they got it right in the end even though there must have been many moments when you doubted that that was achievable." Terracini said he had noticed the aging process on the Chamberlains, though not so much on Tipple. "However, the images struck me almost like a physical blow that you had absorbed so much, endured so much and had emerged victorious with your integrity intact that I felt embarrassed that I had not contacted you before. I am reminded of a quote that I have always used and applied by Harry S. Truman – 'Just about everyone knows what's right, the difficult thing is doing it'. In this case, you saw the wrong and you more than anyone else from what I understand are more responsible for righting it."

Supportive letters and cards came from members of the public, including Teresa Riley, of Narara, NSW, who said she and her late husband, who had been a police officer at the time, had never believed the Chamberlains had anything to do with the death of their baby. Another tribute came from Rod Milton, a retired forensic psychiatrist, who said in a letter on 12th July: "The positive outcome of the recent inquest must have been extremely gratifying for you, a well-deserved reward for your many years of hard work and devotion to the Chamberlains. Please accept my congratulations. Thank you for involving me in the case, and in the many other interesting matters where you requested my opinion. Of the various firms of solicitors which with which I dealt, yours was one of the most professional, and it was always a pleasure to deal with you personally."

In August 2012, Tipple sent a copy of Azaria's death certificate to Andrew Kirkham, who had become involved with the case at the second coroner's inquest 20 years before. Kirkham replied: "I well remember the desperate putting together of Mrs Kuhl's cross-examination and your great contribution to that. Looking back, I think we all did our best in difficult circumstances."

Marshall Perron also wrote a letter, from Buderim in Queensland, on 21st September 2014: "Dear Mrs Chamberlain-Creighton, I write having seen a comment attributed to you in the media a while ago where it was reported you said that you felt sorry for me because I still believe you are guilty of the death of Azaria. Please do not feel sorry for me. I expect the origin of your belief may have come from an interview I did with a half-smart ABC journalist some years ago (I'm sure you have encountered a few of those in the past). Without going into the machinations of the interview, I want to say I do not believe that you harmed Azaria ... that you and your family have suffered monstrously since those tragic events at Ayers Rock all those years ago. My heart goes out to you, Michael and your two boys for what you have endured. If the opportunity arises and you believe there is any point, please pass on my views to all of them."

Perron undoubtedly meant that. In his case, as with others in official positions in the Northern Territory, he was obliged to play a role and carry out his duties as minister for state in a way he perceived fit. There is no easy way out of these things. As Neville Wran, NSW Premier, remarked, someone in a leading position in politics had sometimes to suffer "the blowtorch to the belly". None of them in the NT Government, not Paul Everingham, not anybody, had enjoyed this case.

On 23rd July 2015, Tipple wrote a letter to Boettcher, who had suffered the male problem of losing his head covering: "Dear Bazza, I guess I proved you wrong when you told me you couldn't have both hair and brains. Thankfully you were proved right in everything else. It was truly wonderful to get a finding, that the dingo did it. Couldn't have done it without you. Aidan at the last minute travelled from WA to Darwin to be there for the finding and broke down when he came to my hotel room and we debriefed. Michael is doing it tough. His wife Ingrid has had a stroke and he is now a carer. Life has many twists and turns and we need to seize the day when it comes our way."

In a letter to Malcolm Brown on 21st January 2016, Michael accepted an invitation to speak at a meeting of the Rotary Club of Parramatta City, where Malcolm was president. Addressing the meeting, Michael said: "Probably my current research in 'The Sustainability of the High Intensive Carer on 24/7 Profoundly Disabled Recipients' rather than my 32-year interruption with the NT would be more profitable for all'." He was well received and Brown walked back to Parramatta station with him. All was well between the two of them.

But there was to be no rest for Michael. His biological clock was ticking. He had less than a year to live. Michael was developing a serious blood condition, thought to have been leukaemia or related condition, though it did not manifest itself. Alex Murchison saw him on Wednesday, 4th January 2017 at a Coles supermarket. "He grabbed me and said he appreciated my friendship," Alex said. "I told my wife Dorothy that I had never seen him looking so fit and healthy." But on the Friday, Michael became ill and was admitted to a local hospital. Tipple saw a Facebook post from Michael's wife Ingrid saying that Michael had been admitted to hospital with suspected gall stones. No definite cause of Michael Chamberlain's terminal condition has ever been determined. The nearest description is that it was "a blood disorder". Whatever that was, it was fast-acting. Call it fate or coincidence but on Sunday, 8th January, Tipple felt inspired to pay him a surprise visit. He was shocked when he walked into his hospital room and saw him looking frail and asleep. Tempted to leave him asleep, Tipple gently touched him on the arm. Michael opened his eyes immediately and insisted Tipple sit down. Tipple later described the wonderful time they spent together canvassing the old and new. As he prepared to leave, Tipple asked if he would like him to pray. Michael grabbed his hand and said: "Yes, I would like that very much". Michael never let his hand go until the

Amen and as Tipple walked out, he heard Michael call out: "You are a good man". It was the last words he would ever say to Tipple.

Michael's condition deteriorated rapidly and within a few hours later he was transferred to Gosford Hospital where he was placed in the Intensive Care Unit. His family was alerted and all started making their way to Gosford. Aidan began the journey from Western Australia. Kahlia made plans to fly in from overseas. Michael's condition continued to deteriorate and by midday on Monday, 9th January 2017, was placed on life support. He died later that day. Michael Chamberlain's memorial service was held in the Avondale College Church on 16th January. The yellow Torana Hatchback used in the *Evil Angels* movie was parked outside while the eulogies were given. Ingrid, unable to walk, was wheeled in a wheel chair, with Zahra beside her. Stuart Tipple addressed the mourners and issued a challenge to the NT Government to make the apology Michael died still hoping for. He concluded: "In 1980 there was a sacrifice in the wilderness. Michael's expectation that if you are innocent you have nothing to fear died. That expectation was put on the altar of political expediency and was consumed by rumour, prejudice and incompetence. He will be not rest in peace unless we remember his legacy and continue the fight on his behalf." Also attending the service were Andrew Kirkham and John Byson. Michael was accorded dignity, contrasting with the way he had been treated in life.

Eight days later, on 24th January, the Sydney *Daily Telegraph* carried a story that was adverse to Michael, suggesting that the supposedly "risqué" photos he had taken years before indicated something sinister about the man. For those who knew Michael Chamberlain well, there was nothing sinister about him, and the fact that this was kept for years and apparently selectively leaked to a willing newspaper was the final spit in the face, it might be said, to an innocent man who, along with his family, had been pilloried over an event beyond their control.

Asked for a final word, Tipple said: "We cannot expect our politicians to change or make things better. We must accept the personal responsibility to make sure things are changed. The system got it wrong. Thank goodness there were enough people that got it right and were prepared to do something about it. We need to embrace the observation made in *Historical Trials* by Sir John MacDonnell: 'There is no accepted test of civilization. It is not wealth or the degree of comfort or the average duration of life or the increase of knowledge. All such tests would be disputed. In default of any other measure, may it not be suggested that as good a measure as any is the degree to which men are sensitive as to wrong doing and desirous to right it'."

There was, Tipple said, "still much to do". And indeed, as the following postscript demonstrates, there are numerous instances, not as spectacular as the Chamberlain case, where patient, objective reason and simple observation can nip other potential injustices in the bud.

AFTERWORD

THE FERRY MASTER

HOW STUART AND LES PULLED HIM OUT OF THE SOUP

"

In questions of science, the authority of a thousand is not worth the humble reasoning of a single individual.
— Galileo

Michael and Lindy Chamberlain might be said to have been unique clients. But in the experience of any criminal lawyer, they were far from that. So many things the Chamberlains said went against them, such as Michael's performance in the witness box in the trial. Lindy said in her interviews immediately after Azaria disappeared that she had been wearing a matinee jacket. Because it was not found, she was not believed. When it was discovered, more than five years later, it was powerful support for the contention she had been telling the truth all along? And had not Michael also been telling the truth?

The trouble with so many defendants is, they are not professional criminals, they do not know what to say or do, and what they do say in their muddle and confusion can compound things dreadfully.

Stuart Tipple, in 2012, in the last year in which the Chamberlain case would take up the attention of the judicial system, found a client just like that, a Hawkesbury River ferry master whose boat had snapped the car-ferry cable at Wiseman's Ferry. The ferry master was adamant that he was in the centre of the river, rather than "too close to the shore", as the NSW Roads and Maritime Authority (RSM) asserted. The ferry master told Stuart that his two deck hands could confirm that the ferry was in the centre of the river at the time it hit the cable.

Stuart Tipple took on this case, and in his preparation, fell back on someone who had been of invaluable assistance in the long fight to clear the Chamberlains: Les Smith. Les, always the unpretentious diploma-holder, had discovered the composition of the under-dash spray in the Chamberlains' car, proving it was not blood, and confirmed the capacity of canine teeth to make cuts in jumpsuit fabric. Les's science diploma had previously been held up against the qualifications of acknowledged experts. But he had always fallen back on the basic principle of science established by Francis Bacon: "Have a look!" Or more specifically, cast aside preconceived notions and rely on empirical observation. Anyone can do it, and Smith with his skill in this area would come to the rescue again.

Tipple said that when the ferry master initially approached him, he was "in trouble, big trouble". A conviction could have affected his ferry licence and the loss of livelihood. "He claimed that he was in navigating his boat in the middle of the river when it hit and broke the cable which is stretched across the river and pulls the car ferry and its passengers from side to side," Tipple said. "He had been told that it had caused a very irate politician to be stranded on the wrong side of the river for several hours and heads were going to roll. In particular his head."

After repairs and investigation, the RMS had called the ferry master in, showed him the broken ferry cable and pointed out a copper nail embedded in it. "He was asked if that nail came from his boat," Tipple said. "I still don't know why but he believed the nail was from his boat and he told them so. Had he received legal advice, he would have been told to say nothing and RMS would have had a much more difficult case to run. Armed with his admission, the RMS told him that the location of the nail on the cable had to be the point of impact of the boat and from their measurements it proved the boat was too close to the shore and was definitely not in the middle of the river. He was duly charged with a number of serious navigational breaches.

"He reminded me of the Chamberlains," Tipple said. "He was naive and so convinced he had nothing to fear he never obtained legal advice, cooperated with the authorities and made a damaging admission (that the nail was from his boat) he didn't have to make. He didn't have the financial resources to take on a Government Department but pleading guilty was not an option and a conviction would have serious consequences. I was sympathetic and impressed to help."

The ferry master told Tipple about the two deck hands who could swear that the ferry was in the middle of the river. He also told him that there had been other instances when his boat and other boats had hit the cable. "I prepared his proof of evidence and contacted both of the deck hands," Tipple said. "They both confirmed the boat was in the middle of the river but that no one had contacted them to get their statements. I contacted other boat operators who confirmed they had hit the cable at other times whilst they were in the middle of the river. I telephoned the RMS solicitor and advised her of my client's version of events and requested they contact the two deck hands who could verify the boat was in the middle of the river, and that the charges should be withdrawn. I was told there was no point in contacting the deck hands because there were two witnesses from the car ferry who said the boat was close to the bank and not in the middle of the river. As far as they were concerned, the nail embedded in the cable was irrefutable evidence of the point of impact, proving the boat was too close to the bank."

Tipple then wrote to the RMS confirming his request the deck hands be interviewed before the matter proceeded to a hearing. He was confident that the ferry master and the two deck hands would tell the court that the ferry was in the middle of the river at point of impact. But what about the copper nail? Tipple contacted Les Smith and they travelled together to Wiseman's Ferry. Tipple helped Smith take numerous photographs and take measurements so that Smith could construct his own model to see how a cable would react when hit. "A few weeks later Les rang and said, 'I know what's happened!'," Tipple said. "He later showed me photos of the model he had constructed and demonstrated how when the boat hit the cable, it broke and began revolving at high speed. As it whiplashed the bottom of the boat, it dislodged a number of nails. The copper nail in question had travelled along the cable until it become embedded closer to the bank."

Smith's contribution was "a brilliant and convincing demonstration", Tipple said. The nail had probably come from the boat but the prosecution had not considered whether the nail could have travelled from the point of impact. Tipple did have concerns as to whether Smith would be accepted as an expert. "After all, he only had a diploma and his experience and *cv* looked very ordinary when compared with that of, say, Professor James Cameron in the Chamberlain case," Tipple said. "Cameron's *cv* ran to several pages and was enough to impress anyone. However, I already knew that it was Les Smith who has exposed the truth of what even Cameron had said was an arterial spray in the Chamberlain car."

At the local court hearing, the RMS witnesses gave evidence that the boat was close to the shore when the boat hit the cable. The cable with the nail embedded became an exhibit.

In reply, Tipple called the deck hands, who were adamant that the boat had been in the middle of the river. Tipple thought the odds were now shifting in his favour. Then he called Les Smith. "I had Les prepare his very brief *cv*," Tipple said. "I had him explain to the magistrate how he had worked as a scientific problem-solver for many years with the Sanitarium Health Food Company and how he had assisted and gave evidence at the Royal Commission into the Chamberlain Convictions. The RMS did not object to Les being qualified as an expert witness and the magistrate was clearly impressed as he gave his evidence and demonstrated his model experimentation and how the nail could have travelled along the cable. I thought we were now ahead on points."

Tipple called the ferry master to give evidence and the defence case looked in danger of unravelling. "Under cross-examination he agreed that earlier that day he had sailed too close to the bank and had been warned, something he had forgotten to tell me about," Tipple said. "But worse, for reasons I cannot explain except for nerves, he agreed he couldn't be sure that the boat was in the middle of the river when it hit the cable. It felt like losing after holding a championship point. It was enough for the magistrate to seize on and convict him."

The magistrate reserved her decision for a month. "I had prepared my client for the worst and as we sat in court hearing the magistrate hand down her judgment it was not clear what the verdict would be until the magistrate came to her assessment of my client's evidence," Tipple said. "She pointed out how he had had the opportunity of confirming he was in no doubt he was in the middle of the river and she was impressed that he had not tried to guild the lily. This demonstrated to her he was a truthful and reliable witness doing his best to tell the truth. The evidence of Les Smith was unchallenged."

The magistrate dismissed the charges. As she rose to leave, Tipple got to his feet and made an application. "Prosecuting authorities are usually not ordered to pay costs, even when as in this case the charges were dismissed," he said. "However, if a successful party can show that the prosecution failed to properly investigate, the courts can be persuaded to order costs against them. I tendered the letter I had written to the RMS asking them to interview the deck hands and arguing it had failed to properly investigate. The magistrate agreed and indicated she would make a costs order and then adjourned with the directive for me to discuss and agree with the solicitor for RMS what the costs should be. Wanting to be fair and to avoid another fight, I told the RMS solicitor I would accept $5,000. I saw her go off to speak to her superior on her phone. I could see her becoming agitated before she began making her way back to where I was